MODERN ARCHITECTURE IN A POST-MODERN ERA

For Mateo

MODERN ARCHITECTURE IN A POST-MODERN ERA

ELIE G. HADDAD

LUND HUMPHRIES

First published in 2023 by Lund Humphries

Lund Humphries
Huckletree Shoreditch
Alphabeta Building
18 Finsbury Square
London EC2A 1AH
UK

www.lundhumphries.com

Modern Architecture in a Post-Modern Era
© Elie G. Haddad, 2023
All rights reserved

ISBN: 978–1–84822–595–4

A Cataloguing-in-Publication record for this book is available from the British Library.

All rights reserved. No part of this publication may be reproduced, stored in a retrieval system or transmitted in any form or by any means, electrical, mechanical or otherwise, without first seeking the permission of the copyright owners and publishers. Every effort has been made to seek permission to reproduce the images in this book. Any omissions are entirely unintentional, and details should be addressed to the publishers.

Elie G. Haddad has asserted his right under the Copyright, Designs and Patent Act, 1988, to be identified as the Author of this Work.

Front cover: Neutelings Riedijk, Institute for Sound and Vision, Hilversum, the Netherlands, 2006
Architect: Neutelings Riedijk Architects
Photo: Scagliola Brakkee

Copy edited by Pamela Bertram
Designed by Jacqui Cornish
Proofread by Patrick Cole
Cover design by Paul Arnot
Set in Circular Std and Graphik
Printed in Bosnia and Herzegovina

Contents

Acknowledgements 6
Preface 7
Foreword by Joan Ockman 8

1   **Modernism and its Discontents** 9

2   **The Architecture of** *Béton Brut* 16

3   **Neo-Rationalism** 39

4   **Post-Modern Architecture** 62

5   **Regional Modernisms** 87

6   **The Technological Paradigm** 114

7   **The Continuing Legacy of Modernism** 131

8   **The Project of Deconstruction** 159

9   **Neo-Constructivism, Neo-Suprematism and the Return of the Avant-Garde** 170

10 **Neo-Expressionism in Architecture** 192

11 **The Minimalist Aesthetic** 214

12 **New Directions in Contemporary Architecture** 242

Notes 272
Index 281
Illustration Credits 287

Acknowledgements

The production of this book was partially funded by a research grant from the Lebanese American University (LAU). I would like to thank the University administration for its generous support throughout my academic career, and for making such projects possible.

My thanks to Gwenn Abillama, who assisted me in the production of this work, and assiduously oversaw the process of collecting the illustrations, securing the needed copyrights, and following up with the publisher on other details related to this major task. Also, I wish to thank all the architects, photographers, and friends who supplied us with the illustrations of various buildings and the right to reproduce them.

Thanks to Val Rose, the commissioning editor, for her support and encouragement, and to all the team at Lund Humphries for their professionalism. Also, my thanks to Joan Ockman for writing the foreword to this book.

Finally, I wish to thank the students of architecture at the Lebanese American University who prompted me throughout these years to question some of the received notions, and to attempt to bring some clarity to the diverse manifestations of contemporary architecture.

Preface

This book is the outcome of more than two decades of teaching a course on contemporary architecture at the Lebanese American University. During this time, the course content evolved and was continuously updated and reorganised to account for the diversity of architectural production that evolved since the 1960s. The process of writing a history in continuous flux, and the constant rearrangement of material reminded me of Manfredo Tafuri's famous statement on the work of the historian as an intermittent journey through a maze of paths and provisional constructions, where 'the cards can be reshuffled and to them added many that were intentionally left out' for the game is destined to continue.[1]

The original title for this book was 'Changing Paradigms in Modern Architecture' which was partly inspired by Peter Collins' *Changing Ideals in Modern Architecture*. The title was subsequently changed, yet the original premise underlying this book remained the same, that what took place after the deep 'malaise' of the 1960s, including the major reaction that came to be known as 'Post-Modernism', were a series of paradigm shifts building upon the legacy of the Modernist project. While some movements, such as Post-Modernism, aimed at undermining the very foundations of the Modernist project, others, such as High-Tech, actually took the charge of fulfilling its more radical objectives, that is, the realisation of the ideal of progress through an unwavering faith in technology. This ideal has been revived in our current times through a recourse to new imaging tools, made possible through the information revolution. In parallel, other strands varying from Minimalism to Regionalism, took shape and led to the emergence of buildings and projects that reiterate or adapt some of the formal types of modern architecture. For this reason, I interpreted the developments of the past five decades as being all reactions to, or variations of Modernism,[2] within a Post-Modern era.

The book attempts to chart a middle course between the 'aesthetic' histories that examine architecture solely in terms of its formal aspects, and the more 'ideological' histories that subject it to a critique that often skirts the discussion of its formal aspects. Even though I have attempted to be inclusive of different regions, the task of representing architectural production all over the globe is an impossible task. Yet the projects included testify to the growing impact and dissemination of architecture around the world, with certain themes and constructs appearing in various geographical contexts.

This work was conceived during the COVID-19 pandemic, which allowed me the time to reflect and reorganise my thoughts about recent architectural developments. The aim behind it was primarily to arrange this material into an accessible format for the students of architecture amidst the proliferation of reviews and monographs that address different 'paradigms', often under more exclusive lenses. It was also intended as a reaction to other surveys that brought together different works uncritically under vaguely defined categories, which added to the current confusion.

Foreword

by Joan Ockman

Elie Haddad's survey of architecture in a Post-Modern era begins in the 1960s, a moment when criticisms brewing since the end of the Second World War about modern architecture's flawed ideological foundations came to a head. Among the 'discontents' whom Haddad singles out as progenitors of the ferment were – among others – Bruno Zevi, Aldo van Eyck, Christian Norberg-Schulz, and Christopher Alexander, who respectively introduced ideas of organicism, relational thinking, meaning, and pattern-finding into architectural discourse. Out of the crisis of Modernist belief came the panoply of new approaches that are the subject matter of this book. At the same time, and even amid the success story of Post-Modernism in the 1970s and 1980s, Modernist impulses persisted in complex and hybrid ways, from 'critical' forms of regionalism to technological experimentation to new avant-gardisms. Haddad traces a dozen stylistic directions that architects pursued within the rapidly evolving landscape of late 20th-century global design practice. While not primarily concerned with the larger historical and geopolitical background against which these often-competing new tendencies emerged and took form, he goes beyond the contentious polemics and *partis pris* that surrounded them at the time. Deftly and concisely presenting a very wide spectrum of built works, taking stock of continuities as well as discontinuities, failures as well as successes, he focuses on both canonical and less familiar examples. His taxonomy suggests the diversity and density of architectural production over the last six decades, as well as the rich body of ideas that accompanied it. Inevitably some readers will quibble or quarrel with inclusions and exclusions, and some will want more context. Yet the book's interwoven narratives of aesthetic, intellectual, technological, and ecological innovation will offer students and practitioners a valuable panoramic view of the crowded field of historical and contemporary landmarks that today constitute the expanded territory of architecture.

1 Modernism and its Discontents

The history of modern architecture has been well covered in the classical surveys of Sigfried Giedion, Kenneth Frampton, William Curtis, Alan Colquhoun, and other historians who traced the developments of this major movement that dominated the architectural landscape of the 20th century until the beginning of the 1970s, when a major contesting movement appeared on the scene, labelled as 'Post-Modernism'. The surveys of modern architecture, written by that generation, also ended around that time, while some of them resorted to adding new chapters to their revised editions, covering recent developments.

In writing this book, I was partly inspired by Peter Collins' *Changing Ideals in Modern Architecture: 1750–1950*. As Collins indicated in the introduction to his book, the designation of 'modern architecture' has been applied in principle to cover the architecture of the 20th century, although most historians recognise that its roots go back further in time. The 'ideals' of which Collins spoke covered different themes, all of which had an impact on the development of modern architecture, from Eclecticism to Rationalism and Functionalism. In a similar vein, I have sought to explore the different paradigms that have affected the developments of the past six decades, specifically beginning around the 1960s, when a new wind started to blow from within Modernism, and then led to different reactions and counter-reactions, the effects of which are still felt today. This period has been subject to a multiplicity of approaches in architecture and almost parallels the Eclecticism of the 19th century in its variety. Many architects who are covered in the different chapters do not in fact work within a single repertoire, but like music composers, have shown their skills at handling different projects in different modes, depending on the particularities of varied situations.

The period that preceded the Second World War was marked by the spread of what we now consider to be the ultimate manifestation of 'modern architecture' in Europe – that is, the 'International Style' – and its dissemination to the new continent through the architects who emigrated to the United States, like Walter Gropius, Erich Mendelsohn, and Mies van der Rohe, in addition to the activities of local figures, principal among them Frank Lloyd Wright who realised his masterpiece of Fallingwater in 1936. The famous exhibition on the 'International Style' held at the Museum of Modern Art in New York in 1930 marked the beginning of a period of assimilation of modern architecture in its European version within the American landscape and around the world.

Yet developments after the Second World War, especially during the momentous 1960s, started to indicate a growing malaise within the movement, caused by a dissatisfaction with its reductive tendencies, its institutionalisation into another 'style', its urban disjunctions, and its failure to achieve its original goals of social reform. This discontent would later on take another dimension with the realisation of its failures at the scale of social housing and city planning, and would be echoed among different architects and critics who attempted a 'corrective movement' within Modernism, from Aldo van Eyck to Bruno Zevi.

The period that followed also witnessed the emergence of new voices within architecture, coming from different quarters – from the elitist schools of the East Coast of the United States to the non-conformist areas such as Berkeley on the West. From Princeton there emerged an articulate young architect by the name of Robert Venturi, who pleaded in a gentle manifesto for the recognition of historical continuity, while on the West Coast, Christopher Alexander advocated the search for a metaphysical essence, which should be, in his own definition, based on a common and timeless language that is generated by the local cultures. In what follows I will examine a selection of theoretical positions that paved the way for a reassessment of modern architecture and for its eventual dissipation into various movements and trends.

BRUNO ZEVI: THE RETURN TO ORGANIC ARCHITECTURE

Bruno Zevi was one of the first critics to call Modernism back to its original goals. A fiery anti-academic architect and critic, Zevi was a dedicated believer in the 'organic' ideal of Frank Lloyd Wright, and he saw his role as correcting the misperception and under-valuation of Wright in the European context. Zevi's writings were thus geared towards educating the Italian public in the holistic architecture of Wright, as well as advocating through this a return to the true spirit of Modernism, which is that of an 'organic architecture'. Zevi, who had spent two years during the war at Harvard, where he studied under Walter Gropius, was not so inspired by the European master and the 'classicising' tendency that he saw in the works of European architects such as Gropius, Le Corbusier, and Mies. He was much more impressed by the work of Frank Lloyd Wright and other American architects, as well as Aalto, Scharoun, and Mendelsohn; theirs was an architecture that developed naturally in response to human needs and which promoted, according to Zevi, a democratic and free society.

Towards an Organic Architecture appeared in Italian immediately after the war (1945) and then in an English translation (1949).[1] The first part of the book presented a survey of the development of modern architecture in Europe, from its origin in the Arts and Crafts movement to its later transformation under Le Corbusier, Gropius and others, drawing attention to its 'other' manifestations, specifically the work of Aalto, which indicates a tendency towards 'organic architecture'. An interlude between this first part, and the second, which presents a survey of American architecture and the role of Frank Lloyd Wright, is a chapter titled 'Meaning and Scope of the Term *Organic* in Reference to Architecture'[2] – a manifesto on the principles of a modern, organic architecture. Zevi begins this chapter with a quote from Frank Lloyd Wright in which the master drew a connection between an organic architecture and a free society:

> [. . .] An organic architecture means more or less an organic society. Organic ideals of integral building reject rules imposed by exterior aestheticism or mere taste, and so would the people to whom such architecture would belong reject such external impositions upon life as were not in accord with the nature and character of the man who had found his work and the place where he could be happy and useful because of it. [. . .][3]

This statement sets the direction of Zevi's polemic, his major point of criticism directed towards Giedion, who associated the organic with the 'irrational', presenting it in a duality against the rational/geometric. Zevi, of course, took issue with this limited and erroneous understanding of the organic, arguing instead for a broader understanding of this concept which encompasses some of the best examples of functional furniture, all the way to an architecture that is opposed to the 'theoretic and geometrical, to the artificial standards, the white boxes and the cylinders'.[4] Further, he warned against two fallacies that distort a real understanding of the 'organic': the 'naturalist' fallacy which confuses the organic with an imitation of nature,[5] and the 'biologic' or 'anthropomorphic' fallacy which is at the basis of Expressionism, where a building 'expresses' the feeling or desire of the architect. This, for Zevi, is far from the true significance of the 'organic' which goes far beyond reproducing physical sensations either directly or indirectly.[6] Organic architecture, for Zevi, is not achieved by covering walls with neurotic patterns to express movement, as happened with Art Nouveau, but in the spatial arrangement being designed to accommodate the actual movement of the people who live in that space.[7]

In his other major work, *The Modern Language of Architecture*[8] – which came in part as a reply to Summerson's *The Classical Language of Architecture* – Zevi proposed a 'guide to design' based on seven principles, which he called 'invariables'. To achieve a truly modern architecture, these principles should be followed in the given order, and preferably adhered to as a group, although even in the works of the masters, one does not always find all of these invariables.[9] The last and seventh principle discussed the integration of building, city, and landscape into a dynamic whole, an integration not based on classical static principles, but rather on organic, evolving forms. This may bring to mind the image of medieval towns, but Zevi was thinking of a more futuristic fusion of architecture, city, and landscape, as illustrated by the proposals of Archigram and other groups.[10] This last principle was a direct reaction to the rigid urbanism that was exemplified by Le Corbusier's *Ville Radieuse* (although Zevi did not name it directly), which was applied after the Second World War across the devastated cities and landscapes of Europe:

> The unfinished approach is the goal of the seven invariables, and it is a fundamental prerequisite if architecture is to be involved in the land – and townscape, assimilate its contradictions, and rummage in squalor and kitsch in search of human values that need saving. Sociologists have found that slums, *bidonvilles*, *favelas*, and *barriadas*, have an intensely vital sense of community that is unknown in planned lower-class housing developments.[11]

This statement by Zevi summarised much of the discontent that was brewing as a result of the widespread application of the tabula rasa principle in rebuilding European cities after the war, and in clearing urban slums in America and replacing them with the new 'projects'.

ALDO VAN EYCK: THE CALL FOR REFORM FROM WITHIN

Aldo van Eyck was another major critic of modern architecture, and one of the key players in the movement to reform CIAM, the *Congrès International d'Architecture Moderne*, which for a new generation of architects had come to represent an inflexible and hierarchical institution that betrayed the original objectives of Modernism and most importantly, was unable to cope with post-war realities and challenges. The attempt to reform CIAM eventually failed and the group known as Team X – which included Aldo van Eyck, Alison and Peter Smithson, Jaap Bakema, and Giancarlo de Carlo – precipitated the downfall of the organisation after its last meeting in Otterlo in 1959.[12] Van Eyck did not publish any major theoretical work,[13] yet he was a prolific writer and activist who disseminated his ideas in journals such as *Forum*, where his sharp essays brought to mind the same spirit of the early avant-garde manifestos. In the first issue of *Forum* under the new editorial board of Team X, which van Eyck edited himself,[14] he articulated his position in 'The story of another idea', in which he discussed the new emerging tendencies in opposition to the prevailing priorities of CIAM, which had reduced urbanism to a dogmatic set of parameters such as hygiene and traffic. For van Eyck, the task of urbanism went beyond the simple question of answering the housing needs to the issue of 'inhabitability' – or what Norberg-Schulz would later designate as 'dwelling' – and the response of urbanism to those fundamental human needs that had been totally ignored or misunderstood by modern urbanism. The main goal of urbanism would be to create an environment with which human beings could identify, an environment where one might live with dignity and without losing one's identity.[15]

As Francis Strauven summarised it, van Eyck's 'other idea' was a recognition that the essence of a city or an urban district cannot be defined in terms of functions alone, but should be approached in terms of relations. The built environment is an embodiment of complex interhuman relationships that exist at various scale levels and that comprise a complete range of functions.[16] Van Eyck later introduced the concept of time which does not separate into past, present, and future, as some have done throughout the history of architecture; he saw them all as one continuum. In this way, he argued, artifacts take on a temporal depth without falling into either 'sentimental historicism', 'Modernism', 'utopianism', 'rationalism', 'functionalism', or 'regionalism'. He criticised Western civilisation on the basis of its misunderstanding of this time-continuum that operates well in other cultures, which it dismisses as 'less advanced' or 'primitive'. Van Eyck's text is punctuated by ideas and associations that break the 'logical' order of the narrative to reveal certain images that illustrate his idiosyncratic understanding of things.[17] He concludes this essay with an ominous warning, which seems prophetic in retrospect:

One thing is certain – if society at large fails to come to terms with its people – what a paradox – people will spread over the globe and be at home nowhere, for it is in the nature of the countless pseudo places made today that they are all the same. The same because they are bad in the same way, and different in the wrong way. [. . .] Now who is responsible for that? WHO NOT WHAT! Fetch a mirror, architects, and you will discover again what mirrors are for – and why it is always futile to transfer the cause of failure.[18]

Following this path, van Eyck reached out beyond Western culture, searching for lessons from ancestral communities in Central Africa and North America: the Dogon and the Pueblos, setting a precedent for a renewed fascination with non-Western cultures that would later develop in architectural circles. Those cultures that never followed a 'rationalist' approach in designing their built environment, prompted a number of studies, such as Amos Rapoport's *House, Form and Culture*[19] and Bernard Rudofsky's *Architecture without Architects*, the latter a publication that followed an exhibition on indigenous architecture from various parts of the world, held at the epicentre of the Modernist establishment, the Museum of Modern Art in New York, a few years after the appearance of van Eyck's first article on the Dogon.[20] Van Eyck later reflected on this African experience in 'A Miracle of Moderation', which was followed by two articles by Swiss psychoanalysts who studied the Dogon culture and whom van Eyck had met in Africa during his visit, Paul Parin and Fritz Morgenthaler.[21]

Van Eyck's keen interest in a holistic understanding of urbanism led him to devote a whole issue of *Forum* to an essay by an author unknown at the time, Joseph Rykwert. Rykwert's analysis of 'The Idea of a Town' shed light on the symbolic foundation behind the planning of Roman towns and countered the simplistic readings that reduced planning to a 'rationalist' process based on functional parameters. This essay would develop later into an influential book that put into question the assumptions of modern urbanism.[22] The last major theoretical contribution of van Eyck was a manuscript on *The Child, the City and the Artist – An Essay on Architecture – The Inbetween Realm*.[23] A synopsis of this work appeared in 'The Image of Ourselves'.[24] The notion of 'inbetween' was indebted to the German philosopher Martin Buber and was articulated for the first time by van Eyck at the Otterlo meeting of CIAM.[25] Van Eyck attributed the contemporary condition of decay and disintegration affecting most cities to the lack of 'imagination' and consequently, to the missing of one or more of these constituent elements: the city, the child, or the artist. The city is, like human life, subject to the cycle of time.[26] His plea for a city to be conceived in the light of natural phenomena – a city of rain, snow, coldness, and darkness – is somewhat reminiscent of the early avant-garde's utopian ideals, yet it goes beyond their fascination with technology, glass, or speed.[27] His realisation of the major divide between the multitude which had become transformed in modern society into an anonymous client, and the architect who acts as the professional in charge of the task of building them a 'place', is not too different from the problems that other theoreticians would eventually deal with, namely Christopher Alexander[28] and Christian Norberg-Schulz. The same problem, as Heidegger put it in other terms, of 'dwelling' in modern times.

Similar to Le Corbusier before him, van Eyck saw his role as an advocate who would apply his ideas in real life through practice. Among the realisations that demonstrate this concern for the human dimension in design were his series of playgrounds for children, that he developed out of residual spaces in the city of Amsterdam, which totalled over 700 playgrounds and public spaces.[29] His other major architectural work, which was conceived as a counter-statement to the prevalent monolithic Modernism of the post-war period is the Amsterdam Orphanage, a complex that was designed as a 'settlement', a village of modular units, containing clusters of dormitories for children of different ages, organised around a series of courts. This project was an example of van Eyck's synthesis of three traditions: the Classical, expressed by geometrical order; the Modern, embodying the dynamism of movement through space; and the third tradition, which he called the 'vernacular of the heart', typical of archaic cultures and manifested in the form of a traditional settlement.[30]

THE SEARCH FOR MEANING IN ARCHITECTURE

The structuralist influence on architecture was another one of those major developments of the 1960s and 1970s which attempted to come to terms with the notion of an 'architectural language'. Language, which emerged as a major area of studies within linguistics, filtered into the architectural discourse as a result of this search for a theoretical basis for the understanding of the discipline, as well as a need to come to terms with the notion of 'meaning' in architecture. The question of how, and by what process the meaning of an architectural work is arrived at, how aesthetic judgements are made, could not have come at a more propitious time: when the foundations of the Modern Movement were being questioned and its value system based on functionalism was collapsing in the face of social and urban challenges. The notions of 'text' and 'meaning' both constituted important contributions to the architectural debate, following the reductive discourse of functionalism in the 1930s–1950s. The notion of an architectural text would play an important role in the post-structuralist phase, while 'meaning' occupied a significant place in the structuralist phase, specifically at the level of the 'semantic plane', and later in the development of Post-Modernism.

It is, thus, not a coincidence that a collection of essays appeared in 1970 under the specific title of *Meaning in Architecture*, edited by Charles Jencks and George Baird.[31] In this work, Jencks used the semantic platform to argue for a multiplicity of meanings, and to open the field to certain manifestations that had been repressed by the International Style. He resorted to examples from the whole history of architecture to illustrate the variety of architectural approaches to the question. He would later use the same line of argument to define his Post-Modern agenda for architecture. For Jencks, the immediate interest was to break the rigid categories in which architecture had been caught, that is, the spatial or functional paradigms. For this, he based his argument on the 'architectural sign', derived from the analysis of Ferdinand de Saussure, and analysed its two constituents: the signifier, which he called the 'expression plane', and the signified, or the 'content plane'. According to Jencks, *signifiers* give architecture its expression – that is, form, space, surface, colour, and texture – while *the signified* constitute the set of ideas that they directly or indirectly refer to.[32] For Jencks, the semantic field is a fluid one and this accounts for the change in meaning that some forms undergo over time. Thus, the purist architecture of the 1920s may have connoted functionalism at that time, but could connote something altogether different today. In this sense, Semiotics, or the study of signs, could give a reasonable explanation for the change in value and meaning that different works undergo through time.[33]

Geoffrey Broadbent, in the same book, argued that Semiotics, while unable to define an architectural language, showed at least that abstraction was not an end in itself in language and certainly did not lead to an architecture of signification.[34] He confirmed the assumption that the signifier in architecture would refer to the building, while the signified referred to a concept.[35] The Saussurian system may have limited relevance in architecture, but it could help in understanding some of the underlying structures of an architectural language. Thus, the opposition between *langue* and *parole* may be translated as an opposition between the concept of architecture as 'style' – that is, a socially constructed system – and *parole* which would refer to the particular expression of a certain work. As an example of that, Broadbent referred to the Schroeder House, which, despite its ingenuity and its effective response to the client's needs, ignored the 'social contract' at the time and was misunderstood even by some of the proponents of Modernism.[36] He further stressed that architecture could not be a signifier for some abstract meaning, but rather the 'signified of some pervading philosophy', whether that happens to be the 'spirit of the times' or other ideas.[37]

Another major voice in the discussion on meaning was the Norwegian theoretician Christian Norberg-Schulz. While Norberg-Schulz began his theoretical studies with a structuralist investigation of architecture, he later moved to adopt phenomenology as a framework for architectural interpretation and as a means to reclaim the historical role of architecture as a humanist and cultural construct. Norberg-Schulz elaborated this theory in his major opus, *Genius Loci*,[38] which came as a sequel to his previous two works in architectural theory. *Genius Loci* was perhaps the most influential of Norberg-Schulz's writings, as it came out at a time when questions of meaning, history, and mythology assumed greater importance in architectural discourse, in a Post-Modern climate that gave back relevance to such themes. And unlike his previous studies, this one was more explicitly concerned with the interpretation of phenomenology in architecture, as clearly stated in the introduction that acknowledged the debt to Heidegger, particularly the essays collected in *Poetry, Language, Thought*.[39] In this illustrated essay on architecture, with images ranging from the macroscopic scale of idyllic landscapes to the microscopic scale of architectural details, Norberg-Schulz proposed to elaborate the constituting elements of a 'phenomenology of place'. The phenomenological challenge lies in reviving a poetic dimension in architecture and in re-establishing the lost connection between the various elements that constitute our world. Specifically, he stressed the connection between the man-made world and the natural world, historically evident in various places and environments, and attributed to Heidegger's concept of 'gathering'. Its last phase, symbolisation, plays a more crucial role in the concretisation of meaning in a place, and in the realisation of the concept of 'gathering'.

In his follow-up work, *The Concept of Dwelling*, the author selected examples of appropriate dwellings such as the Hill House by Mackintosh, the Hvitträsk complex by Gesellius, Lindgren and Saarinen, Behrens' house in Darmstadt, Hoffmann's Palais Stoclet, and Wright's Prairie houses which share little in common but were nevertheless identified as fulfilling the main purpose of dwelling: to reveal the world, not as essence but as presence, as material and colour, topography and vegetation, seasons, weather, and light. Yet this time, the critique of the 'modern house' was more explicit. The author recognised its failure to arrive at a satisfactory solution to the problem of dwelling, as it lacked what he termed as the 'figural quality'. Hence, what seems to be the problem is simply the inability of the modern house to look like a house, and not, as Heidegger had alluded to, the inability of modern man to dwell. Norberg-Schulz expressed the hope that the revival of this figural quality, as evident in many Post-Modern works, would again make dwelling possible.[40] Despite a cautionary remark against a fall into Eclecticism, the book ended on an optimistic note that the recovery of the figural quality would lead to a recovery of dwelling, in which phenomenology would play a major role as the catalyst for the rediscovery of the poetic dimension in architecture.[41]

CHRISTOPHER ALEXANDER: THE 'OTHER' VOICE IN ARCHITECTURE

Christopher Alexander emerged as one of the most radical voices of the 1970s, putting into question the whole architectural enterprise, including the commissioning process leading to the construction of buildings. Alexander advocated a return to the essential qualities which can be discerned in places and times where the activity of building had been firmly rooted within the life of a culture. Alexander's new worldview was expressed through his published works from *The Oregon Experiment* to *A Pattern Language* and *The Timeless Way of Building*.[42] His books gained him a cult following since the 1970s, extending beyond traditional architectural circles. His theories also influenced the development of 'New Urbanism' in the 1990s, by architects such as Andreas Duany and Elizabeth Plater-Zyberk, among others.

For Stephen Grabow, who wrote an authoritative study on Alexander, his work constituted nothing less than a major paradigmatic change in the history of architecture.[43] Following modern architecture's recognised failures in addressing certain fundamental issues in the generation of meaningful environments, Alexander addressed these issues through a scientific approach that investigated the fault lines and proposed a comprehensive theory to reclaim those essential qualities. Proceeding from a systematic analysis, Alexander noted that the actual substance out of which the environment is made consists of relations or patterns, rather than individual elements or things, and those patterns are generated by the implicit system of rules that determines their structure.[44] Furthermore, the meaningful or 'holistic' environments invariably contain a certain 'quality' which constitutes the enigmatic element that he sought to identify, which he referred to as 'the quality without a name', and in other instances associated it with the 'organic order' of things. Building upon D'Arcy Thompson's theory of form,[45] Alexander stressed the importance of the generative process in the development of forms, implying the model of an organic order as a basis for a new architecture. Alexander followed an empirical approach to arrive at the constituent elements of a general aesthetic theory that would offer communities the possibility to design, on their own, a meaningful environment, where different constituent elements would be interrelated and composed within a significant whole.

Alexander put his theory to the test through multiple projects all over the world, starting with small projects such as the Linz Café in Austria (1980), to more elaborate works like Julian Street Inn Shelter for the Homeless in San Jose, California (1988), Eishin University Campus in Tokyo (1989), and the West Dean College Visitors Centre in Sussex, England (1995). While his work always emphasised the participatory approach to design, including the input of the community, it is clear that the stylistic direction was somewhat inclined towards a revival of the local vernacular, imbued in some cases with Post-Modern accents. Alexander's philosophy was perhaps best expressed in the Mexicali Housing project in Mexico (1976) commissioned by the Mexican government, where the architect and his team had to develop a series of low-cost units, working directly with the local population to build them. This constituted the first opportunity for Alexander to put his ideas into practice, applying the 'pattern language' which, according to the architect, worked beautifully and allowed them to realise a project that avoided the normative prescriptions of modern architecture. Organised around a series of patios, alleyways, and public spaces, the different units form a new village, built on a modular template of varying patterns, employing a new material consisting of small blocks of soil-cement rather than concrete.[46]

Alexander aimed throughout his life to uncover the underlying order of things and to reveal the principles of order and harmony in the environment. An interesting debate that was indicative of the opposite tendencies at the time took place at Harvard between Peter Eisenman, advocate of an intellectual approach to architecture, and Christopher Alexander, searching for what may properly be termed as the true 'phenomenological' approach that would overcome the constraints of a positivistic paradigm.[47] While Alexander approached the problem from the perspective of a scientist searching for the properties that lead to the creation of beauty, Eisenman was clearly preoccupied with the translation of philosophical ideas emanating from French circles, referring to 'post-humanist' themes. Later developments in architecture confirmed the resilience of architectural culture to radical change, with Alexander's paradigm becoming marginalised and his influence restricted to a group of followers who remained committed to the development of a 'pattern language'.

All these developments that were taking place throughout the 1960s and into the 1970s nevertheless indicated a deep malaise within modern architecture, which led to the formulation of new approaches to tackle the problem of re-enchanting architecture, or re-establishing its connection to people, places, history, and culture in general. This would eventually lead to the major counter-revolution of Post-Modernism, which would take place in parallel to other variations on the Modernist paradigm. And while Post-Modernism would dominate the centre-stage of architecture during the 1980s, it would later subside to be replaced by the different trends and variations that will be explored in the following chapters.

2   The Architecture of *Béton Brut*

The designation of Brutalism has been associated with the use of *béton brut* – concrete – as a material of choice, not only for structural components, but as a finish material. This aesthetic move towards *béton brut* was initiated by Le Corbusier before the Second World War, and continued in his later works, from the Unité d'Habitation in Marseille, to the Millowners' Association Building in Ahmedabad and the Monastery of La Tourette in Lyon. These projects would have a long influence on the work of many architects who saw in this material both a possibility for creating new formal structures as well as an expression of the 'spirit of the times'.

'New Brutalism', while not related to Le Corbusier's version of Brutalism, was often confounded with it in later histories. The term was coined by Peter and Alison Smithson to describe their own work, specifically Hunstanton School, which was conceived as a bare structure using a steel frame construction with glass facades, for a middle school that was supposed to illustrate the benefits of basic construction, in response to social and economic constraints. All internal fixtures, including plumbing, were installed like 'found objects', without the customary finishing and detailing.

The critic Reyner Banham promoted this tendency in architecture. In one of his essays, while drawing a connection between 'New Brutalism' and Le Corbusier's use of *béton brut*, as well as with contemporary artistic manifestations – namely the art of Jean Dubuffet – Banham stretched the definition to extend to the work of Louis Kahn, particularly his Yale Art Gallery. He still stuck to the Smithsons' representation as the most expressive of the new trend due to its 'ineloquence' and 'ruthless logic'. Compared to Kahn's Gallery, the Smithsons' work did not revel in the sophistication of details nor in the composition of elements. Instead, Banham saw three main characteristics as defining the new architecture: its memorability as an image, clear exhibition of structure, and valuation of materials 'as found', that is, as raw materials. Banham extolled another example that went even further in expressing these ideas: the Smithsons' unrealised competition for Sheffield University, an informal composition of blocks, unified by circulation routes, with 'graceless memorability'.[1] Robin Hood Gardens (1968–72) (fig.2.1), a project that came into being fifteen years after Banham's article, may have accurately reflected his designation, more so than Sheffield. Yet for all its 'memorable' qualities, this large housing complex – with its famous streets in the air, and despite all its good intentions – eventually proved to be a failure. Yet it is perhaps this example by the Smithsons, with its large-scale concrete structure and array of precast concrete mullions, that stuck to the popular imagery of what New Brutalism came to stand for, more than Hunstanton: a mega-structure of *béton brut*, used as an expressive structural material, and left bare without any cladding.

2.1   Alison and Peter Smithson, Robin Hood Gardens, Poplar, London, UK, 1968–72

2.2 Van den Broek and Bakema, Delft University Auditorium, Delft, the Netherlands, 1959–66

In Europe, the Brutalist aesthetic, which originated with Le Corbusier's Unité d'Habitation, and was confirmed in later works such as the Monastery of La Tourette, continued to develop with a number of large projects of institutional character, such as the Delft University Auditorium (1959–66) (fig.2.2) by the architects Van den Broek and Bakema, who also relied on the use of cast concrete in major projects. The Auditorium building took the form of a monumental structure cantilevering above the main entrance, supported by large triangular pilotis. On the other side of the building are located smaller lecture halls, also cantilevering above the ground and marked by a rhythmical sequence of pre-stressed concrete beams and columns, which express the roof structure.

Denys Lasdun's Royal National Theatre (1963–76) (fig.2.3) represents a major landmark of Brutalism in the United Kingdom. Built on the South Bank of the Thames, this theatre does not betray its function as other theatres do, but appears as a composition of horizontal layers that spread around the site, punctuated by the fly tower of the theatre, all rendered in the characteristic concrete, marked by the imprint of the wooden planks used as formwork during construction. On the riverside, a series of foyers compose the main public areas which become an extension of the public realm. The complex accommodates three theatres of different sizes, with the largest one occupying the central space.

Brutalism found another interpretation in Germany with Gottfried Böhm, whose church in Neviges (1964–8) (fig.2.4) is a masterpiece of *béton brut* in an Expressionist style. Böhm won the competition to design the Pilgrimage Church in this small town in Germany in 1964. The

17

above
2.3   Denys Lasdun, Royal National Theatre, South Bank, River Thames, London, UK, 1963–76

right, exterior and interior
2.4   Gottfried Böhm, Pilgrimage Church, Neviges, Germany, 1964–8

competition called for a large space that could accommodate 900 seated worshippers in addition to 3,000 standing, with additional chapels, administrative and ancillary spaces. The architects created a monumental structure in rough concrete, with a towering profile composed of multiple peaks that evoke the distant mountains. The 'crystalline' interior of the church reflects the sculptural forms on the exterior, interspersed with clerestories that bring light into the space. On the left side of the church are located two chapels, one of which hosts the sacred relic. The concrete surfaces are punctuated with panes of brilliantly coloured stained glass, designed by the architect himself, in an abstract Expressionist manner.

Contemporaneous to his masterpiece in Neviges, Böhm also designed the Town Hall in Bergisch Gladbach-Bensberg (1962–71) (fig.2.5), a civic structure that straddles the foundation walls of a medieval castle that lay in ruins. The complex was conceived as an organic, necklace-shaped arrangement of offices that culminates in the town's council chamber, which is enclosed by a surviving section of the medieval wall. The whole complex, composed of a staggered layering of eight floors of different functions, punctuated by the symbolic stairway towers, is rendered in rough concrete, giving it a sculptural quality that integrates well into the medieval site.

BRUTALISM IN AMERICA

In Massachusetts, the master himself, Le Corbusier, designed the only building to be

2.5 Gottfried Böhm, Bensberg Town Hall, Bergisch Gladbach-Bensberg, Germany, 1962–71

realised in North America, the Carpenter Center for the Visual Arts (1963) (fig.2.6), on the campus of Harvard University. In marked contrast to the traditional red-brick buildings on campus, the new centre featured Le Corbusier's favourite material, with the deep-case windows that had been previously adopted in hotter climates, such as those in the Millowners' Association Building in Ahmedabad. Accessible via a wide ramp that cuts through the building and connects it to two parallel streets, it was characterised by its rough concrete and its curvilinear forms that mimic two kidneys placed in opposition, intersected by the ramp. The building floats on pilotis at the basement level. This project was realised with the assistance of Josep Lluís Sert, Dean of Harvard's Graduate School of Design at the time, who played an important role in securing this commission for the Swiss master.

Josep Lluís Sert, a committed Modernist who had emigrated to the US from Spain in 1939, also left a number of buildings in a hybrid Brutalist genre, mixing rough concrete with other materials. His most iconic buildings, post-1960, were also realised on the campus of Harvard University, as well as the neighbouring Boston University. At Harvard he designed the Science Center and the Holyoke Center (1960–66) (fig.2.7), an administrative building that also included retail operations on the ground floor, while for Boston University he designed the Law School tower and the Mugar Memorial Library.

The Holyoke Center represents the Modernist ideals of urban planning at the time, resolving the need for high-density structures by devising a strategy that splits the programme into two parts: a low-scale volume that mediates between the scale of the neighbourhood and the new building, and a high-scale element that towers above, usually receding from the main street, to reduce its impact. Here, Sert divided the administrative functions into two towers, connected by another transversal wing, producing an H-shaped configuration, and appended at the lower levels by two-storey volumes, containing retail functions that connect with the street. The other element of interest that Sert introduced was an internal pedestrian street, lined by shops that provide a connection between the main and back streets.

2.6   Le Corbusier, Carpenter Center for the Visual Arts, Cambridge, Massachusetts, USA, 1963

The whole complex is rendered in *béton brut*, with metallic louvres that mediate sun exposure.

Another master of Modernism, Marcel Breuer, adopted the *béton brut* aesthetic for much of his later work of the 1960s and 1970s, most of which was realised in the United States. His preference for rough concrete for its sculptural qualities was well expressed in one of his statements, where he mentioned the move away from a more abstract

2.7   Josep Lluís Sert, Holyoke Center, Cambridge, Massachusetts, USA, 1960–66

conception of space, in the 1930s, to one that favoured a more sculptural approach:

> After we did some of these spaces, on account of some inner need which you call the development or change of the spirit of the time, mass appealed to us, gravity, solidity, a wall you can lean against and not just a glass wall, which limits your movement. And this change has pushed architecture into what we call a more sculptural concept of architecture.[2]

In addition to the iconic Whitney Museum in New York (1966) – a concrete shell clad in granite – Breuer realised a large number of structures in concrete in the 1960s, among which is a complex of five buildings for New York University at University Heights (1959–70) that includes the central Begrisch Hall (1959–61) (fig.2.8), an elevated structure containing the auditoria, with a distinctive cantilevering profile. Although later associated with the work of Paul Rudolph, it was Breuer who actually pioneered the use of bush-hammering on rough concrete in the 1950s, exposing the aggregate to give the surfaces a distinctive texture. This was first tested on his Grosse Pointe Public Library in Michigan (1952). Among the celebrated examples of Breuer's sculptural architecture is the complex for the Monastery of St. John in Minnesota, which comprises an imposing trapezoidal church and a free-standing bell-tower that takes the shape of a sail, or a bell banner. The structural potentials of concrete were once again

above

2.8 Marcel Breuer, Begrisch Lecture Hall, New York, USA, 1959–61

right

2.9 Marcel Breuer, Church of St. Francis, Muskegon, Michigan, USA, 1964–6

exploited here to offer a free span interior, with the concrete pillars exposed and connecting to the roof beams of the interior. The work on St. John's in Minnesota led to another commission for a religious project, the spectacular Church of St. Francis in Michigan (1964–6) (fig.2.9). As Hyman notes, this is considered one of Breuer's most dramatic and Expressionist buildings, inside and out, with windowless side walls revolving and twisting into hyperbolic paraboloids. The background wall of the altar is composed of an exposed ribbed concrete structure that evokes medieval cathedrals.[3]

Although most critics would put the work of Louis Kahn in a category all of its own, and would reject the designation of 'Brutalism' in characterising his work, there are some legitimate reasons to consider his work in this chapter as well, as Banham alluded to. Kahn's adoption of concrete as a material of choice, which was elegantly expressed in projects such as the church in Rochester, New York, the Salk Institute in La Jolla, California, and the monumental parliament complex in Dhaka, all reinforced the appeal of this new material in architecture, especially in its American context. The impressive manipulation of geometric forms and the play of volumes within volumes would mark Kahn's particular approach to architecture where light would play a major role in sculpting the interior spaces.

The First Unitarian Church and School in Rochester, New York (1959–62) provides us with a clear indication of Kahn's mature style, which consisted of enveloping the primary function, whenever the space requirements would allow it, within an arrangement of secondary functions that would form a buffer zone from the outside and turn the internal function into a well-protected 'cocoon'. In this case, the envelope consisted of the school and ancillary functions, articulated through a repetitive order of vertical elements and windows, uniformly clad in brick. The main church space would have no windows to the outside, but would receive light from above, filtered through four main turrets at each corner, which would turn the ceiling into a cruciform-shaped structure. This element becomes the main form-giver of the space below, and as Robert Mc Carter would describe it:

The inward-folding, downward-sloping form of the ceiling is lowest and darkest at the center of the room, with light coming into the space at the corners. In this way, Kahn's ceiling is the exact opposite of classical church domes, as well as his beloved Pantheon, which are highest and brightest at their centres. Along with the room's layered outer edges, the ceiling and its light-filled corners impart an expansive, boundless character to the sanctuary space, creating a powerful sense of place, of a world within, distant from the outside world.[4]

This important feature of the building was articulated in cast concrete marked by the imprints of the wood-board formwork, and supported at the edges by a set of slender columns, and surrounded by concrete block walls, also left bare to express their materiality. This refined work of architecture may be described as an example of a 'hybrid Brutalism' where cast concrete is used alongside brick, concrete blocks, and wood panelling, all in their natural condition, to project an alternative approach in architecture.

In contrast to the above, the Salk Institute (1959–65) (fig.2.10) was more radical, in that it would employ two materials only – cast concrete and wood panelling – to create another masterpiece overlooking the Pacific Ocean. Conceived originally as part of a larger complex, which would have included an evocative agglomeration of volumes designed as a 'Meeting House', the project was reduced to the essential laboratories, composed within two rectangular volumes facing the sea, with an open court in-between. Appended to the two elements are vertical towers, five on each side, containing the researchers' individual studies on alternating floors, with a tilted wall section to offer a view of the sea. The whole complex is rendered in a refined cast concrete, with a meticulous attention to the details of the formwork, to ensure a smooth finish, with carefully detailed joints between the plywood panels. Within the framework provided by concrete walls and slabs, the studies were enclosed by teak wood panels, serving as insulating walls, openings, and shading devices. Yet as one enters the plaza between the two parallel blocks, one can see only a sequence of concrete walls, tilted at an angle,

2.10 Louis Kahn, Salk Institute for Biological Studies, La Jolla, California, USA, 1959–65

2.11 Louis Kahn, National Assembly Building, Dhaka, Bangladesh, 1962–83

and finely rendered to form a perspectival frame for the horizon beyond.

Kahn's magnum opus was without question the monumental parliament complex in Dhaka, Bangladesh (1962–83) (fig.2.11). This major project – which included a number of institutions, among them the assembly building, the secretariat, and the hospital complex – was laid out as a constellation of elements, with the assembly building occupying a central prominent position. And as in previous projects, Kahn once again employed for this most symbolic structure, the typological format of the introverted central space, surrounded by a sequence of independent volumes of squarish or rectangular format, that contain the supporting functions – in this case, the offices of the parliamentarians, as well as the prayer hall, distinguished by its orientation as well as its cylindrical towers. The central assembly hall, in its circular form, is thus protected by a collage of volumetric elements, in pure forms of cast concrete, accentuated by the horizontal and vertical infills of marble strips that add a textural accent to the austere concrete. The elemental shapes thus appear like historic precedents, owing to Kahn's fascination with the Roman baths of Caracalla, among others. Large circular and triangular openings through the rough concrete allow light to filter into the spaces indirectly. The interior spaces located in the interstices between different elements – containing the stairways and passageways, and also cut through by large circular openings – further accentuate the monumentality of this complex, and highlight the beauty of its rough matter, while the assembly hall projects the symbolic image of a 'world within a world'. As McCarter observed: 'The assembly hall itself is truly a "world within a world" – in both its powerful monumentality and stark simplicity, it is a glorious central, top-lit space as close to his idealised Pantheon as any Kahn would ever realize.'[5]

One of the most controversial projects to be realised in this new style was the City Hall in Boston (1969) (fig.2.12) designed by Kallmann, McKinnell, and Knowles. The three architects were faculty members at Columbia University, and winners of the competition to design this major landmark

THE ARCHITECTURE OF BÉTON BRUT

2.12   Kallmann, McKinnell, and Knowles, Boston City Hall, Boston, Massachusetts, USA, 1969

on the newly created Government Square, part of a major 'urban renewal' plan that saw the erasure of an entire neighbourhood, an example of the tabula rasa that was applied to many cities around the world. The project was controversial not only due to this unpopular decision of radical urban transformation, but for what people saw as an overbearing edifice that showed no affinity or relation to the place, its history, and building traditions. The building in itself is a well-thought-out and finely articulated complex, designed as a singular, monumental block that rises above thick pilasters on the plaza level, opening to the public and allowing visitors to enter its large monumental atrium. The volume is subtracted at the lower levels, to allow for a playful contrast of solids and voids, while at the top, it is crowned by a continuous ring of two office floors, with a monotonous rhythm created by deep fortress-like windows.

The work of Paul Rudolph also attracted great attention in the 1960s and 1970s, as he developed his personal style from a mainstream Modernism, as in the classic Milam Residence in Jacksonville, Florida (1961), to a Brutalist aesthetic first manifested in the Yale School of Architecture (1958–64) (fig.2.13). The Yale School became quite emblematic, displaying a mature style in the treatment of rough concrete into a

2.13   Paul Rudolph, Art and Architecture Building, Yale University, New Haven, Connecticut, USA, 1958–64

2.14 Paul Rudolph, Boston Government Service Center, Boston, Massachusetts, USA, 1962–71

textured material. The building appears to owe its articulation to wood-frame construction, with the concrete posts, pillars, and beams emulating the trabeated construction system, expressing the structural relationships between elements. The rectangular volume was marked at the four corners by vertical elements, containing the stairwells as well as other supporting facilities, and anchoring the building in its context. On the interior, these elements frame the central atrium space, which extends over two floors above ground and looks over the main exhibition space, carrying the studio spaces above. Clerestories in the roof allow for light to enter this atrium space, while the offices and studios benefit from large glazing areas that offer a view of the surroundings. The main characteristic of this building, besides its articulation of elements, was the finishing, whereby the ribbed vertical arrises of concrete were accentuated by manual hammering, a technique that was introduced by Marcel Breuer.

Paul Rudolph's approach was not always well received, and his project for the Boston Government Service Center (1962–71) (fig.2.14) became symptomatic of the lack of sensitivity that modern architecture exhibited in urban contexts. There, the large complex occupying a trapezoidal block, appeared like a bunker turning its back to the city, centred around a large internal plaza.

The gymnastics of this large complex, with its anthropomorphic details, failed to relate to its context and became one of the eyesores of the new development around Government Center, sharing much criticism with its distant neighbour, Boston City Hall. The project was designed to house three main departments: Health, Welfare and Education, Employment, and Mental Health. The first department, which was to occupy a 23-storey tower, was never built, while the two other departments would occupy the offices, arranged like a necklace over six floors around the plaza, spreading out into a labyrinth of footpaths, interspersed with green spaces. Similar to the Yale School of Architecture, Rudolph used the same technique of chiselling the rough concrete, and even a similar articulation of the horizontals and verticals, although given here a much freer form than the geometrically ordered school building.

The modern 'settlement' of Habitat 67 (1963–7) (fig.2.15) in Montreal by Moshe Safdie constitutes another landmark project. The complex, developed as the Canadian pavilion for the World Exhibition of 1967, outlasted its intended life cycle, and continues to serve as a residential complex. Composed of 354 stacked concrete boxes that form 158 apartments, spread over a twelve-storey height, the apartments are serviced from the back, through elevator cores and flying passageways, with their

2.15 Moshe Safdie, Habitat 67, Montreal, Quebec, Canada, 1963–7

fronts open towards the view of the river and the landscape. Safdie's proposal, which originated from his thesis at McGill University, titled 'A Case for City Living', was intended to project a new way of living in urban or suburban contexts, avoiding the typical towers, and also pioneering the use of prefabrication in residential architecture. The prefabrication process took place on-site, with the basic modular shape moulded in a reinforced steel cage. Once cured, the concrete box was transferred to an assembly line, to be fitted with electrical and mechanical systems, insulation, and windows. Modular kitchens and bathrooms were installed and finally, each unit was lifted to its designated position. Despite its use of concrete as a raw material, Safdie himself described this project as a reaction against Brutalism. His intent, through the use of modular architecture and the arrangement of volumes, was to give a more 'humanist' character to modern urban dwelling, offering each apartment its own balcony and views, inspired no doubt by the traditional vernacular architecture that became popular at the time through the publication of Bernard Rudofsky's *Architecture without Architects*.

BÉTON BRUT IN LATIN AMERICA

The appeal of *béton brut* was quite pronounced in Latin America, as witnessed in a number of projects that all espoused this material as a form of expression, and as a symbolic statement of the 'modernisation' process that these countries were intent on undertaking. This interest in the expressive materiality of concrete started with one of the first modern towers, the Ministry of Education and Public Health, in Rio de Janeiro (1936–44) on which Lucio Costa collaborated with Oscar Niemeyer, Alfonso Eduardo Reidy, and with Le Corbusier as a consultant. It later continued in the work of Niemeyer and Costa on the new capital of Brazil, which became emblematic of a new monumentality. Niemeyer, however, transcended the confines of Brutalism to forge his own individual style, which will be addressed in another chapter.

Also in Brazil, Lina Bo Bardi's distinctive style produced some of the masterpieces of the period, among them her Social Service of Commerce in São Paulo (1977–86) (fig.2.16). Located in a

2.16 Lina Bo Bardi, Social Service of Commerce, São Paulo, Brazil, 1977–86

decommissioned industrial site, Bardi rehabilitated part of the industrial complex, adding two structures that stand at an angle to each other, connected by flying bridges at different levels. The existing warehouses were reconfigured for cultural facilities, while the main tower, largely opaque and marked by organic cut-outs that expose the brick colour under the concrete skin, would house sports facilities on its five storeys. The other tower contains additional facilities, as well as the vertical circulation.

In São Paulo, Paulo Mendes da Rocha designed one of his masterpieces, the Brazilian Museum of Sculpture (MuBE) (1986–95) (fig.2.17). Conceived as one element of a large park design, the museum consisted of a main concrete canopy, 60 metres in length, covering the open space under which the museum was tucked, divided into two zones below the pavement, taking advantage of the slope. A more recent project by da Rocha is the impressive 'Cais das Artes', or 'pier of arts', which is a museum and theatre complex located in Vitoria, Brazil (2008). The complex was designed to accommodate a large museum and a theatre on a site that offers inspiring views of the landscape around the large bay. The architect developed the project around two separate blocks, a cubical element containing the theatre, anchored to the ground, and a long, extended slab that houses the museum spaces, suspended over the terrain, to allow for unrestricted views of the landscape. To realise this challenge, the engineers had to conceive of a system of pre-tensioned concrete beams, seven metres in height, that connect to the ground at very limited points.

In Brazil also, João Batista Vilanova Artigas' School of Architecture and Planning at the University of São Paulo (1961) presented a more ascetic facade to the street, with a large concrete canopy, carried by fourteen tapered columns, providing the defining volume to the spaces within, arranged around a top-lit covered court.

In Argentina, the sculptural articulation of concrete found another master in Clorindo Testa, whose Banco de Londres of 1966, in Buenos Aires, presented a playful manipulation of solids and voids, within an exoskeletal structure that shows a mastery of the process of construction beyond simple functional and programmatic requirements.

In Chile, Juan Borchers' Electrical Cooperative (1965) presented a complex set of elements, arranged within a 'rational' framework of a rectangular concrete box. Yet the interior surprises the visitor with its expressive forms, internal ramps, and brise-soleils that filter the light coming in. There is no question that Le Corbusier's work was a direct influence here, specifically his Millowners' Association Building in Ahmedabad. Also in Chile, Emilio Duhart's CEPAL Building in Santiago (1966) – with its elegant horizontal slab of concrete, elevated above the ground, and marked by the spiral of the assembly hall which projects above the slab like a turret or a campanile – recalls Le Corbusier's work in Chandigarh, albeit on a smaller scale.

In Latin America as a whole, the fascination with Brutalism continued unabated, with the old masters as well as younger ones continuing to favour concrete as a material of choice, for structure as well as envelope, well into the new millennium. The School of Economics and Business at the Diego Portales University in Santiago, Chile by Rafael Hevia, Rodrigo Duque Motta, and Gabriela Manzi (2013) presents another example of a new interpretation in concrete. Rather than

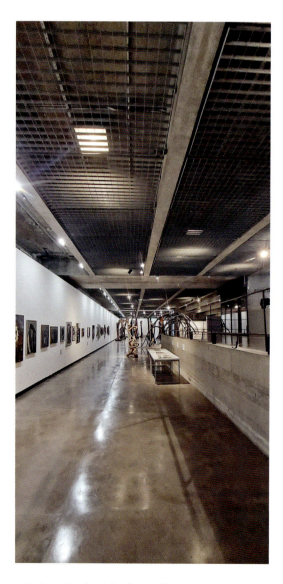

2.17 Paulo Mendes da Rocha, Brazilian Museum of Sculpture (MuBE), São Paulo, Brazil, 1986–95

relying on the typical office block to house the new function, the architects split the programme into two blocks, one rectilinear, the other cubical, joined by a plaza which also accommodates basement functions such as auditoria. The rectilinear volume is marked by alternating rhythms of concrete louvres on the southern facade, lined by the service corridors, and articulated by different colour patterns on each floor. The main element, housing the offices and classrooms, is a cubical volume, raised above the plaza through a 'carving out' of its ground floor, which renders that space into a sculptural form. The irregular openings on the facades put into emphasis the rough texture of the concrete surfaces. As Tom Wilkinson noted in *The Architectural Review*, these buildings 'hark back – as only South American architecture does today – to the glory days of Brutalism, revelling in the possibilities of concrete without, however, wallowing in mere nostalgia'.[6]

Foreign architects working in Latin America also resorted to concrete as a material of choice. Grafton Architects' recent landmark for the University of Engineering and Technology in Lima, Peru (2015) (fig.2.18) brings to mind the work of Clorindo Testa, although the architects mentioned other sources of inspiration, namely the ruins of Machu Pichu and the natural peaks of Skellig Michael off the coast of Kerry.[7] The large structure with its stacked floors and interconnecting voids, was composed as a series of vertical concrete plates perpendicular to the main avenue, which carry the various functions of classrooms, laboratories, and ancillary spaces. The architectural concept revolved around the idea of creating an artificial cliff that responds to the natural context, with green areas interspersed within the various floors. From a distance, the complex appears like a giant sculpture, with its play of solids and voids, all rendered in concrete. Composed on an irregular site, the trapezoidal floor plan adjusts to the constraints while providing a spacious interior featuring a large atrium space that extends over several floors, with flying staircases connecting the different floors, and allowing much of the natural light to percolate through the space. In a sense, the architects succeeded in creating a vertical campus with a stimulating internal experience.

2.18   Grafton Architects, University of Engineering and Technology, Lima, Peru, 2015

BRUTALISM IN THE FAR EAST

In Japan, the Brutalist aesthetic found a number of protagonists, among whom figures Arata Isozaki, an architect whose career would move across different styles. His first commissions, such as the Oita Medical Center (1960) and the Oita Prefectural Library (1962–6) (fig.2.19), were imposing structures of concrete that demonstrate a particular version of Brutalism, inspired by the Metabolist movement.

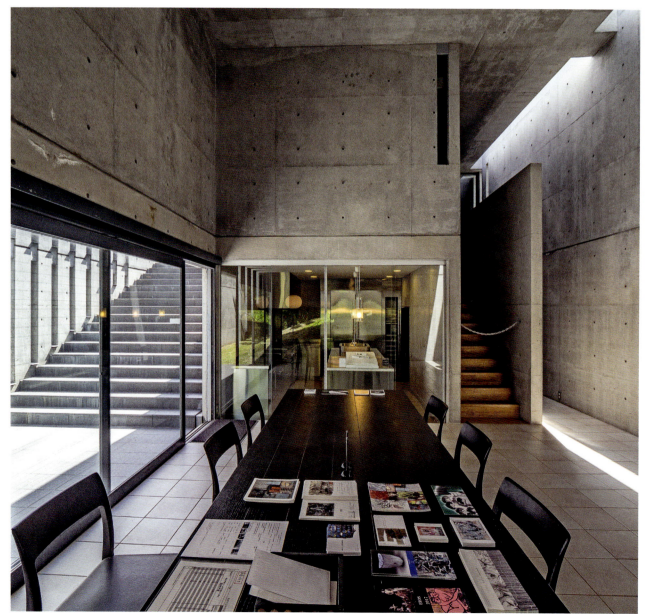

left, top
2.19   Arata Isozaki, Oita Prefectural Library, Oita, Japan, 1962–6

left, bottom
2.20   Tadao Ando, Koshino House Ashiya, Japan, 1979–84

A more refined version of Brutalism in Japan appeared in the work of Tadao Ando, whose approach was sometimes described as 'Minimalist'. Starting with his first solo commission, the Tomishima House in Osaka (1973), Ando displayed his main architectural strategy based on the use of simple geometric forms, in this case a rectangular form that occupies the whole site, with limited openings to the outside, while allowing light to enter the house through a roof skylight. The rendering of this simple box in rough concrete further accentuates his ascetic approach. The articulation of concrete structures continued with later projects, though in a more refined way, as in the Koshino House in Ashiya (1979–84) (fig.2.20) where two parallel elements form the body of the house, separated at ground level by an external stairway, and connected underground through a passageway. The passageway links the first element, which contains the living, dining, and master bedrooms, with the second which contains a row of six bedrooms for children and guests. While the main living room space has a wide window opening towards the garden, its double height space is washed by the light coming down through a corner slit running along the wall, revealing the tapestry-like texture of the concrete wall.

Another jewel in the series of houses by Ando is the Izutsu House in Osaka (1982), located in the midst of a dense urban fabric composed of shops, factories, and houses, beneath their typical, pitched roofs. Here, Ando installed his concrete box, with its walls around the site perimeter, divided into two halves: on one side, an open courtyard with a stairway serving the three levels of the house, while in the other half are located the main functions. Ando used the same formal strategy on other functions, specifically religious structures, of which he designed quite a few. The church on Mount Rokko (1985) is, again, a concrete box with an adjoining bell-tower. The interior is ascetically rendered: a composition of concrete walls, one of which is glazed from floor to ceiling, while the main altar wall presents a simple surface, with light percolating through a slit in the ceiling.

Among the public institutions designed by Ando, the Chikatsu-Asuka Historical Museum (1991–4) in Osaka occupies a special position. Designed to exhibit the artifacts found in the tombs of the Kofun culture, the building is actually conceived as an extension of the landscape: a wide forum of terraced steps serving as an outdoor amphitheatre, underneath which are integrated the exhibition spaces. Distinct elements punctuate this wide field, in the form of three squares, one of which serves as a small campanile, while the others introduce light to the underground spaces.

CONTEMPORARY BRUTALISM

Following its destitution in the 1970s, with the rise of Post-Modernism and the return to a more symbolic and less monumental architecture, Brutalism witnessed a comeback in recent years, with many architects from all over the world exploring again the potentials of this material. The evolution of a 'Neo-Brutalist' language over recent years has produced a number of refined works that cross the boundary towards 'Minimalism', and project interesting contrasts between the roughness of the material and the natural landscape. Among the many examples of this approach one can mention the work of Wang Shu and Vector Architects in China; Hevia, Duque Motta, and Manzi in Chile; Zakarian and Navelet in France; and Bernardo Bader in Austria.

Vector Architects' Seashore Library in China (2014–15) (fig.2.21) is a masterpiece in concrete, sitting over the sand, close to the ocean. It contains a large reading room with stepped floors and additional spaces for stacks, administration, and archives. The language is based on a clear articulation of components, creating a sculptural volume with multiple viewpoints. Their Seashore Chapel (2015) is an equally evocative and poetic structure, raised on pilotis and accessible by a ceremonial stairway leading to a sparse interior

Exterior and interior
2.21 Vector Architects, Seashore Library, Beidaihe New District, China, 2014–15

2.22 Wang Shu – Amateur Architecture Studio, Ningbo History Museum, Ningbo, China, 2008

with a framed view of the sea. The building stands on the shore like an abandoned ship, with its sharp gable roof, built of concrete and whitewashed walls.

On a more monumental scale, the project by Wang Shu for the Ningbo History Museum (2008) (fig.2.22) – which was characterised by several critics as representing a new direction in Chinese architecture with a regional accent – may also be considered as representative of another version of 'Brutalism'. This contemporary work blends raw materials, from concrete to bricks, in a rough interpretation of a vernacular way of building. The large-scale museum, which appears upon approach as a vast rectangular block with an irregular facade of various materials, takes the form of a canyon of 'valleys' and 'caves' upon reaching the upper platform, where open courtyards meander through the different carved-out blocks. The building sits like a fortress, or an artificial mountain with external walls of cement mixed with bamboo, with broken tiles collected from the destroyed houses that have been cleared in the area, adding more texture to these monumental, abstract walls.

In Mexico, the work of Alberto Kalach also merits attention. His Jojutla School (2019) (fig.2.23) was conceived as a rectangular grid of eight bays around two open courtyards, carried by a structure of concrete arches spanning in two directions. The arches support a coffered ceiling of concrete, while the interplay between the concrete structure and some elements of brick – such as the partition walls and the cylindrical tower that rises slightly above the single-storey structure – bring to mind the work of Louis Kahn. Internally, the classrooms are all arranged along the two sides of the plan, with lattice-wood partitions providing partial enclosures and allowing for air circulation.

In the European context, a number of recent projects have also favoured a return to concrete, left in its raw materiality and sometimes combined with other materials such as granite or wood. The Crematorium Siesegem in Belgium by KAAN Architecten (2013–19) (fig.2.24) is a case in point, with concrete used for the overall form and structure, yet complemented on the interior with panels of marble, cut into large sections that clad the walls of the main assembly hall. The polished concrete presents a marked contrast to the textured marble, resulting in a rich interior space that befits the function of a memorial hall. Zakarian and Navelet's Place du Village House in Giens, France (2015–19) (fig.2.25) presents a simple composition of two rectangular elements, parallel to each other, and framed by a third, squarish volume. This composition delivers a contextual house, while providing an open-air courtyard that blends with the surroundings. Located on a promontory overlooking the Mediterranean, this small house is built of

2.23 Taller de Arquitectura X (Alberto Kalach and Roberto Silva), Jojutla School, Jojutla, Oaxaca, Mexico, 2019

2.24 KAAN Architecten, Crematorium Siesegem, Aalst, Belgium, 2013–19

2.25 Zakarian-Navelet Architectes, Place du Village House (Maison à Giens), Giens, France, 2015–19

2.26   Bernardo Bader, Klostergasse Studio, Bregenz, Austria, 2017–19

in-situ poured concrete, its texture marked by the fir planks used for the formwork.

The office designed for the architectural firm of Bernardo Bader presents another exquisite example of a refined Brutalist work on a small scale. The Klostergasse Studio (2017–19) (fig.2.26), located in the centre of the city of Bregenz in Austria, is a slender rectangular structure that comprises the offices of the firm spread over four floors, with alternating windows distributed over the facade to break the monotony, as well as to offer different views. The whole building is rendered in a dark grey concrete, from floors to walls and ceilings, left untreated to feature the textural quality of the material. The stairway presents an additional point of interest, with its carved-out, organic pattern creating an element of contrast to the plain rectilinearity of the office spaces.

If these projects from diverse parts of the world confirm anything, it is that Brutalism never really died with the late works of Le Corbusier, but rather took on various forms and continues to exert its appeal in different contexts, with its association to Minimalism in some cases, and to more monumental forms in other cases.

3 Neo-Rationalism

Neo-Rationalism was started as an Italian movement, known as La Tendenza, by a group of young architects in Italy in the 1960s, who were trying to find their own way out of the Modernist orthodoxy, while not necessarily breaking with Modernism. As the affiliation indicated, they were historical heirs to the 'rationalist' movement of Gruppo 7 of the 1920s–1930s. The group was an informal gathering of young architects, formed around Ludovico Quaroni, Ernesto Rogers, and Giuseppe Samonà, comprising the emergent voices of Aldo Rossi, Giorgio Grassi, Guido Canella, Vittorio Gregotti, and Carlo Aymonino.

One of their main goals was to re-inscribe the architectural project within its urban context. The importance of re-orienting the architectural discourse towards the city had, as one of its principal goals, to anchor the architectural project within the larger dimension and reaffirm its broader extension into the realms of history, sociology, and economics. The architectural project would therefore be reconsidered under a new set of criteria, drawn from the theoretical discourse of the Enlightenment all the way to early modernity, including the questions of typology and morphology. Besides Aldo Rossi, Giorgio Grassi also played a key role in the new movement, drawing on the lessons of the German Modernists, as a means to elaborate a 'rationalist' agenda, based on research into constant types and norms.[1]

Neo-Rationalism did not remain restricted to its Italian context, but spread throughout Europe and the rest of the world. Its multiple variations, which took many forms, expanded from the context of Italy to Switzerland (where Rossi left an impact through his teaching at the ETH in Zurich), and to Germany, the UK, and other countries. Eventually, Neo-Rationalism came to embody a certain approach that reaffirms architecture as the art of building, based on a 'rational' method that counters both the expressionistic and eclectic design tendencies that permeated architectural production in the Post-Modern period. In certain contexts, this was based on classical principles of organisation, proportion, and hierarchy, without resorting to historicist or symbolic associations.

NEO-RATIONALISM: THE ITALIAN ORIGINAL

Aldo Rossi played a prominent role, both as a theoretician and a practising architect, in the elaboration of the Neo-Rationalist agenda. In his main thesis, *The Architecture of the City*, he developed a framework for the investigation of the city as a human construct through time. Rossi's intent was to present a 'scientific' (one could say structuralist) theory of the city, based on an analytical approach that would incorporate quantitative as well as qualitative criteria. The structuralist influence is perceptible through the first reference that he made to Ferdinand de Saussure and his own attempt to follow Saussure's linguistic model and translate it into a 'program for the development of an urban science: description and history of existing cities; research on the forces that are at play in a permanent and universal way in all urban artifacts; and naturally, delimitation and definition of the field of study'.[2] Intertwined within this structuralist framework are other notable influences: Marxist references to the political aspects of urbanism as influenced by class struggle; anthropological references to the role played by ritual in the founding of cities and their continuity; and ontological references to the Greek City as a model.

Aldo Rossi's role within the Tendenza movement definitely left an impact on his theoretical approach to architecture, which did not prevent him from developing his own idiosyncratic style: a mix between the Neo-Rationalist approach marked by a revival of classical typologies, and a poetic tendency that would remain personal.

NEO-RATIONALISM

left, top

3.1 Aldo Rossi, Gallaratese Quarter 2, Milan, Italy, 1969–73

left, bottom

3.2 Carlo Aymonino, Gallaratese Quarter 2, Milan, Italy, 1969–73

below

3.3 Aldo Rossi, Elementary School in Fagnano Olona, Varese, Italy, 1972–6

This approach was always marked by two poles: on the one hand, the legacy of the Enlightenment architects and theoreticians such as Boullée, Durand, and Ledoux; and on the other, the work of early modern architects, specifically Adolf Loos. In his early projects, one can trace the influence of Loos,[3] as in the Villa ai Ronchi (1960), where the arrangement of simple cubical elements defines the habitation, without any ornamental features.

The same formal approach that Rossi took in his early work, continued with his major commission for a residential block in the Gallaratese district of Milan (1969–73) (fig.3.1). This project constituted one element of a larger complex, designed by Carlo Aymonino. The contrast between Aymonino's irregular composition of multiple units (fig.3.2) and Rossi's solitary block facing them in a stoic manner, reaffirms its particularity. The 200-metre-long slab refers to the 'urban block' that is common in the suburbs of Italian cities, but takes it to an extreme. Composed as a set of two storeys of apartments raised above a covered portico, rhythmically punctuated by repetitive vertical 'fins', the apartments open up to the outside through square windows. The rectilinear composition of square windows, tall and thin pilasters, and cylindrical markers gives this complex a distinctive character, allowing for a very complex sequence of paths and meeting areas that form a public space on the ground level.

With the Elementary School in Fagnano Olona (1972–6) (fig.3.3), Rossi moved on to adopt specific typologies as an organisational system for the architectural project. Centred around an internal courtyard, which becomes a recurrent feature

41

MODERN ARCHITECTURE IN A POST-MODERN ERA

NEO-RATIONALISM

3.4 Aldo Rossi, Friedrichstadt Housing Block,
Berlin, Germany, 1981–7

in many of his public projects, a series of wings extend laterally from the public space to contain the regular, squarish classrooms, organised along longitudinal corridors. Fronting the whole composition is the main pavilion, comprising the administrative offices and the canteen, while the internal court is marked by two elements: a large stairway that doubles as an amphitheatre, facing the cylindrical volume housing the library. This cylindrical element is given a distinctive feature, a lightly conical roof, covered in metal sheets, with a rooftop skylight. The combination of rectangular blocks with cylindrical elements, all platonic solids, becomes a marker of the Rossian language.

The transformation in Rossi's work, from the 'purist' phase to a more 'historicist' phase can be clearly seen in the contrast between the housing in Gallaratese and the one designed for the IBA project in Berlin (1981–7) (fig.3.4). Despite his claim to 'contextualism', Rossi here adopts a language that is not particularly common in the context of the city – namely the combined use of red bricks and exposed metallic profiles. Given that his projects respect the notion of 'perimeter' and the adjoining urban fabric, this one articulates its distinctive presence by using a colourful palette of materials, and through the insertion of the steel lintels that frame the windows and the glass curtain walls, a clear reference to industrial structures. The complex is further articulated by the steep, pitched elements that crown the circulation towers and mark the rhythm of the facade. At the corner of the two streets, Rossi inserts another element that would become one of his 'signatures', a large cylindrical column that recalls Filarete's column on the Venetian canal. The same element reappears in his Residential Building in the Vialba district in Milan (1985).

The poetic approach of Rossi is perhaps best expressed in the Teatro del Mondo, created for the Venice Biennale (1980). This temporary structure was built out of wooden planks on a steel frame, as a floating theatre for the exhibition *Venezia e lo spazio scenico*. It was towed across the sea in the summer of 1980 to participate as a 'visiting' architectural project in other cities, as in the Theatre Festival of Dubrovnik. The Theatre of the World, explained Aldo Rossi, is characterised by three facts: it has a precise yet undefined usable

43

3.5 Aldo Rossi, Bonnefanten Museum, Maastricht, the Netherlands, 1990–94

space; it figures as a volume following the form of Venetian movement; and it is on the water: 'It appears obvious that being on the water is its primary characteristic, a raft, a boat: the limit or boundary of construction in Venice.' A poetic interpretation was offered by Daniel Libeskind who perceived it as a 'hieroglyph' that alludes to emptiness as a main element in architecture. This theatre, according to Libeskind, offers an insight into the 'fragile connection that subsists between space and architecture, between a body and its spirit'.[4]

Another project by Rossi that showcases his rational/poetic approach is the Bonnefanten Museum (1990–94) (fig.3.5) in Maastricht. The typical E-shape plan culminates here at its middle wing in a cylindrical tower, crowned by a zinc-plated elliptical dome that features an open belvedere, providing an element of contrast to the plain facades of red brick walls. One enters this building at the central wing, into a foyer that is marked by a telescopic, ziggurat-shaped tower that draws light into the interior, and then proceeds onto a ceremonial stairway, framed by brick walls, and covered by a simple pitched roof with an exposed wood truss-construction, culminating in the large, domical space. A composition of pure elements that carries specific connotations for Rossi:

> The foyer leads directly to the living part of the building: the essence of the museum. This essence is difficult, if not impossible, to define: is the museum a collection of memories of life? Is it itself part of our life? Our architecture leaves the question unanswered, referring it to a more general appraisal. The essence of the museum nevertheless continues to constitute the beginning and the end of our cultural decline.

Now we climb the stairs which are steep and belong to an old Dutch tradition and are tied to the Gothic world of Shakespearean taverns as well as to the staggering characters of Conrad's novels and to all the northerners shipwrecked in southern seas. We have tried to represent the essence of this world, in the knowledge that beyond geometry there is only the shipwreck.[5]

The building projects an industrial appearance, which relates to the history of Maastricht, emphasised by the zinc-clad dome. The dome was intended as a reference to Europe's classical architecture, specifically the work of Alessandro Antonelli in Turin, but it also connotes grain silos and industrial architecture.

A second major commission in Berlin would offer Rossi an opportunity for the deployment of historical quotations. Here, at the Schützenstrasse (1992–7) (fig.3.6) the architect was faced with the challenge of re-stitching a whole block of the city, of which only one Neo-Classical building remained standing. Incorporating this lone fragment in the composition, Rossi resorted to a polychromatic collage, combining different materials (brick, stone, metal, concrete) in different tones and textures, to reconstitute a section of the city, while avoiding the monotony of singular blocks. The large block was subdivided into smaller sections, arranged around three internal courtyards: one square, one rectangular, and one octagonal, containing a diverse mix of functions: residential units, hotel, offices, and retail.

Giorgio Grassi's approach towards architecture was more radical in the sense of adhering to the strict geometry of specific types, repeated without any concern for variations or embellishments. Whereas Rossi's style was more varied and nuanced, Grassi's rigorous discipline prevailed over other considerations, which earned him a particular position in the Neo-Rationalist camp. In his analysis of the work of Grassi, the Spanish architect Ignasi de Solà-Morales summarised the characteristic traits of his architecture:[6]

Thus, for Grassi, the repertoires of clear and elemental solutions are permanent. Reinforcing the synchronic character of his structuralist focus through formal typological analysis, he tends to downplay the notion of historical change, privileging in turn the permanence and immutability of types. A certain metaphysical, if potentially schematic, conception of basic forms seems to run through his thinking, opposing the experimentalism of modern architecture.[7]

And further on:

In contradistinction to the ever more personal and autobiographical tone in Rossi's architecture, immersed in the heights and depths of dream, and the nostalgic *trompe-l'oeil* re-creations of the bourgeois city in the work of Leon Krier, Grassi's work maintains a stripped-down dryness, a quality which one also encounters in the best Minimalist artworks of this period.[8]

Grassi's project for Student Housing in Chieti, Italy (1979), is exemplary in this regard: composed of two arcaded elements facing each other across a well-proportioned street, they recall to some extent Neo-Classical compositions such as Weinbrenner's Royal Avenue in Karlsruhe, Germany. The uniform street frontage and the full-height open gallery make a symbolic architectural statement that reaffirms the social dimension of student housing. The project is divided into three blocks on each side, containing the dormitories, and two blocks containing the public functions, such as the cafeteria. Each dormitory block culminates into a communal living room that overlooks the public colonnade.

The Public Library in Groningen (1989) further articulates this typological method. The library complex fits well into its context of traditional row-houses by respecting the same rhythm along the street, the scale of the houses, and the materials, without emulating their historical form. Grassi divided the building front into two equal slabs, separated by a void that maintains the street rhythm and incorporates an alleyway that leads to the entrance. One slab is for offices, while the other houses the library, which expands at the back side of the plot, occupying a large section of the site. The whole complex is rendered in plain brick, avoiding any ornamentation or mannerism.

MODERN ARCHITECTURE IN A POST-MODERN ERA

3.6 Aldo Rossi, Schützenstrasse, Berlin, Germany, 1992–7

As mentioned above by Solà-Morales, the strict observance of the rules of construction brings the work of Grassi close to that elementary quality of Minimalism.

Vittorio Gregotti is the rather odd character in the Tendenza movement. Despite his active presence in it, Gregotti's agenda seemed to veer more towards a 'structuralist' analysis of the city, and by extension the 'territory', rather than a 'typological' or 'rationalist' approach to form as interpreted by Rossi. His concept of the 'territory' owes much to Giuseppe Samonà, who first introduced it into the architectural discourse of post-war Italy.[9] Gregotti published his seminal *Il Territorio dell'architettura* in 1962,[10] in which he articulated a conceptual framework that positions architecture within the larger context of the territory, as well as within a multi-layered historical framework.[11] Gregotti occupied a number of key positions throughout his career, serving on the editorial board of *Casabella* under the leadership of Ernesto Rogers, and later becoming its editor-in-chief, from 1982 to 1996, as well as playing an important role later as director of the Venice Biennale (1974–6), effectively introducing architecture to this major event.

In one of his essays, Gregotti provides a complex explanation of his vision of the concept of territory as environment, which carries within it the layers of history, and the role that the architectural project is bound to play in this context:

> The physical spirit of history is the built environment which surrounds us, the manner of its transformation into visible things, its gathering of depths and meanings which differ not only because of what the environment appears to be, but also because of what it *is* structurally. The environment is composed of the traces of its own history. If geography is the way in which the signs of history solidify and are superimposed in a form, the architectural project has the task of drawing attention to the essence of the environmental context through the transformation of form.[12]

One of his major works, the University of Calabria (1973–9) (fig.3.7), illustrates his approach to the

3.7 Vittorio Gregotti, University of Calabria, Arcavacata, Cosenza, Italy, 1973–9

concept of the territory, by laying out an axial system stretching two kilometres over the whole site, organising it into a sequence of blocks, each dedicated to a separate academic department. Similar in some ways to Le Corbusier's project for Algiers, the complex floats over the territory, with minimal incursion over the topography below it. Gregotti explained his concept in these terms:

> The project also attempts to bring about an interaction between the morphological and functional systems. The first system consists of a linear succession of university departments running across the hill system to the plain of River Crati. The blocks housing the departmental activities accommodate the varying levels of the land and are laid out on a square plan on the axis of a bridge. The second system considers the morphology of the hills, the succession of their slopes and peaks (which carry the local road system) and their relationship to the fabric of the low-tiered houses along the northern slope intended as university residences. Since the southern slopes are cultivated with olive trees, an alternating succession of residential units and natural spaces results.[13]

This interplay of nature/architecture appears to owe more to structuralist tendencies of the period than to any notions of type or typology. In the initial drawings submitted for the project, the buildings appear like mechanical components, clad in prefabricated panels,[14] bringing to mind the early projects of James Stirling, such as the Olivetti Training School (1969–72). The buildings were realised later in a more subdued tone, with painted concrete blocks and plain wall surfaces rendered in an earthy colour, contrasting with the steel panels of the passageways, bridges, and external stairways.

The work of the Tendenza architects was not limited to these figures, but included other major architects such as Gianuggo Polesello and Guido Canella. Among the realised works of Polesello is the complex for the University of Las Palmas in the Canary Islands (1988–91), a project that attempts to reinvent a classical architectural language by using new technologies, with concrete pillars forming the structure that carries the circulation elements, connecting bridges and glass walls, within an overall 'scheme' that carries elements of composition derived from Greek and Roman types.

Guido Canella designed the Pieve Emanuele Civic Centre in Lombardy, Italy (1971–81), which assumes the allure of a medieval castle with cylindrical brick towers, connected by a cantilevered, metal-clad slab that owes more perhaps to Brutalism than to mainstream Neo-Rationalism.

NEO-RATIONALISM: THE SECOND WAVE

A second wave of Neo-Rationalism appeared as an offspring of the Italian movement of the 1970s, spreading mainly in the European context, with the brothers Rob and Léon Krier in London, Oswald Mathias Ungers in Berlin, and later joined by Mario Botta and a contingent of Swiss architects, who were no doubt influenced by the teachings of Aldo Rossi at the ETH in Zurich.

The brothers Krier played an important role in giving the Neo-Rationalist agenda another direction, by focusing their studies on the important notion of 'urban space', analysing in a methodical manner the failures of modern architecture, and proposing to re-establish the connections with the historic traditions of the 18th and 19th centuries, especially in the context of the European city. Rob Krier's publication on this topic, *Stadtraum*, which appeared in 1975, bore a direct connection to Camillo Sitte's *Der Städtebau nach seinen künstlerischen Grundsätzen* (1889). It was translated as *Urban Space*,[15] and given an enthusiastic foreword by Colin Rowe, the main theoretician behind the revival of the notion of urban context in architecture.

Rob Krier's book was more like an illustrated manifesto, with a clear pedagogical presentation of the main principles and patterns of proper urbanism and an analysis of the morphologies and typologies of urban spaces. After introducing the premises of his argument, Krier proceeded to review the 'erosion of urban space in 20th-century town planning' and then proposing alternatives for remedying this condition that came as a result of the combined war destructions and so-called 'urban renewal' projects. While Rossi discussed the notions of morphology and typology at a theoretical level, Krier was the one to provide an illustrated guidebook, articulating a set of directives on how to re-design public spaces that would reaffirm the continuity of historic cities.

In practice, the Krier brothers' agenda was geared towards a revival of the 19th-century European city which veered into a revival of Neo-Classicism. This can be seen in several of their proposed urban rehabilitation projects, as well as projects for new towns, such as Rob Krier's masterplan for Leinfelden in Germany (1971), the urban proposal for Altona-Nord in Hamburg (1978–81), and the several urban proposals for Berlin which led to the housing complexes such as Schinkelplatz (1977–87) with its assorted units organised around a large public square, and the housing on the Tiergarten (1980), a composition of urban 'villa types' around a rectangular court, framed at one end by a brick-clad crescent building with two campanile towers at either end.

Léon Krier in turn proposed his own version of architecture with a revivalist agenda that takes its cues from regional and historicist influences, as in his project for a new town in Poundbury, England (1993–) (fig.3.8), commissioned by Prince Charles as an antithesis to the Modernist city and its abstract blocks. The individual units of this planned town would be commissioned to different architects, to ensure variety within a set of guidelines that re-introduce traditional forms and materials, pitched roofs, and Victorian details. The design of the town around informal piazzas and pedestrian paths and alleys was also inspired by Sitte's theory of town planning, rejecting wide avenues and axial patterns.

NEO-RATIONALISM

Neo-Rationalism in Germany took other forms, with several players reinterpreting the tendency towards the revival of historic types, but in an even stricter version, more in line with the work of Giorgio Grassi. Among the main actors in this movement were Oswald Mathias Ungers and Josef Paul Kleihues.

Oswald Mathias Ungers' legacy in architecture was largely as a theoretician and an educator. After completing his architectural studies at Karlsruhe in 1950, he set up his practice first in Cologne and later in Berlin, then in Frankfurt and back to Karlsruhe. During his time in Berlin, he also began an academic career at the Technical University, serving as Dean of the school from 1965 to 1967. He later accepted a position at Cornell University, from 1969 to 1975, returning to Germany in 1976. Notable among his students were Rem Koolhaas, Max Dudler, Hans Kolhoff, and Christoph Maeckler.

Ungers advocated a revival of historic types, re-composed and subjected to transformations to suit contemporary requirements. Among the several projects that he designed, although not realised, the project for Hotel Berlin illustrates a methodology of reinterpreting basic typologies, in this case the 'topos' of a circular drum within a rectangular form. The rectangle is divided into two sections: a square that contains the circular form and the remainder section which acts as a formal entry to the interior. The perimeter block contains the rooms of the hotel, elevated above a portico, which would simulate a city wall.

Among the realised projects of Ungers, the Museum of Architecture in Frankfurt (1979–84) (fig.3.9) consisted of the restoration of an existing mansion on the riverfront, where the architect played on the notion of a house-within-a-house, leading to an upper level where the 'original hut' is symbolically re-created. The methodology employed consisted of building another armature within the house, a three-dimensional grid of columns that carry the museum floors, reaching to the top. The whole site is enclosed, allowing an outdoor space at the back, also framed by a set of columns, through which nature infiltrates, offering the architect the opportunity to create a dialectic between a geometric order and natural elements.

3.8   Léon Krier, New Town, Poundbury, UK, 1993–

51

left, top

3.9   Oswald Mathias Ungers, Museum of Architecture, Frankfurt, Germany, 1979–84

left, bottom

3.10   Oswald Mathias Ungers, Baden State Library, Karlsruhe, Germany, 1991

right

3.11   Josef Paul Kleihues, Archaeological Museum, Frankfurt, Germany, 1984–8

The Baden State Library in Karlsruhe (1991) (fig.3.10) gave Ungers another opportunity to respond to a large programme within a historic context, in this case, Karlsruhe, a Neo-Classical city realised according to the plans of Friedrich Weinbrenner, and marked by several of his buildings. The new library would replace the one that was demolished during the Second World War, and would be re-composed on a rational grid, occupying a whole quadrant.

Josef Paul Kleihues's greater impact was in the direction he gave to the reconstruction of several sites within the western section of Berlin, before unification, as part of the IBA programme. Between 1979 and 1987, Kleihues was appointed as head of the IBA, which was conceived as an 'international exhibition' on architecture. Besides his role as head of this agency and his active role as theoretician, critic, and educator, he had to his credit a number of projects, many of which were not realised. Among his realised works is the Archaeological Museum in Frankfurt (1984–8) (fig.3.11), part restoration of an existing cloister with its church, and part addition of new administrative quarters, rendered in a planar style of polished travertine, with exquisite detailing. Another example by Kleihues is the Museum in Kornwestheim, a collage of a skewed rectangular element with a semi-circle that adapts to the site, the whole rendered in travertine. The rectangular pavilion features a roof of repetitive skylights, reminiscent of industrial structures, but ennobled here by the stone cladding.

At the intersection of Swiss, Italian, and American influences, we can locate the special case of Mario Botta. Botta received his education at the IUAV

MODERN ARCHITECTURE IN A POST-MODERN ERA

left

3.12   Mario Botta, Single-Family House in Riva San Vitale, Switzerland, 1971–3

below

3.13   Mario Botta, BSI Bank (formerly Gottardo Bank), Lugano, Switzerland, 1982–8

in Venice, and during that time met Le Corbusier, Carlo Scarpa, and Louis Kahn. The influence of Kahn on Botta is quite noticeable in the majority of his works, which rely on clear geometric compositions, and in some cases reiterate the concept of the room-within-a-room, and the interrelation between served and serving spaces.

From his early works, such as the Single-Family House in Riva San Vitale in Switzerland (1971–3) (fig.3.12), Botta exhibited this interest in pure forms, rendered with polished stones, concrete, and/or brick layers. This particular house, built on a hillside overlooking Lake Lugano, has the appearance of a cubical campanile, a subtracted volume of concrete blocks accessible via a steel bridge from the upper level of the site. The carved volume allows the architect to embed the openings in the form of glass curtain walls within the enclosure, avoiding direct openings to the exterior. A few years later, Botta used a similar approach at the house at Ligornetto, Ticino (1976),

which appears as a marker in the field, a boundary that is almost opaque to the exterior, covered by alternating bands of coloured stone. The house is composed of a rectangular slab, sliced in the middle by a passageway that separates the two halves into the public and private spheres. It consists of three floors, with the ground floor used for services and parking, while the first-floor acts as a piano nobile. A geometrical cut-out is subtracted from the rectangular block at the upper floors to introduce light into the various spaces, again avoiding any traditional openings.

One clear example of Kahn's influence on Botta is the BSI Bank (formerly Gottardo Bank) in Lugano (1982–8) (fig.3.13), which applies the principle of repetition to create a monumental composition. Instead of one continuous block, the architect divided the programme into four interconnected blocks, based on a V-shape plan that culminates into a rectangular element, and linked to a 'datum' line of offices and passageways. The articulation of elements, and the conceptual framework, bring to mind Kahn's approach, specifically his design for the dormitories at Bryn Mawr College.

This desire for monumentality also finds its translation in larger institutional and religious projects, such as the San Francisco Museum of Modern Art (1989–95) (fig.3.14), conceived as a simple geometric volume, a large multi-layered podium of brick, perforated at its centre by a cylindrical tower wrapped in bands of black and white stone. The top of the cylinder is truncated at an angle and sheathed in glass, creating a giant oculus that brings in natural light to the interior. Around the same time, Botta designed the large cathedral of Evry in France (1988–95) which also features a large cylinder containing the church itself and admitting light through its large oculus. The cylindrical space is wrapped on three sides by a U-shaped rectangular volume that accommodates auxiliary functions, the whole clad in brick, which is rendered on the interior of the church into exquisite courses of alternating bands, recalling the details of Scarpa. This propensity towards the 'Gesamtkunstwerk', with a particular attention to craftsmanship, finds its culmination in the design of all furnishings, such as benches and altar, the latter rendered into a refined composition of Carrara marble blocks.

3.14   Mario Botta, San Francisco Museum of Modern Art (MoMA), San Francisco, California, USA, 1989–95

NEO-RATIONALISM: THE THIRD WAVE

Some historians may object to the notion that Neo-Rationalism extends to our contemporary period, and would only restrict it to its original Italian context, or its close derivatives in Germany and the United Kingdom. Yet the influences of that movement – either directly through the generation which studied under Aldo Rossi or Oswald Mathias Ungers, or indirectly through the survival and dissemination of ideas – warrant the designation of such works in the same lineage. This new version of Neo-Rationalism spread beyond the original foothold of Italy and Switzerland, and later Germany, to inspire other architects around the world, who adopted a more restrained architectural approach in contrast with the efflorescence of the more 'Expressionist' tendencies of others, like Frank Gehry and Zaha Hadid. It is as if the old dichotomy between 'standardisation' and 'artistic will' – which was at the heart of the debate of the Werkbund on the eve of the First World War, and which then

3.15 David Chipperfield, Am Kupfergraben, Berlin, Germany, 2003–7

3.16 David Chipperfield, Museum of Modern Literature, Marbach am Neckar, Germany, 2001–6

pitted Hermann Muthesius against Henry van de Velde – came back to life in a new form.

It is in this context that one could view the work of David Chipperfield. Chipperfield, who studied at the Architectural Association in London and then practised under Norman Foster and Richard Rogers, forged his own way later on, adopting a more 'conservative' approach than Foster and Rogers, and attempting to address the question of context in a more dialectical way, taking into consideration the historical dimension of architecture. As he stated:

> As architects, we cannot avoid the influence of context, both physical and social. Sometimes this context can give us inspiration, but invariably the challenge for architecture lies in those situations where the location gives us few clues. The evaluation of architectural typology and forms must be part of our self-imposed context, a context not imposed on us by authorities, but by our own conceptual process. [. . .]
>
> While we are tempted to see postmodernism in architecture as an embarrassing phase, it potentially offered a new departure. Not only a new style, but also a realisation that architecture is an affair not primarily of individual buildings, but of an entire constructed environment and that it must establish what we might describe as empathy. The desire for empathy demands that architecture cannot be an autonomous, self-referential activity, but must engage its context; physical, social and historical.[16]

Perhaps Chipperfield's best example of this dialectical relationship with history, which translates into an empathic engagement with its context, is his design for the corner building Am Kupfergraben (2003–7) (fig.3.15) which houses an art gallery over three floors in Berlin's historical Museum Island. Here, the architect surgically inserted a modern building that responds to its 19th-century neighbours through a stimulating dialogue, matching their heights and filling the empty void in the site, while presenting a contemporary facade that asserts its distinctive presence. The facades are clad in off-white bricks, marked at certain points by stone consoles with large openings of natural wooden sashes, irregularly placed at specific points in relation to interior functions, giving the building its character.

The design for his own summer house in Galicia, Spain (1996–2002), provides another illustration of contextuality, with a composition that ties in with the neighbourhood, while distinguishing itself slightly by its formal organisation and its material finish. The house nestles into its site, articulated on a solid base that provides a platform for the glazed piano nobile, with a full view of the ocean, while the upper level houses the private areas, with apertures framing the views to the landscape.

In his Museum of Modern Literature in Marbach am Neckar (2001–6) (fig.3.16), Chipperfield created a modern temple. Composed of two floors, the uppermost floor projects above ground from the main entrance side, while the lower floor is integrated within the site. The new structure stands elegantly next to the Schiller Museum of 1903, a Neo-Classical building with a central lobby crowned by a circular dome. Embedded in the topography, the building responds to the steep slope of the site, offering an intimate, shaded entrance on the brow of the hill facing the old museum, with a series of tiered platforms facing the valley below. On the highest terrace, the building appears as a pavilion, providing an austere entrance marked by the slender concrete columns that articulate the facade. The route through the entrance pavilion and down towards the exhibition galleries gradually adjusts from daylight to artificial light, designed to respond to the preservation of old manuscripts. The walls and ceilings of the interior are in fair-faced concrete, with limestone used for the floors as well as in the pre-cast concrete posts of the facade.

Whereas the site in Marbach provided the architect with several indices to work with, the Museum in Naga, Sudan (2008), is an example of a project in a desolate environment, which offered no direct references. Here, the architect designed a simple rectangular structure on a Neo-Classical plan, with a sequence of spaces proceeding from the main portico, mimicking pre-historic post-and-lintel constructions with wide slabs of concrete resting on beams, and ascending as a broad stairway following the slight slope of the site. On the inside, the thick posts and walls of earthen

above and left
3.17   David Chipperfield, Neues Museum, Museum Island, Berlin, Germany, 1993–2009

tone, carrying the white painted roof beams and panels, with modest clerestories introducing light into the interior, provide an atmosphere of serenity and repose. Chipperfield succeeded here in creating a modest, yet modern, temple that enters into dialogue with the site without mimicking any historic style.

Chipperfield's tour de force was his restoration of the Neues Museum (1993–2009) (fig.3.17), a project that put the architect to the test of responding to the sensitive issue of restoring a historic structure left largely in ruins after the Second World War. This museum occupies an important site on Museum Island in Berlin. The strategy used was to complement the existing ruins, meticulously restoring what was left and re-configuring the 'form & figure' of the original by inserting new components that recreate the original design, centred on a main entrance foyer, and a central 'nave' flanked by two wings composed around two internal courtyards. The James-Simon-Galerie on the same Museum Island in Berlin (1999–2018) (fig.3.18) confirmed Chipperfield as a master in the art of classical composition. While the original proposal, which

NEO-RATIONALISM

3.18   David Chipperfield, James-Simon-Galerie, Museum Island, Berlin, Germany, 1999–2018

won the first prize in the competition, left a little to be desired and led to a campaign against the proposed project, the final version displayed what can be labelled as the best example of the architect's mature 'Neo-Rationalist' style. In order to fully appreciate what Chipperfield was able to realise in this project, one has to compare his final design to what other competitors had proposed.

The new structure acts as a nexus to the Museum Island ensemble, standing on the site of the previous Tax Administration building designed by Schinkel, which was destroyed in 1938. It was designed to become the main entrance to the series of museums around it, accessed through a monumental external stairway, surrounded by an imposing colonnade on a stone plinth, and

left, top

3.19   Max Dudler, Jacob and Wilhelm Grimm Centre, Berlin, Germany, 2006–9

left, bottom

3.20   Emilio Tuñón, Museum of Contemporary Art Helga de Alvear, Cáceres, Spain, 2014–20

incorporating various public facilities for museum visitors. The stone plinth reinforces the bank of the water canal, and acts as a public forum, accessible at all times. The colonnade that surrounds the building forms an extension to Stüler's colonnade that originates at the Neues Museum. Arriving at the 'podium' level, visitors are led into the foyer of the building, which provides direct access to the Pergamon Museum. On the level below are located cloakrooms and other facilities, while at the lowest level the auditorium is tucked beneath the grand stairway. In his essay on this major work, Adrian von Buttlar drew connections between this modern masterpiece and other examples from the past – from the Propylaea of Pericles in Athens to the Brandenburg Gate in Berlin – postulating the correspondence with Schinkel's design for a royal palace on the Acropolis in Athens, as well as some analogies to recent works, such as Giorgio Grassi's Student Housing in Chieti. Yet beyond all these possible references, this work presents a distinctive piece of architecture, as von Buttlar states:

> Nevertheless, despite these complex references and analogies with architectural history, the James-Simon-Galerie reproduces nothing. It is not a metaphor, a symbol or an image, but rather a precisely thought-out, functional structure [. . .]. Seen in aesthetic terms, it is a monumental sculptural construct formed of bodies, connecting elements, space, light, materiality and colour – calculated on the basis of the kinaesthetic perception of the viewer.[17]

In line with the direction set by Ungers and Kleihues, one can position the work of Max Dudler. His Jacob and Wilhelm Grimm Centre in Berlin (2006–9) (fig.3.19) is quite exemplary in this respect. Conceived to house the largest open-shelved library in Germany, in addition to a computer centre, administration facilities and meeting areas, the whole structure presents an imposing facade to the exterior, marked by the regular rhythm of the arcade on the ground level, and the openings above, all rendered in marble. In line with the building code that restricts building heights to 22 metres (excepting public buildings), Dudler composed the library in two interconnected elements, with one segment of the building respecting the neighbouring height limit, while the other exceeds it to mark its presence as a public institution. From the forecourt, one arrives at a two-storey foyer, which forms a prelude to the heart of the building – the great reading room. The reading room was arranged into multiple, receding levels, like terraces, covered by a skylight that allows for an unobstructed view of the sky. The debate over whether it would have been better to have one central reading room or a number of smaller decentralised rooms ended with the decision to have both: all items in the library collection are accessible from the multi-levelled hall; reading areas are spread over the tiers of the great room, among them computer work areas. The interiors exhibit a reduced colour palette of white surfaces and cherry wood. Special areas such as the reading rooms and alcoves were covered with wall panelling in a veneer of cherry wood, giving them a natural warmth.

Recent examples of architecture confirmed the continuing influence of Neo-Rationalism on a number of contemporary architects around the world. In Spain, as an example, Emilio Tuñón's Museum of Contemporary Art Helga de Alvear (2014–20) (fig.3.20), like Chipperfield's Museum of German Literature, is a statement of classical principles, rendered in a restrained style. The museum sits on a restrictive site, adjoining the historic Casa Grande, within the perimeter of the old city walls of Cáceres. The cubical form of the main building, actually closer to a parallelepiped, connects back to the Casa Grande through another wing, the whole wrapped by a colonnade of white concrete columns that create a uniform pattern on the facade, punctuated at select points to allow for window apertures. The last floor of the columns does not support the wall behind it, but actually reveals an open frame, enclosing a roof terrace. The mastery of this composition translates into neutral internal spaces, where light reveals the spaces left in their bare materiality, contrasted by the wood panelling of doorways and window frames.

4 Post-Modern Architecture

Post-Modernism emerged in the Humanities and the Social Sciences as a reaction against the limitations of Modernism as a project based on the philosophical framework of the Enlightenment. In this sense, it embodied a reaction against the Modernist teleology of progress and the various 'meta-narratives' that accompanied it. In architecture, Post-Modernism designated an attempt to overcome the dogmatic imperatives of the Modern Movement through a return to history, with the aim of restoring the lost or missing dimension of 'meaning' in architecture. The main proponent of this tendency in architecture was the critic and historian Charles Jencks, whose series of books on this theme established him as the main advocate of the movement.[1]

In the Humanities, there was no such return to history, but rather an attempt to go forward beyond the limits and ideological constraints of Modernism. One of the main figures of this interpretation was Jean Baudrillard, whose essays revel in the new condition of Post-Modernity, simultaneously criticising and celebrating it, a condition that he characterised as one of 'simulations', that is, dominated by the image (mass media), which becomes more real than reality itself, something that is epitomised in contemporary reality-TV shows. The Post-Modern condition engenders a world of simulacra, of signs which have blurred the distinction between the object and its representation, the manifestations of which pervade all fields from art to politics.

Jean-François Lyotard is credited for having drawn the philosophical framework for this new direction in *La Condition postmoderne*.[2] Commissioned originally as a study on the condition of education in Quebec, the study developed into a critique of knowledge in the 20th century, which Lyotard separated into 'savoir' and 'connaissance'. 'Savoir', which is the general condition, would be reduced to 'science' (or connaissance) according to Lyotard, and knowledge should not be divested of the 'narrative form' which admits of a plurality of language plays, unlike scientific knowledge which was reduced to its denotative function and relegated to institutions, rather than allowed to develop within the broader social realm.[3] Lyotard concluded his study by diagnosing the 'Post-Modern condition' as one where recourse to 'meta-narratives' such as progress, the emancipation of humanity, or the dialectic of the spirit as a means of legitimising the scientific discourse would be excluded in favour of smaller narratives, that is, non-systematic discourses, where the principle of 'consensus' in defining such legitimacy would also be superseded.[4]

This general approach of re-evaluation of cultural and educational frameworks found its own translation in architecture in the wave of discontent that spread in the post-war period, manifesting itself in the break-up of the CIAM organisation, as well as in the emergence of new variations on modern architecture, which finally led to a more radical reaction against Modernism. Among the positive aspects of this reaction was a reclaimed sensitivity to issues of historical continuity, context, identity, and a change of outlook in urbanism. The attack on modern architecture appeared like a coordinated move on two principal fronts, the American and the European, with significant manifestos emerging on the two continents that ushered in the new style.

From this perspective, it becomes clear that Post-Modernism in architecture took a different course from the same movement in the Humanities. And whereas in architecture, it focused primarily on the revival of a 'classical' language, no similar attempts were undertaken in other artistic fields, from literature to film, to resuscitate older forms or 'genres'. The development of Post-Modernism in architecture can be seen therefore as a 'reactionary' development, which led some critics, such as Terry Eagleton and Fredric Jameson, to admonish its architectural manifestations within a general critique of 'late capitalism'. Yet one could detect a certain differentiation between a Neo-Classical Post-Modernism, as advocated by Charles Jencks and represented by the works of Venturi, Graves, and Stirling, and a more 'contemporary' Post-Modernism, which inherently assimilates the notions of 'simulation' and 'simulacra', best represented by the work of Rem Koolhaas, which will be discussed in another chapter.[5]

Jencks' enthusiasm for the new direction of architecture at the beginning of the 1980s, supported by the seminal work of Graves, Moore, Stirling, and Hollein, reaffirmed the attribution of the 'Post-Modern' epithet to this particular brand of 'Neo-Classical' architecture. Thus, he would come back to define Post-Modernism as 'an eclectic mix of traditional or local codes with Modern ones', celebrating the conversion of major figures such as James Stirling to the new creed. And whereas he had previously been critical of some architects, like Charles Moore, he later lauded his Piazza d'Italia in New Orleans as a 'major monument' of Post-Modernism.[6] As Post-Modernism progressed through the 1980s, newer buildings would occupy the centre stage as eminent examples of the new style, superseding previous examples. Thus, Stirling's Stuttgart Museum and Graves' Portland City Hall and Humana Headquarters in Kentucky became the main icons of this movement, comparable to the Bauhaus in Dessau and the Villa Savoye in Poissy for Modernism.[7]

Paolo Portoghesi also played a key role in promoting the new tendency in Italian and international circles. In addition to his book, *Postmodern: The Architecture of the Postindustrial Society*,[8] he curated the Venice Biennale of 1980 which became one of the major manifestos of the new movement. Portoghesi argued for a critical involvement with history, not a naïve return to an idealised past, nor an eclectic sampling of historic traditions; yet, his survey included much of the historicist eclecticism that became a trademark of the movement. The 'Post-Modern' in architecture thus came to connote this paradigmatic shift in architecture towards, on the one hand, a contemporary Neo-Classicism, and on the other, an eclectic mixture of Modernist and historicist tropes – a shift that appeared as a betrayal of Modernism by some of its well-known figures such as Michael Graves, James Stirling, and Arata Isozaki, in addition to the emergence of a new group of masters, like Robert Venturi and Paolo Portoghesi.

CARLO SCARPA: A POST-MODERNIST AVANT LA LETTRE?

Before tackling the main figures of the new movement, it is important to note that some architects were already exploring new forms and approaches to architecture that did not follow the dogmatic principles of Modernism, but rather, put the whole idea of a functionalist architecture in question. One major figure to appear on the scene in the 1950s, and who would be re-discovered later in the 1990s, was the idiosyncratic Carlo Scarpa. Scarpa cannot be categorised in any particular movement, although his early work was clearly inspired by Frank Lloyd Wright and by the legacy of the Arts and Crafts movement. Some critics even read in his work a similarity to complex literary authors, as Francesco dal Co suggested: 'Like (Karl) Kraus's words, Scarpa's design contains differences. His craft evokes ancient meanings, reinventing them. His fragments grow up from deep roots. His forms house and renew secrets that have become indecipherable.'[9]

Evoking the connection to Frank Lloyd Wright, Manfredo Tafuri still distinguished the particular approach of Scarpa, who drew from the American master a fascination with detail and with the art of discontinuity (without its associated ideology), which led the Venetian master to develop his own language, drawing on historical and personal sources.[10] Yet Scarpa's celebrated attention to detail and his revival of ornament was in itself a reaction against Modernist dogmas and the 'grand schemes' associated with it. His works expressed this historical continuity which nevertheless was intent on situating each project within its present time. His projects, which spanned from the 1930s to the 1970s, could be seen as a transition within this historical continuum between the two major movements: Modernism and its antithesis, Post-Modernism. A case in point is his design for the extension of the Banca Popolare di Verona (1973–8) (fig.4.1) which features a planar facade that unifies the different sections of the building. Yet this

4.1　Carlo Scarpa, Banca Popolare di Verona, Verona, Italy, 1973–8

facade is in itself an exercise in ornamentation, featuring two types of openings: rectangular bay windows contrasting with circular ones, crowned at the top by a glazed loggia. The rectangular bay windows project slightly beyond the facade and are carried on a plinth that extends into a T-shaped, inverted ziggurat, an ornamental signature of Scarpa. On the rear facade, the same treatment is applied, yet the facade terminates at one corner into an irregular composition which displays the 'twin pillars' motif carrying the steel beams of the upper loggia.

Scarpa's surgical approach to architecture was best expressed in his restoration of the Castelvecchio in Verona (1958–74) where he displayed his mastery of operating through the multiple layers of this historic complex, removing certain parts to reveal older layers, and adding new elements that engage a dialogue with the existing parts. His careful staging of the displays adds another element of interest, as does his daring removal of certain sections to reveal the original parts or to create a space for his intervention. The materials used, such as concrete inlaid with local stone, steel, brass, and wood, testify to Scarpa's mastery of the arts of craftsmanship.

POST-MODERNISM IN AMERICA: ROBERT VENTURI AND MICHAEL GRAVES

Robert Venturi, a young architect who graduated from Princeton in 1950, led the charge in America with his 'gentle manifesto' titled *Complexity and Contradiction in Architecture*, published in 1966, in which he advocated diversity in architecture and criticised the elimination of history as an archival resource. His illustrated book resuscitated examples from the architecture of the Renaissance, the Baroque, as well as the 19th century, alongside those by modern architects, notably Wright, Le Corbusier, Aalto, and Kahn, and examples from vernacular architecture, to show the validity of certain principles across different times and places.

Venturi started his professional career with two public projects at different scales: the Guild House, an elderly housing project in the centre of Philadelphia, and the Nurses Association in a

4.2   Robert Venturi, Vanna Venturi House, Philadelphia, Pennsylvania, USA, 1959–64

suburb of the same city, both completed in 1961, followed by his mother's house, in 1964. The Vanna Venturi House (1959–64) (fig.4.2), took on a special significance, as it concretised several of the principles that he expressed in his manifesto. This pseudo-traditional house is approached through a long axial path, which reveals at the end a quasi-symmetrical composition with a simple pitched roof. Yet upon closer inspection, one detects several idiosyncratic details, from the unusual entrance to the crooked stairway that leads to the upper level, to the combination of different types of windows: square windows and horizontal ones. With this project, Venturi was making a clear statement in favour of an architecture that is pluralistic and diverse, responsive to human needs; an architecture that does not seek to make a heroic statement nor to overthrow traditional types; and most importantly, an architecture that could take on a symbolic significance and 'communicate' with the larger public. The Venturi House was a landmark in the history of architecture, as it provided a counterpoint to the canonical example of the 'Modern House' represented by Villa Savoye. In comparison to the latter, the Venturi House did not aim to represent ideal principles or project a radical new vision of living, but simply to propose a new version of the historical type that was prevalent in this context. Associated with this revisionary attempt, and certainly influenced by it, were the emerging discussions on 'architectural language' and the necessity of architecture to 'communicate' through recognisable symbols and signs.

4.3 Robert Venturi, Guild House, Philadelphia, Pennsylvania, USA, 1961–6

4.4 Robert Venturi, Dixwell Fire Station, New Haven, Connecticut, USA, 1967–74

In the Guild House (1961–6) (fig.4.3), Venturi presented an example of what he advocated as a 'banal and ordinary' architecture, in opposition to the 'heroic and original' projects promoted by the Modern Movement. The Guild House stands unassumingly on a prominent urban block, as a rectangular composition of symmetrical units spread over six floors, with a segmented opening at the top floor, offering the collective living room a panoramic view. The building uses simple brick construction due to budget constraints as well as the intention of the architect to resort to common construction systems, which anchor the building in its context. The composition is nevertheless given a symbolic expression through the accentuation of the symmetry on the street facade, the large graphic sign above the entryway, and the massive column that marks the entrance. The historian Stanislaus von Moos noted the possible references of this modest 'urban palazzo', relating it to the villas of Palladio, which feature a comparable treatment of the facade.[11] In contrast to his 'ordinary' building, Venturi gave the example of the 'heroic' project by Paul Rudolph, Crawford Manor, a building designed for a similar function but articulated in a different way, with an obvious lack of concern for its relation to context.

Other examples testify to Venturi's ability to handle different projects in a contextual way, yet always giving them a particular accent. In the Dixwell Fire Station (1967–74) (fig.4.4), the architect provided an example of a 'typological' interpretation that follows the normative organisation of a fire station, in a composition that wraps around the site corner, providing a minor inflection as a mannerist accent to the facade. In the Fire Station in Columbus, Indiana, he again made a play on the theme of the square and longitudinal windows, in a building that reiterates the notion of complexity of details within a simple composition. The firehose tower in this case becomes the main marker – a modern campanile in the centre of a rectangular composition. In both cases, graphics play a part, as a 'pop culture' application to the traditional building.

Venturi distinguished himself in playing different tunes to respond to different contexts. On the campus of Princeton University, his projects were neither banal nor ordinary. The Gordon Wu Hall (1980–83) (fig.4.5) is an exquisite building that occupies its site with a sense of classical decorum, acting as a 'hyphen' connecting the dormitories of Butler Hall. Its main entrance is emphasised by a symbolic facade of marble and grey granite cladding, which contrasts with the red-brick walls, displaying in two-dimensions a secular version of a church facade, recalling that of San Miniato al Monte. At both ends, it is marked by a prominent semi-circular bay window, which contains at the entrance side the ceremonial stairway, with high-risers on one section that double as a seating area. Inside, the wood veneers and the brick walls contribute to create a warm atmosphere that befits a dormitory within a historic university.

On another site in the same campus, Venturi was called upon to rehabilitate and embellish the facade of an existing structure, the Lewis Thomas Laboratory (1983–6) (fig.4.6), a building that had been designed as a research lab for molecular biology. Here, he resorted to a playful composition of different courses of bricks, alternating with bands of cast-stone framing the windows and the entryway. The entrance is marked by a cast-stone arch profile that is not supported by any post or column, clearly expressing its symbolic and non-bearing role. The building facade thus becomes the main point of interest, crafted to make the structure fit within its context.

Another major project of interest by Venturi, was his addition to the National Gallery in London (1986–91) (fig.4.7). After a competition that yielded a project by Ahrends, Burton and Koralek (1984), which became the centre of a controversy spearheaded by Prince Charles, the commissioning body resorted to a second competition that was won by Venturi, who proposed a project that would better negotiate the transition between the historic museum and the new addition. His proposal manoeuvred quite astutely the requirements for the new addition, the Sainsbury Wing, by elaborating a rhythmically playful facade facing Trafalgar Square; its repetitive pilasters and columns turning the corner and making a gesture towards the historic museum, while the lateral side of the museum featured a glass curtain wall, bringing light into the grand stairway. The playful rhythm of columns on the facade recalls other examples of Renaissance and Baroque architecture, such as Santa Maria

4.5 Robert Venturi, Gordon Wu Hall, Princeton University, New Jersey, USA, 1980–83

4.6   Robert Venturi, Lewis Thomas Laboratory, Princeton University, New Jersey, USA, 1983–6

Assunta in Venice where the motif of condensed columns marks the facade. Entering from the main street side into a rather low ceiling floor, where the main lobby and administrative functions are located, the visitor accedes to the right onto the grand stairway to the upper level. On that 'piano nobile', the main gallery spaces are laid out in a sequence, with an enfilade of archways leading from one to the other, as if in a sacred space. The interiors (fig.4.8) are rendered in subdued colours, with stucco surfaces appropriate for the display of ecclesiastical works. The new wing is connected to the old museum through a bridge, marked by a cylindrical drum, acting like a pivot.

Two architects who expressed most radically the shift from Modernism to Post-Modernism were Michael Graves and James Stirling. Michael

above and right

4.7 & 4.8   Robert Venturi, Sainsbury Wing, National Gallery, London, UK, 1986–91

MODERN ARCHITECTURE IN A POST-MODERN ERA

above

4.9   Michael Graves, Snyderman House, Indiana, USA, 1972

below

4.10   Michael Graves, Villa Plocek, New Jersey, USA, 1977

Graves started out as one of the members of the informal group known as the New York Five, which initially proclaimed a return to the roots of modern architecture, specifically the 'white period' of the 1920s. One of his early works, the Benacerraf House addition, was an interpretation of the Corbusian free facade, breaking it up into its constituent elements, and dissolving it even further in the Snyderman House (1972) (fig.4.9), where the separation between structure and envelope is further accentuated in a formal composition that evoked the two-dimensional purist paintings of Père Corbu. A few years later, Graves made a radical shift towards a personalised language of Neo-Classicism, with a return to the principles of symmetry, hierarchy, ornamentation, and a clear reference to the classical orders. An example of this contrast between the early Graves and the later one can be seen in comparing the Snyderman House with Villa Plocek (1977) (fig.4.10). While the former

is characterised by its structural expression, its lightness and permeability, the latter dominates the site by its heaviness, an example of a re-interpreted Italianate villa with all the 'gravity' that it entails. The Plocek House is a classical composition: the three storeys of the house are laid out in a manner that recalls classical precedents: a rusticated base, overlaid by the main floor, the piano nobile, and capped by the last floor. In the floor plan the two organisational axes, the main entry axis and the one perpendicular to it, intersect at the centre, while the stairway is inscribed within a ceremonial square niche around which the different rooms are laid out. The classical language adopted by Graves is nevertheless manipulated and transformed in a mannerist way, by exaggerating certain details, such as the keystone or the pediment, and in some cases, removing certain key elements from the composition in an ironic twist. Graves' shift translated also into a shift in representation techniques, from the colourless axonometric drawings that characterised his early work, to polychromatic pencil drawings on yellow tracing paper that became his signature mark.

This change in style crystallised with the winning scheme for the Portland City Hall (1979–82) (fig.4.11), a public building that was celebrated as an icon of the new movement, and featured on the cover of Charles Jencks' fourth edition of *Post-Modern Architecture*. The Portland City Hall stood for everything that Boston City Hall did not: a building that represented 'civic' architecture, with an ability to express its public function symbolically through a recourse to a well-assimilated architectural language. Despite its monumentality, the breakdown into different sections – emphasised by the dignified base, the polychromatic facade and the infusion of ornamental features – made this building 'speak' more directly in a language that would be supposedly understood by the majority of people. At a time when 'semiotics' were popular in academic circles, the attempts to establish a relation between this new field of studies and architecture seemed to open new paths for the development of a more culturally open practice. The building was designed on a square plan, set on a two-storey greenish base, almost cubical in volume, with several floors of office space. A sculpture of a woman, baptised

4.11   Michael Graves, Portland City Hall, Portland, Oregon, USA, 1979–82

Portlandia, executed by the artist Raymond Kaskey, crowns the entrance. A typical cross-axial system subdivides the plan into four quadrants, with the entrance located on the main axis, incorporated within a giant keystone-cum-pilaster gateway motif that spreads across the whole facade; marked by a brown-stone cladding, it is distinguished from the rest of the facade, which displays a uniform pattern of small square windows.

This version of architecture was quickly appropriated by the new corporate culture of the 1980s, finding in it an appropriate signifier for its new, and more global, outreach. Following the Portland City Hall, Graves was commissioned to design the Humana Building in Louisville, Kentucky (1982–5) (fig.4.12), a corporate headquarters which attempted in some ways to respect its context by splitting the building in two components: a frontal pavilion, with a pediment-capped

POST-MODERN ARCHITECTURE

left

4.12 Michael Graves, Humana Building, Louisville, Kentucky, 1982–5

below

4.13 Michael Graves, San Juan Capistrano Library, California, USA, 1983

loggia that attempts to relate to the scale of the adjoining structures, while the rest of the structure recedes back and soars to the required height to accommodate the programme in its mid-rise tower. The building is once again clearly articulated into three main sections: the base, consisting of the front portico; the middle section, punctuated by the small square windows and interrupted in the centre by the vertical glass curtain wall; and culminating at the top in a cantilevering belvedere that offers a view of the city.

Graves displayed a particular sensitivity to regional contexts, as can be seen in his project for the Clos Pegase Winery in Napa Valley, as well as the public library of San Juan Capistrano. There, the architect adopted the Spanish Mission style, to meet the programmatic demands without excessive ornamentation. The San Juan Capistrano Library (1983) (fig.4.13) was designed on a rectangular plan layout, with an off-centre axis leading from the main entry porch, marked by a set of ceremonial pilasters topped by a segmental arch, the whole composed around a central rectangular courtyard. In the first quadrant, leading from the main foyer, is a sequence of square rooms dedicated to reading areas, culminating in a lounge. On the external side of this main quadrant are also located the stacks. The second quadrant, to the right of the entrance, is dedicated to the children's section, while the third quadrant, on the opposite side of the court, encloses the main auditorium. The fourth quadrant is framed by five cubical elements, three of which are gazebos for outdoor reading. The classical peristyle that surrounds the courtyard provides a screening layer between the indoor and outdoor, thus reducing the effect of direct light. It also leads through another portico to a smaller courtyard with a reflecting pool, somehow reminiscent of the sequence of courtyards in Alhambra.

The Clos Pegase Winery (1984–7) (fig.4.14) is another example of Graves' immersion in the classical idiom, and his adoption of the notions of ritual in a contemporary reinterpretation of Roman models. The winery was designed as part of a complex that includes the owners' house at the top of the hill, with the winery located on the site below. The design, won through a competition, featured a main rectangular pavilion at the entrance side, punctuated at its centre by a large square

75

4.14 Michael Graves, Clos Pegase Winery, California, USA, 1984–7

portico, marked with a symbolic Doric column that figuratively carries the lintel under a segmental archway. This entry pavilion contains the foyer as well as the administrative offices and ancillary functions. A rectangular garden, screened by trees on both sides, leads the visitor to the main tasting room at the end of the cardinal axis, which also leads to the main wine storage areas. On the east side of the path are located the large spaces for fermentation and processing. Originally conceived to have a sculpture park on the western side, designed as an open-air circular pantheon where visitors could be initiated into the wine rituals, this part of the programme had to be sacrificed. The language of Graves in this project consisted of an assembly of different elements and components, in a rather homogeneous way, without resorting to any ornamentation.

A number of prominent architects also adopted the Post-Modernist gospel, and participated in this 'revisionary' approach to architecture, among them Philip Johnson, who as a young architect collaborated with Mies van der Rohe on the Seagram Building. In his AT&T headquarters in New York City (1984), Johnson in fact repudiated the Modernist principles by creating one of the iconic landmarks of the new movement, with its classical details, stone cladding, and 'Chippendale' crowning pediment. Robert Stern, in turn, started off his career with a number of mannerist interpretations of historical styles, as in his Wiseman House (1967), to fall back later on a revival of traditional styles, as in the Neo-Georgian House on Lake Michigan (2009) which is emblematic of a number of commissions that Stern realised for wealthy clients.

THE ENIGMATIC CASE OF JAMES STIRLING

James Stirling was one of the last architects expected to abandon the Modernist ship and shift to the new style in vogue. Stirling had written a critical account of Le Corbusier's chapel in Ronchamp, criticising it as a reactionary development because it indicated a shift from the 'rationalist' project of the 1920s.[12] His early work expressed his penchant for a technological architecture, combining high-tech elements with traditional brick cladding, as in his University of Leicester Engineering building (1957–63) (fig.4.15) which appropriately took the appearance of a large factory complex. The University of Leicester building was composed of a main tower with a glass curtain wall, soaring above a horizontal slab containing the laboratories and covered by a distinctive skylight roof that emulates industrial structures. To complete the composition, a cantilevering volume housed the auditorium, somewhat reminiscent of the work of Konstantin Melnikov and Moisei Ginzburg.

Granted, Stirling had a distinctive approach towards modern architecture, especially in the early phase of his career, as argued by several critics. He attempted to combine different sources and influences, adapting architecture to its context, and rejected being categorised in any way, either as a New Brutalist or as a Post-Modernist.[13] Yet, his early formal strategies were fundamentally 'Modernist' in spirit, as evidenced by a number of projects, from the Cambridge History Faculty building (1964–7) to the Residential Complex at St Andrews University (1964–8), to the Olivetti Training School (1969–72). Several years after this early phase, Stirling's abrupt change of direction came through the competition for a museum in Dusseldorf (1975). There, for the first time, the architect shifted to a composition of primary solids, arranged in a contextual manner to respond to the historic site. The composition featured a large cubical volume with an open cylindrical drum at the centre, appended to a smaller element in the middle of a wide plaza, which acts as an entrance pavilion to the museum. Stirling's architecture shifted from being an 'assembly' of modular and prefabricated units to a composition of primary forms, featuring polychromatic materials in an overtly classical idiom. One of the catalysts of this move may have been the young Léon Krier, who joined Stirling's practice towards the end of the 1960s. Although this project never saw the light, its successor in Stuttgart, the Staatsgalerie (1977–84) (fig.4.16), winner of the competition, was realised. Yet this work raised major questions on what some regarded as an inappropriate symbolism. Günther Behnisch, who lost to Stirling and came third,

4.15 James Stirling and James Gowan, University of Leicester Engineering Building, Leicester, UK, 1957–63

lambasted the proposal as an unwelcome revival of totalitarian architecture. A more sympathetic analysis was written by Anthony Vidler, who argued that the architect had effectively managed to create a building which, while 'losing its face' as Colin

4.16   James Stirling, Michael Wilford & Associates, Staatsgalerie, Stuttgart, Germany, 1977–84

Rowe had remarked rather negatively, succeeded in avoiding the pitfalls of history and in managing the problematic question of 'monumentality' in post-war Germany. Stirling's ambivalent attitude may be explained, according to Vidler, in this way:

> In the first place, of course, this would be attributable to the modernist rejection of what Sigfried Giedion called the pseudomonumentality of the nineteenth century, the routine 'misuse' of shapes from the past, the devaluation of traditional language, a loss of monumentality attributable to no 'special political or economic system'. In the second place, in the German context, however, Stirling's resistance to traditional monumentality stemmed evidently from his opposition to a specific variety of pseudomonumentality, that of the Third Reich. The memory of Nazi 'misuse' of Schinkel's neoclassic forms rendered a direct and 'postmodern' quotation of Schinkel, or any other classic image, immediately suspect.[14]

The competition posed the problem of expanding the old museum, which dates back to the middle of the 19th century, which the architect resolved by avoiding both the imitation of historic styles and a straightforward Modernist building, choosing instead to combine elements from the historical repertoire, starting with Schinkel and extending to Le Corbusier. The new addition was based on the typology of the old museum, taking the U-shaped plan as its basic template, but elaborating it substantially while avoiding its most prominent feature, the central temple front with its Neo-Classical portico, substituting it by a network of ramps leading to the main entrance. The wide ramp leads to the main entrance, covered by a painted steel canopy; it continues onwards on the exterior of the building, circling the open-air central drum garden, culminating at the back street on the higher plateau. This face-less building that uses travertine and sandstone as cladding, marked by pink and blue steel balustrades, thus avoids classical

4.17   James Stirling, Michael Wilford & Associates, Staatsgalerie interior, Stuttgart, Germany, 1977–84

monumentality while presenting an overture towards the main avenue (fig.4.17). As Vidler and others noted, its reference in plan to Schinkel's museum in Berlin finds an echo in the central drum, invisible from the street and only revealed through the 'promenade architecturale'. Other elements, such as the 'piano-shaped' entrance lobby, recall the gestures of Le Corbusier, while the mushroom-tapered columns in some of the interior spaces refer simultaneously to Egyptian motifs as well as to Frank Lloyd Wright's early works.

POST-MODERNISM AROUND THE WORLD

This selective survey of the main advocates of the new movement, namely Venturi, Graves, and Stirling, does not, of course, do justice to a number of architects who were equally influential in spreading the new gospel, from Robert Stern, Quinlan Terry, and Terry Farrell, to Alessandro Mendini and Ricardo Bofill, to a number of other architects in Latin America, the Near East, and Southeast Asia, where in some cases the Post-Modern reaction took the form of an uncritical revival of historical types.

Ricardo Bofill left his mark on the development of a Post-Modern language in Spain and other countries. Of his early work, the Muralla Roja (1968–73) (fig.4.18) was an impressive housing project in Spain's Calpe region. Taking its cues from the Arab vernacular of the casbah, the whole complex of solid walls, turrets, and labyrinthine alleys is rendered in tones of red, pink, and blue stucco, and culminates at the rooftop levels into open spaces with water pools and recreation areas.

A more overt essay in Post-Modernism, his Arcades du Lac in Saint Quentin-en-Yvelines in Paris (1974–82) (fig.4.19), takes a more monumental character, with large-scale buildings arranged to form a symmetrical composition around an artificial lake. This project, which appears to take its cues from the theoretical propositions of the Krier brothers with their language of 'street, square, and blocks', is composed of two main elements: the 'Arcades' organised around four main quadrants, fronted by a linear set of longitudinal blocks four storeys in height; and the 'Viaduct', a linear volume that extends into the lake. The Arcades comprise around 400 units, while the Viaduct houses around 80 units, all built in cast-in-situ concrete, featuring prefabricated ornamental panels of terracotta, lending the ensemble an 18th-century Baroque character. This expressive monumentality found further translations in other 'grand' projects such as the Espaces d'Abraxas in Marne-la-Vallée (1978–82) (fig.4.20) and the Echelles du Baroque in Paris (1979–85). In other instances, Bofill showed a more restrained Neo-Classical approach, as in the Shepherd School of Music at Rice University in

4.18 Ricardo Bofill, La Muralla Roja, Calpe, Spain, 1968–73

4.19　Ricardo Bofill, Les Arcades du Lac, Saint Quentin-en-Yvelines, Paris, France, 1974–82

4.20   Ricardo Bofill, Les Espaces d'Abraxas,
Marne-La-Vallée, Paris, France, 1978–82

above

4.21   Ricardo Bofill, Shepherd School of Music, Rice University, Houston, Texas, USA, 1991

left, exterior and axonometric drawing

4.22   Arata Isozaki, Kitakyushu Central Library, Fukuoka, Japan, 1973–4

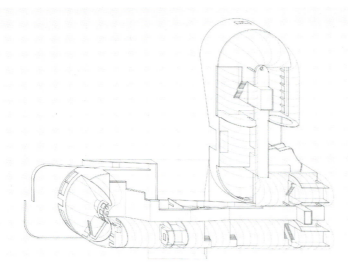

4.23 Arata Isozaki, Museum of Contemporary Art, Los Angeles, California, USA, 1981–6

Houston (1991) (fig.4.21), a project that distinguishes itself by blending into its institutional context, adopting a language of brick, with a longitudinal element that evokes a Greek Stoa punctuated by a colonnade.

In Japan, previous infatuations with 'Metabolism' gave way, under architects like Arata Isozaki, to a particular version of Post-Modernism, blending the taste for the futuristic with the revival of historicist types. In this sense we can read Isozaki's Kitakyushu Central Library in Fukuoka (1973–4) (fig.4.22) as a playful articulation of the barrel-vault typology, stretching it and bending it to result in a hybrid building: historicist in its recollection of certain typologies, and futuristic in its manipulation of concrete to the limits of plasticity. Afterward, and in one of his first international commissions, Isozaki went further in adopting the Neo-Classical language in the Museum of Contemporary Art in Los Angeles (1981–6) (fig.4.23) where the complex was composed of different volumes, arranged around a sunken courtyard that leads to the galleries. The main elements that protrude above ground are the administrative wing, configured within a floating, barrel-vaulted space, framing the entrance portico to the plaza and underground galleries. The adjoining volumes around the plaza are covered by pyramidal skylights that bring light into the interior spaces, and provide an additional accent to the whole complex, clad in a deep-red sandstone.

TWO POLES OF POST-MODERNISM: BERLIN AND MIAMI

The success of Post-Modernism was not limited in the end to the historicist revivals of ornamental features on public buildings, or to the resurrection of historical types, but concretised on a more urban level in the rehabilitation of the concepts of 'urban fabric' and 'context', which had been overlooked in the object-centred Modernist approach. The rejection of the CIAM principles of planning that created disjointed urban ensembles after the Second World War led to a reconsideration of the historical city, which formed a common denominator between the Post Modernists and the Neo-Rationalists, that is, Robert Venturi, James Stirling, Léon Krier, and Aldo Rossi.

One of the main experimental grounds for this new direction in urbanism was the city of Berlin, which became, under the active stewardship of Josef Paul Kleihues, a testing ground for the new ideas on urbanism, which centred on the rehabilitation of several urban voids within the city. In this context, the residential projects of Aldo Rossi, Léon Krier, Hans Hollein, Oswald Mathias Ungers, Vittorio Gregotti, Arata Isozaki, and many others, were realised as urban ensembles that complemented the urban fabric of the 19th-century city, respecting its scale, typology, and urban patterns. Kleihues' initiative translated into a major urban design initiative titled 'Internationale Bauausstellung' or IBA (International Building Exhibition). This initiative consisted of organising a series of competitions on public and private sites that required development, with a large focus on replenishing the urban housing stock of the city, in contradistinction to the Modernist urbanism of CIAM, as manifested in the previous project of Interbau (1957), which consisted of developing the Hansa quarter in the city. Back then, the Modernist idiom reigned and the site was parcelled into different sections, with each architect producing their signature building as part of this modern city of towers in a park. Kleihues' gamble paid off and several of the projects that were selected found their way to execution by private developers, contributing to a new direction of urban planning which continued after re-unification. This new direction also set another modus operandi: the idea of bringing together 'star' architects along with local ones to work within strict guidelines and to collectively participate in the reconfiguration of the city. In this way, the IBA of 1978–87 brought together Peter Eisenman, Aldo Rossi, Martorell/Bohigas/Mackay, Arata Isozaki, Kollhoff/Ovaska, Jourdan/Muller/Albrecht, and others.

In counterpart to the projects in Berlin, Post-Modernism was to take another turn, with a more frivolous approach, exemplified by the projects for the Disney Corporation in Miami by Michael Graves. Even Charles Jencks, the apostle of Post-Modernism, noted that these projects would signal the end of the style as they verged on 'kitsch'. This fear of the end prompted Jencks to preface his 1991 edition of *The Language of Post-Modern Architecture* with the ominous essay 'Death for Rebirth', in which he refuted the detractors who had been announcing the imminent death of Post-Modernism.[15] Jencks conceded that movements are bound to reach an end, and that Post-Modernism would not escape this predicament, but unlike Modernism, its death could be a liberating event which would free it once again from any dogmatism. For him, the central ideology of Post-Modernism remained 'pluralism', which continues to express the condition of the present times.

5 Regional Modernisms

'Regional Modernisms' is used here in a general sense, and in the plural, to designate the multiple and different manifestations of architectural projects that have adopted a 'modern language', including new building methods and materials, yet were designed to respond to the specificities of particular places and cultures, and to engage them in a dialectical way, avoiding any vulgar imitation. Some historians used the epithet of 'critical regionalism' to describe such works, which they referred back to the early phase of modern architecture, with Alvar Aalto as one of its leading pioneers.[1]

In their theoretical proposition for a 'critical regionalism', Alexander Tzonis and Liane Lefaivre differentiated between 'regionalism' as a tradition that is simply restricted to a certain region, and a more engaged 'critical regionalism', which draws on Mumford's synthesis of the local and the global and which includes a variety of approaches from around the world. It is this understanding of regionalism which allows for the possibility, according to them, for a more significant contribution of local cultures in the process of their self-representation, while also avoiding a lapse into regionalist clichés or nationalistic tendencies. Writing during the heyday of Post-Modernism, Tzonis and Lefaivre clearly saw this approach as a 'third way' that would respond to some of the criticism waged against Modernism, without falling into the eclecticism of Post-Modernism.

Tzonis and Lefaivre's definition was considerably wide-ranging, accommodating Wright's and Aalto's work as well as some of the projects by Richard Neutra, Oscar Niemeyer, Ernesto Rogers, Aldo van Eyck, and a number of other architects. Thus, in their compilation of examples of 'critical regional' works, the two authors included in their survey Aalto's Town Hall in Saynatsalo, Neutra's Kaufmann House, Safdie's Hebrew Union College, even extending it to MVRDV's Hageneiland and Calatrava's Winery in Alava, Spain.[2] Some architects were recognised for the first time, namely Dimitris and Suzana Antonakakis, whose work in Greece was exemplary, as they sought a balance between new techniques and local methods and materials. Their house and atelier at Oxylithos (1977), for example, articulates the programme into three units, irregularly composed around the open court, with the 'atelier' acting as a wind barrier facing the sea; while the Archaeological Museum of Chios (1965) respects the scale of the small town by breaking down the programme into modular units of reinforced concrete, wrapped with local stone walls, arranged organically around a central open court.

In the same vein, Kenneth Frampton appropriated the notion of critical regionalism to propose a direction that would avoid the opposite poles of prevailing architectural practice at that time: one geared towards technique, the other towards 'commodity' or what he called 'scenography'. For Frampton, critical regionalism seemed to provide the means to mediate the 'impact of universal civilisation' (or globalism in today's terminology) with 'elements derived indirectly from the peculiarities of a particular place'. This did not mean a retreat into hopeless attempts at a revival of the vernacular nor an escape into a 'populism' that based itself on the notion of 'communicative' or 'instrumental' signs. In his opinion, this would imply a constant challenge, that is, to commit to a process of 'double-mediation': on the one hand deconstructing the spectrum of world culture, while on the other, reaching a critical synthesis of universal civilisation. This process was, simply put, a dialectical approach to resolving the opposition between local culture and universal civilisation, that is, the specific and the general. The main characteristics of buildings satisfying this synthesis would be their sensitivity to natural surroundings – to factors of climate, topography, and context – as well as their attention to the tactile and visual qualities of form, without privileging the latter over the former. The seminal example that expresses such qualities for Frampton is Aalto's Saynatsalo Town Hall.[3]

5.1   Reima and Raili Pietilä, Dipoli Student Residence, Otaniemi, Finland, 1966

From the related positions of Tzonis/Lefaivre and Frampton, a certain understanding of 'critical regionalism' emerges which is principally centred on the desirable synthesis of the universal and the local, the attention to context, and the specificity of place, without a lapse into pre-determined 'formal' recipes of 'nationalist' overtones or abstract principles.[4] Following this definition, but with a preference for a less loaded term, I will survey in this chapter a variety of examples of 'regional Modernisms', that show a continuing interest among a growing number of architects to seek this middle ground between generic abstraction and regional character with projects that display sensitivity to context, respect for the cultural, social, economic, and climatic specificities of the place, while blending new technologies with existing building methods within a general framework of production that remains, nevertheless, 'modern'.[5]

EUROPEAN INTERPRETATIONS

Following in the footsteps of Alvar Aalto, who became a father figure for a new wave of Scandinavian Modernism, other architects also attempted to strike the proper balance between nature and architecture in their work. Reima and Raili Pietilä designed the Dipoli Student Residence in Otaniemi (1966) (fig.5.1) as an 'organic' composition. The building integrates itself within the site, using local materials like pine wood and natural rocks, in construction as well as finishes. Similar in its approach to Aalto's compositions, the large student centre incorporates an auditorium, meeting and entertainment spaces, and offices. A regular grid at one corner of the site accommodates offices, while the other functions take a more irregular, organic layout that wraps around the grid.

Jørn Utzon, famous for the design of the Sydney Opera House, showed a great affinity for the particularities of place when it came to designing his own retreat house in Mallorca, Can Lis (1971) (fig.5.2). Located at the top of a cliff overlooking the sea, the house was built as a composition of four elements, each containing one set of functions in a clustered organisation. Blending concrete with local yellow stone, the house fits naturally in its context, opening to the landscape through different windows, allowing the light to flood indirectly and directly into the interior.

Sverre Fehn, the architect of the famous Nordic Pavilion (1962) at the Venice Biennale – a work of exquisite abstraction formed by a set of thin beams that provided a canopy to an open interior space, interrupted only by trees that cut through the roof – showed his regional affinity when it came to design in his native Norway. The Villa Schreiner in Oslo (1963) was called an 'Homage to Japan' as its rectilinear geometry blends with the surrounding nature. With sliding, wide-bay glass doors and windows, the house exhibits the characteristics of Japanese houses, while the building material reaffirms its belonging to the Scandinavian environment. In a different way, the Villa Busk in Bamble (1990) straddles a ridge near a valley. The plan is arranged along a linear spine running east to west, with a concrete retaining wall. The house is mainly built of wood, its overall appearance recalling vernacular farmhouses.

Another direction in regional Modernism was taken by Spanish and Portuguese architects from the early 1970s onwards. The work of the great Catalan architect Josep Antonio Coderch inscribes itself within this line of sensitive Modernism, a Modernism that responds to place and culture, as can be seen in his Rozes House in Girona (1962), reminiscent in its simplicity of the work of Dimitris and Suzana Antonakakis. Perched on top of a natural site, the building negotiates its position with a series of repetitive modules for a sequence of bedrooms, organised on a diagonal and culminating in the main living areas. His earlier apartment building, La Barceloneta (1951), with its irregular units and its

5.2   Jørn Utzon, Can Lis, Mallorca, Spain, 1971

lively facade, already revealed his inclination towards a more responsive Modernism. One of his last projects, the expansion of the School of Architecture in Barcelona (1978) relied on a language of curved brick walls, in an organic arrangement.

One of the main figures in the 'Spanish Renaissance' that brought modern architecture within the gambit of contextualism is the architect Rafael Moneo. Two of his major works show us different interpretations of the question of context: the Museum of Art in Merida and the Town Hall in Murcia. Both examples are located in Spain, although the influence of Moneo and his works eventually extended well beyond his native country. In the National Museum of Roman Art in Merida (1979–86) (fig.5.3), Moneo was faced with the challenge of building in a historic setting over existing Roman archaeological ruins. Rather than produce a generic

89

5.3 Rafael Moneo, National Museum of Roman Art, Merida, Spain, 1979–86

building that spans the site, the architect chose to engage with the site by imposing another layer of construction, a grid of columns that enter into a dialogue with the archaeological strata, while keeping the underground level accessible as an open 'crypt' for visitors. Above it the museum was conceived like a cathedral, with a central nave flanked on both sides by transepts, one of which encompasses a series of rooms for the exhibition of artifacts.

As stated by the architect:

> The first intention of the project was to build a museum that would offer to people the opportunity to understand the lost presence of the Roman town. Moreover, it was important that the museum building achieve the character and presence of a Roman building: thus the prominence given to the construction as the expression of the architecture itself [. . .] The walls are constructed by a procedure not far from the Roman manner – a massive masonry bearing wall infilled with concrete – a manner of building that allows the materiality of the Roman brick wall to become, finally, the most important feature in the architecture of the museum.[6]

The extension to the Murcia Town Hall (1991–8) (fig.5.4) presented a different challenge. Facing an imposing ensemble of historic buildings on the main town square, including the 16th-century cathedral and the Episcopal Palace, Moneo saw this task as a facade problem, that is, mainly to design a building that would present a concordant facade in that historic plaza. The facade thus reappears here as a major task, and for this the architect deployed several attempts before settling on a 'musical score' that plays on the rhythm of the pilasters, while presenting an abstract elevation devoid of any ornamental features. As noted, the historical allusions relate to several references, from the altarpiece common in all cathedrals, to the backdrop of Roman theatres. The playful facade, clad in local sandstone, affirms its 'modernity' while also paying respect to the scale of the other historic buildings.

Juan Navarro Baldeweg's work, similar to Moneo in certain aspects, is grounded in a phenomenological approach that emphasises the importance of light, gravity, and the sensorial qualities of space. His approach to architecture was

5.4 Rafael Moneo, Murcia Town Hall, Murcia, Spain, 1991–8

also influenced by his artistic experiments, which translated into significant installations such as Wheel and Weight (1974), Swing Piece (1976), and the Five Units of Light (1974), the latter conceived as a set of boxes functioning like resonance chambers that record in different ways the effects of light onto specific surfaces. Baldeweg thus brings to architecture the affinity of an installation artist with a particular sensitivity to the parameters of light, gravity, and spatial perception. In his own words he describes architecture:

> Architecture, which can be construed as an interposition along this continuum between two spheres, external and internal, acts as a 'box' to enlarge or filter the threads of its uninterrupted, encompassing basic fabric. An image that I always find seductive is that of the room or built space as a resonance chamber, a transformer of foreign signals which translates and adapts them into receptible terms, as imposed by organic nature and culture. In other words, this is a way of understanding architecture as part of nature, an abstract landscape inferred from the natural world and, what is more, directed at establishing

an indissolubly powerful alliance with the body as a whole.[7]

This description suitably applies to one of Baldeweg's masterpieces, the Altamira National Museum and Research Centre in Santander (1994–2000), built close to the historic Altamira cave where the earliest prehistoric cave art was discovered in the middle of the 19th century. The flux of visitors imperilled the original site, so the authorities took the decision to build a replica of the caves, including reproductions of the artwork on the walls, in addition to a museum and research centre. Baldeweg masterfully reproduced the situation by embedding the project into the terrain, with horizontal terraces that extend across the site. The design separated the programme in two parts, locating the cave replica under the eastern side beneath a canopy roof, while on the western side, the terraces that form an extension of the landscape enclose the research centre and administrative functions. Through the clerestories, light percolates to the different levels. The whole complex does not seek to impose its presence on the site, but rather to dissolve within it, to become a part of the landscape.

An earlier project by Baldeweg, the Castilla y Leon Convention Centre and Exhibition Hall in Salamanca (1985–92) also attests to the architect's sensitivity to a historic urban context. Located at the perimeter of the walled precinct of the city, the new convention centre was commissioned to house two auditoria. The building programme was divided into two sections: a large volume containing the auditoria, covered by a domical structure; and a separate pavilion that makes the connection with the street, with a public stairway cutting between. The two sections are connected at the basement level, providing additional public spaces for the exhibition hall and access to the smaller auditorium. While the larger volume presents an opaque facade to the street, clad in stone and laterally open

5.5   Schneider and Lengauer, The Cemetery and Wake Room, East Tyrol, Austria, 2011

through a large archway to the stairway access, the other pavilion features a Modernist profile, with the base in stone, surmounted by an elegant steel and glass structure. The building thus presents a modern extension to the historic site, and blends well within its surroundings.

In Austria, Switzerland, and southern Germany, other projects adopting a syncretic approach between Modernism and local Alpine traditions of construction have also been realised, sometimes veering into a Minimalist tendency, as in the work of Peter Zumthor, which will be discussed in another chapter. The Cemetery and Wake Room by Schneider and Lengauer in East Tyrol, Austria (2011) (fig.5.5) is one example of this direction. Perched on a sloping site next to the old church, this meeting room, consisting of a rectangular space, blends gracefully into its context with its concrete structure clad with local quarry stone. The opaque solid volume is capped by a clerestory that draws light into the interior, while presenting a horizontal accent to the structure. The interior walls are all lined in larch wood, with simple wooden benches arranged along the edges, contributing to the solemnity of this sacral interior.

REGIONAL MODERNISM IN NORTH AMERICA

Antoine Predock charted his own course, drawing on the lessons of the masters, specifically Frank Lloyd Wright and Alvar Aalto, but with a particular sensitivity to the region in which he lived and practised – the American Southwest. Predock's architecture is characterised by certain essential qualities, mainly an attention to light and climate brought into emphasis through the use of platonic, or one could even say archetypal, forms. Predock created his works with a keen eye towards the landscape, attempting to bring it into the composition, in a dialogue with architecture. As Geoffrey Baker puts it, Predock's search for an authentic architecture was promoted by a certain 'earthing of emotions':

> This 'earthing of emotions' within a 'universal frame' occurs in Predock's work by the way he packs his buildings with archetypal references that range from gateways to towers, bridges to tunnels, terraces to pyramids. Primordial themes involve water and the hearth, inventively transformed to take on new meanings that, to quote Sylvia Lavin, 'search for shared experience that can transcend the vagaries of time and place'.[8]

One of his earliest projects, the housing settlement of La Luz in Albuquerque (1967) encapsulates this attention to the landscape, and most importantly, to the necessary qualities that make a settlement turn into a viable 'community' of different housing units interspersed by sheltered outdoor spaces, alleys, and courtyards, a vision that transcends the dogmatic principles of modern town planning. Here, on a semi-arid plateau near the Rio Grande, the settlement of individual townhouses was designed on the higher level of the land, forming a close-knit community, designed with particular attention to climate and landscape. Each unit is a two-storey house, with private bedrooms on the upper level, and a slightly depressed living area to meet the natural ground on the river side. The houses are built of earth-coloured adobe walls that reduce heat transfer, with thick external walls providing protection from the winds.

Following this early experiment, Predock continued with several commissions for public institutions, such as the Rio Grande Nature Center and Preserve in Albuquerque (1982). After the acquisition of a large site which was turned into a protected natural reserve, Predock developed the master plan and designed the exhibition centre, which consists of a triangular-shaped complex intersected by a circular space at the edge of the water pond, acting like a periscope that gradually allows the visitors to view the landscape in its variety. His Nelson Fine Arts Center at the Arizona State University (1989) is an example of a new type of monumentality, drawing on a combination of different forms, clustered around a series of courts. The large complex contains a museum, theatre, dance halls, and art galleries extending to shaded terraces, forming an open matrix of pathways. The interplay between inert solids of concrete with shaded terraces and planted areas gives this complex a particular character, reflecting a special relation with the desert context. The interiors, equally monumental with their trabeated

5.6 Antoine Predock, American Heritage Center and Art Museum, Wyoming, USA, 1986–93

architecture and high ceilings, with light filtering through skylights and clerestories, add another element of mystery to the complex.

Another important marker in Predock's rich itinerary is the American Heritage Center and Art Museum in Wyoming (1986–93) (fig.5.6). A project designed as an artificial mountain, conical in shape with few openings, this monumental complex provides a welcome contrast to the plains beyond. The central atrium, open to all levels, separates the two halves of this 'mystic mountain': one part dedicated to the museum, the other to the heritage centre. Attached to it is a low-rise extension of modular units that contain the archival and administrative spaces. Like his other works, the clear articulation of elements, the roughness of the main structure, and the play of light provide the visitor with an architectural experience that connects in a particular way to its context.

Charles Moore, working with Richard Whitaker, Donlyn Lyndon, and William Turnbull Jr., initiated a vernacular approach to modern architecture with his Sea Ranch Condominium in California (1964–5). Conceived as part of a master plan to develop a large site with ocean views, in collaboration with landscape architect Lawrence Halprin, the project was part of an ecological agenda to implement housing in this zone, a site that included low hills and a forest, while attending to prevailing winds, microclimates, and local flora and fauna. The first in a series of residential developments, Condominium 1 by Moore and his associates became a model for the 'Sea Ranch' type that would develop later. The continuous shed roof follows the slope of the terrain, embedding the complex in the topography. The redwood siding, as well as the timber-frame structure, further puts the architecture in tune with the environment. The asymmetrical plan, with interior courtyards and protected gardens, constitutes a clear deviation from the orthodoxy of the Modern Movement, with a complex that embeds itself into the landscape, responding to ecological factors.

Moore's sensitivity to the context was highlighted further in another project that provided an alternative to the prevailing norm in campus architecture, the Kresge College in Santa Cruz, California (1965–73) (fig.5.7). This small college campus was designed as a village cluster with traditional structures laid out irregularly to constitute alleys, pathways, and small plazas, allowing for a variety of public spaces, much like an Italian hill town. These informal spaces, framed by the neighbouring buildings, which have been celebrated and alternatively criticised as being 'flimsy' theatrical facades – colourful cardboard-like screens – actually provide a welcome contrast to the natural landscape of redwood trees that surround them. Kresge College provided an alternative model for campus design around the world, in clear contrast to the other model epitomised by the vision of Mies for the Illinois Institute of Technology campus in Chicago.

LATIN AMERICAN MODERNISM

There is a tendency among architectural historians to consider the work of Oscar Niemeyer as the progenitor of a 'regional Modernism' in Latin America. The important figure of Niemeyer, whose career spanned a century, cannot be easily relegated to a single tendency, as his work, like that of all great architects, challenges any simple categorisation. His work, in fact, spanned across different periods and continents, testifying to a more general and less specific architectural idiom, whether the buildings were designed for Brasilia, Paris, Constantine in Algiers, or Tripoli in Lebanon.

The work of Luis Barragán in Mexico earned him a particular place in the context of a regional Modernism. His long career, which began at the end of the 1920s with restoration projects as well as historicist revivals – as in the Efrain González Luna House in Guadalajara (1928) – evolved in the 1930s to take on a Modernist character, before moving into a mature phase, where a synthesis is

5.7 Moore, Lyndon, Turnbull and Whitaker, Kresge College, Santa Cruz, California, 1965–73

achieved between the particularities of place and the language of Modernism. This appears distinctly in his own house in Mexico City (1947), composed like a puzzle, with rectangular elements of open and closed spaces within an enclosure that defines the house. Inside, the main living room opens up to the garden through a large picture-frame window. The walls, rendered in light tones of terracotta, contrast with the natural wood of the floor and the abstract paintings on the wall. The whole space exudes a sense of serenity that became one of the hallmarks of the architect. As Antonio Toca Fernández remarks:

> With their courtyards, walls, gardens, fountains, and spaces, the elegant poverty of Barragán's buildings succeeds in capturing the vitality of Mexican culture. Barragán was able to identify and absorb what was worth learning from foreign architecture and incorporate it into his personal mode of expression in a manner appropriate to the Mexican climate, lifestyle and sensibility.[9]

The Egerstrom House with the appended San Cristóbal Stables (1966–8) (fig.5.8) constitutes perhaps Barragán's most famous work, which takes a larger dimension than his more modest houses, given the additional stables that form a part of the complex. Here, the whole setting is designed with the equestrian function in mind, providing generous open spaces punctuated by screening walls and water pools. The house sits at the entrance to the rectangular enclosure, composed of rectangular rooms arranged in a pinwheel fashion around a central court. The white adobe walls of the house contrast with the colourful palette of the enclosure and the garden, giving the whole its distinctive character. This work of Barragán is quite representative of a regional Modernism, infused as it is by the palette of colours that the architect attributed to the Mexican landscape, as well as to the natural elements of plants, flowers, and fruits. Yet another reading is also possible: to see in Barragán one of the early masters of a modern Minimalism, which composes with abstract elements, stripped walls of different colours, a setting that would provide an adequate background for a theatre of silence. His various designs, with

5.8   Luis Barragán, Egerstrom House and Stables (Cuadra San Cristóbal), Atizapán de Zaragoza, State of Mexico, 1966–8

REGIONAL MODERNISMS

their rich palette of violet, pink, and orange hues also evoke a De Chiricoesque landscape.

A close disciple of Barragán, Ricardo Legorreta developed a similar approach in architecture, based on a juxtaposition of colourful elements and forms, using warm textures and natural materials, and incorporating delicate details. The Camino Real Hotel in Mexico City (1968) (fig.5.9), one of Legorreta's first large-scale projects, exemplifies his architectural approach. Restricting the scale of this large hotel to six floors, the architect organised the guest rooms in a rectangular block occupying half of the site, within interconnected wings arranged around courtyards; other functions are clustered around a central courtyard, with an imposing water pool by Isamu Noguchi and pink-coloured lattice-screen walls designed by the artist Mathias Goeritz. The colourful interiors and public spaces give a distinctive accent to the design, which was conceived to shield the interior from the urban context.

With many international commissions around the world, Legorreta always sought to search for the particularities of the place. His Hamad Ben Khalifa University Student Center in Qatar (2011) (fig.5.10) is a complex that includes student dormitories, in addition to recreational areas, a sports centre, and other facilities. The different functions are arranged in clusters on an axial plan, within the introverted complex that filters light into the interior through a variety of screens. This variety is also reflected in the different spaces, each given its own colourful rendering and identity. The cubical volumes on the exterior are clad in polished stone, giving the complex a regional character.

Similar to Predock's approach towards the natural setting is the work of Peruvian architect Luis Longhi. His Pachacamac House in Lima (2006–10), located in a hilly region of orchards and plantations, submerges itself within the hilltop site, its stone cladding making it appear as a natural extension of the landscape. The apertures

5.9   Ricardo Legorreta, Camino Real Hotel, Mexico City, 1968

5.10   Ricardo Legorreta, Hamad Bin Khalifa University Student Center, Doha, Qatar, 2011

of the different rooms are like tunnels cut through the ground, bringing light to the interior spaces. The house, with an irregular composition that responds to the topography, takes the form of a medieval castle buried in the terrain, with massive walls of local stone contrasting with sections of cast concrete.

The Archaeological Museum of Paracas in Peru by Barclay and Crousse (2008–12) (fig.5.11) presents a similar attempt to integrate the architectural project in its landscape, through material and formal strategies. Built on the ruins of a previous building destroyed in the earthquake of 2007, the museum was conceived on a geometrical pattern that mimics traditional Peruvian textiles. The bright interiors, with their carefully modulated temperature and lighting, contrast with the rough texture of the exterior, rendered in reddish Pozzolan cement, which gives the building a textural quality that recalls the exhibited Pre-Columbian ceramics. The turrets incorporated in the design recall traditional solutions for natural ventilation in hot climates.

The Terreno House in Valle de Bravo, Mexico (2018) (fig.5.12) by Fernanda Canales presented an opportunity to create a work that blends into the surroundings, yet mediates the harsh climatic conditions through a structure of concrete and brick walls on a mountainous plateau. The house is composed of a series of bedrooms, arranged in a linear fashion around a central courtyard, and partly

5.11   Barclay & Crousse, The Archaeological Museum of Paracas, Paracas, Peru, 2008–12

REGIONAL MODERNISMS

left and above
5.12   Fernanda Canales, Terreno House, Valle de Bravo, Mexico, 2018

framed on the other side by the living quarters. The bedrooms are each covered by a shallow domical roof of concrete, covered by brick on the outside.

Another example of Modernism tuned to the requirements of the region is the recent project by Alberto Kalach for a school in Mexico, following the 2017 earthquake. The Jojutla School (2019) (fig.5.13) was designed as a prototype that would resist future earthquakes and provide a new type for educational buildings. It is composed of two main elements: the classrooms unit, configured as a rectangular slab with two inner courtyards; and an activities pavilion, square in form, leading to a roof garden and covered by a tensile structure. Both elements feature a grid of bi-directional concrete arches, which creates an imposing frame, while allowing a flexible arrangement of spaces. The combination of concrete with wooden components, used for lattices and pergolas, as well as brick walls for internal partitions and circulation towers, gives a regional accent to the project which was also conceived to allow natural ventilation through the open spaces and skylights.

THE VIEW FROM DOWN UNDER

In Australia, Ken Woolley is often mentioned as a leading figure of a regional movement referred to as the Sydney School, which combined several influences in their approach. His Woolley House (1962) and Baudish House (1964) are examples of this style, the latter presenting an irregular composition of free-flowing spaces, exhibiting a rich palette of natural materials, with windows and doors of reddish-brown wood, while the pine-wood ceilings rest on natural clinker brick walls. The whole ensemble blends with the natural environment and presents a domesticated version of modern architecture.

A more contemporary version of this regional Modernism can be seen in the work of Glenn

5.13   Taller de Arquitectura X (Alberto Kalach and Roberto Silva), Jojutla School, Jojutla, Oaxaca, Mexico, 2019

5.14 Glenn Murcutt, Simpson-Lee House, New South Wales, Australia, 1988–93

Murcutt, whose architecture has also been recognised for its technical sophistication and environmental responsiveness. The Simpson-Lee House in Australia (1988–93) (fig.5.14) is composed on a linear path connecting a garage/studio to the living pavilion. Entry is via a vestibule, providing bracket-glazed openings to the living areas. The vestibule accommodates a series of sliding screens, allowing a glazed wall to completely disappear and the living room to be experienced as an open veranda. The house exemplifies Murcutt's philosophy of 'touching the earth lightly', using industrial materials to realise a Minimalist architecture that blends into the landscape.

Renzo Piano's efforts to relate his buildings to the specificities of location and 'culture' found one of its most expressive forms in the Jean-Marie Tjibaou Cultural Centre (1991–8) (fig.5.15) designed for the Kanak community in New Caledonia, off the coast of Australia. Attempting to blend his expertise and technical skills with the particular building traditions of the place, Piano resorted to a detailed study of Kanak culture and their typology of habitations. The whole complex was devised as a 'settlement', composed of ten huts that rise to different heights, each one based on a circular plan. These separate huts, connected by a path, are organised primarily into three different villages. The first, at the entrance, is dedicated to exhibitions, with a sunken auditorium for major events. The second contains the administrative functions, while the third village, at the end and slightly apart, is dedicated to creative and pedagogical activities. These hut-like structures act like wind-breaks, with adjustable louvres that respond to the prevailing winds, framed by structural systems that enclose the spaces within. Using laminated wood, concrete, glass panels, and steel, as well as tree barks, the architect assembled this project as a 'composite' of different materials, with a keen interest in making it blend naturally into its surroundings, while also symbolically relating it to the local culture.

CONTEMPORARY EXAMPLES FROM ASIA

The Japanese architect Kengo Kuma – notable for a number of works, from the Nezu Museum in Tokyo (2009) to the Exchange in Sydney (2020) – has also completed a series of projects that exemplify his approach in negotiating the particular materials and techniques of the region. This is especially true of his projects that are located in small villages or non-urban contexts, where the affinity to the locale plays a more important role.

Kuma's design for a market and hotel in Yusuhara, Japan (2009–10) (fig.5.16) represents this regionalist tendency in his work. Conceived as a large indoor market with a small hotel, the building combines modern materials like concrete and glass, with traditional ones such as wood and thatch. The ground level of the market opens to the street with wide glass bays, while the structure of the internal hall is composed of tall wooden posts, bearing a ceiling of wooden beams. On the other side of the open atrium space lie three floors accommodating the hotel rooms. The exterior of the complex is covered by panels of thatched straw

5.15   Renzo Piano, Jean-Marie Tjibaou Cultural Centre, Noumea, New Caledonia, 1991–8

which insulate and shade the interior space. The architect synthesises here two different aspects of architecture: a vernacular approach which uses materials from the local culture 'as found'; and a modern approach with more polished and industrial materials like glass and concrete.

In China's Yunnan province, Kuma designed the Yunfeng Spa Resort (2016) as a series of terraces with individual units straddling the topography, clad in local stones of different colours ranging from light beige to dark grey, and arranged as a three-dimensional mosaic. The architect explained this composition as a way to relate to the site and beyond, to the mountain of Yunfengshan, a sacred place in Taoism. The houses were thus arranged to follow the spiritual path of the mountain. Unlike the individual resort units that face the public paths with a somewhat opaque stone facade, the centrepiece of the resort – a communal building housing the main entertainment and spa functions – is a large space with wide bays of glass opening up to the landscape around it. Its multi-tiered roof structure is also covered in stone cladding, like the individual units, ensuring a closer rapport with the natural context.

In China, the first Chinese architect to win the Pritzker Prize, Wang Shu, founded with his wife, Lu Wenyu, the Amateur Architecture Studio,

MODERN ARCHITECTURE IN A POST-MODERN ERA

104

which is credited with a large number of projects, most of which insert themselves in a sensitive manner in their context. As part of his self-training in architecture, Wang Shu went to work with craftsmen to gain experience in actual building construction. The first projects he undertook were mainly renovations of old buildings, which led him later on to favour the use of recycled materials in construction. The Academy of Art in Hangzhou (2007) (fig.5.17) stands out as an example of this synthesis between new and old methods of construction. The organisation is based on the typical concept of enclosure, with courtyards and gardens playing a central role in the composition. The complex is composed of several buildings, with the main functions located in a linear composition that turns and twists in response to the site. These large buildings, built of concrete, are characterised by their undulating traditional roof. Other individual buildings complement the composition and articulate their own presence on the campus. All the functions were carefully accommodated with regard to views, wind, sun, and relationship to the site. The base of the buildings and most of the external walls were all composed of recycled stones, which came from the demolitions of existing houses, while the units facing the internal courtyards were faced with large panels of wood.

Founded by the architect Zhang Ke, the firm Standard Architecture, established in 2001 in China, has also to its credit a number of inspiring works that fall within this spectrum of regional Modernism. As the architect states, his work aims to consciously distance itself from the typical work of his generation, with a focus on creating buildings that are rooted in their historic and cultural settings. Two of the firm's recent works stand out particularly as examples of this regional Modernist approach: the Tibet Visitor Centre (2008) and the Yarlung Boat Terminal (2014).

The Tibet Namchabawa Visitor Centre (2007–8) is located in a small village in the southeastern part of Tibet's autonomous region. The building serves as both a visitor and town centre for the villagers nearby; it includes a medical station, meeting rooms, and service areas. The concept generator is the series of massive stone walls set into the slope, like retaining walls that form an extension to the landscape. Following a footpath, the visitors

5.16   Kengo Kuma, Community Market and Hotel, Yusuhara, Kochi, Japan, 2009–10 find their way into the main hall of the building, a long rectangular slab, from where they proceed to the other spaces, all laid out in parallel strips to the main hall. The interiors provide a stimulating contrast between the rough stone of the walls and the white-painted concrete of the floors and ceilings. Few openings are articulated within these spaces, offering a view to the mountains beyond.

The Yarlung Boat Terminal (2014) is also a small structure located on the bank of the Yarlung Tsangpo river, in Tibet. Working with a small building programme, consisting of a lounge, a ticket office, an emergency dormitory, and public amenities, the architect designed a building that blends well into its natural context while asserting its presence, with one wing projecting above the land and offering a view of the river, like a belvedere. The L-shaped structure is accessed through ramps that lead to the main spaces. The walls and roofs are built of local stones, executed by local masons from the region. The interior spaces provide a rich contrast between the natural stone and the floors and ceilings of timber.

The Indian subcontinent provided a fertile ground for its own versions of regional Modernism, which started with the work of the pioneers, who were influenced by Le Corbusier, Kahn, and other Modernists, yet who had already charted their own way towards a regional style. Among these pioneers, two main figures stand out: Charles Correa and Balkrishna Doshi.

After completing his bachelor studies in Mumbai, Charles Correa went to Michigan and then MIT, where he received his master's degree. Despite studies with Buckminster Fuller in Michigan, Correa opted for a more traditional approach, combining some of the features of Modernism with local traditions and materials. His Gandhi Memorial (1963) is a case in point. The building incorporates a museum and archives in a modest structure of modular concrete units, topped by brick-covered pyramidal roofs. Some units are enclosed by brick walls, while others are open-walled. The plan is organised in an irregular way around a large, outdoor public space, mimicking the organisation of traditional Indian villages.

5.17   Wang Shu – Amateur Architecture Studio, The Academy of Art in Hangzhou, China, 2007

Balkrishna Doshi, another pioneer of modern architecture in India, is often referred to as a 'Brutalist', given his association with Le Corbusier, in whose office he worked, and whom he assisted on the Ahmedabad projects. However, his Sangath Office in Ahmedabad, India, (1981) clearly articulates his attempts at synthesis between Modernism and regionalist tendencies. Sangath incorporates the architect's office, in addition to a research centre, all sunk into the ground, with a prominent roof system of barrel vaults covering the different volumes, built of low-cost and recycled materials. The complex is organised in a modular way, around an open court that doubles as an amphitheatre.

Carl Pruscha, an Austrian architect who devoted much of his life to working in Asia, developed a regional style that also made use of brick as a basic material for construction. The Taragaon Hostel in Nepal (1971–5), located on the route between India and Tibet, is intended for use by pilgrims to the nearby Buddhist sanctuary of Boudhanath. It is an example of a mature work which makes use of traditional construction methods impregnated by a Modernist approach that simplifies forms, and puts emphasis on tectonics over other aspects of design. The hostel was composed of a series of units housing dormitories, arranged around a number of courtyards and alleyways, with two main buildings at the centre comprising the communal facilities. The double-layered brick barrel vaults allowed for better climatic performance.

Anupama Kundoo received international recognition for her revival of traditional crafts, and her exploration of economical and sustainable methods of construction. Her buildings feature traditional craftsmanship while also doubling as experimental case studies, as in her own house, Wall House (2000), situated on the outskirts of Auroville in India. There, the architect conceived the house as a composition of parallel linear catenary vaults, built of hollow clay tubes for additional insulation, and walls of local bricks. While the building features a solid wall on one side, it opens itself to the surroundings on the other sides, integrating the building within its natural context. Kundoo's Nandalal Sewa Samithi Library in Pondicherry, India (2018) was also built of local bricks, yet projects a distinctive institutional character through its overall composition and playful roof shape, which alludes to an open book. The roof canopies, in plastered and painted masonry, create an element of contrast to the brick walls, detailed in distinctive brick courses. The interior of the building provides extensive reading areas, while the roof also offers a generous space for collective activities.

Another architect who further carries the message of regionalism is Bijoy Jain of Studio Mumbai. Jain's work does not follow any prescribed rules, but instead tries in different ways to create an architecture that blends with its surroundings, while reviving craft techniques and using traditional materials. His several works, in India and abroad, testify to a 'timeless way' of building, assuming a very subdued character. The Palmyra House in Alibag, India (2005–7) (fig.5.18) is an example of restrained elegance. Conceived as two linear elements, separated by an outdoor patio with a pool of water, the house is submerged in its landscape of palm trees. The two elements are both based on a wooden structure, with louvres made of palm trees filtering the light through. Similar in composition, they both feature a double-storey public function opening onto the common patio, with a mezzanine level containing the bedrooms. The tall wooden louvres on the patio side can slide open, further erasing the boundaries between interior and exterior.

The Copper House II in Chondi (2011–12) was designed on a U-shaped plan, mixing concrete and wood-frame construction and topped by copper panels for the roof and wall cornices. The interiors, with their rhythmic repetition of wood studs, contrast with the plain concrete surfaces, exuding a feeling of serenity. Similar effects can be discerned in the Carrimjee House in Satirje (2011–14) (fig.5.19), a composition on a rectangular plan of nine principal rooms, connected by a patio and arranged around two principal courtyards. The complex is built of bricks and lime, with a plywood roof. The character of the work harks back to 'Oriental' examples, especially Katsura, for its complex simplicity, and its distinct way of incorporating nature into architecture. A more sophisticated example of the use of brick can be found in the Ahmedabad Residence in Gujarat (2011–14), an introverted structure centred around three dwelling units, arranged around a large courtyard, for a multi-

REGIONAL MODERNISMS

left, top

5.18   Studio Mumbai Architects – Bijoy Jain, Palmyra House, Alibag, India, 2005–7

left, bottom

5.19   Studio Mumbai Architects – Bijoy Jain, Carrimjee House, Satirje, Maharashtra, India, 2011–14

generation family. The use of thin brick elements, produced on site, in combination with concrete for the structural elements, gives this project an affinity to the work of Kahn. But unlike Kahn, there is no effort spent here on geometrical transformations, or on articulating spaces within spaces. The outcome is more subdued, again suggesting a phenomenological approach to form-making.

AFRICA AND THE MIDDLE EAST

In the Middle East and Africa, similar efforts were made to come to terms with Modernism, by adopting its lessons while adapting them also to the cultural and climatic factors of the region.

One of the first pioneers of a distinct architectural style in the Middle East is the Iraqi architect Rifaat Chaderji. Chaderji has several projects in Iraq to his credit, built during the early years of the new republic, such as the Administration Offices for the Federation of Industries in Baghdad (1966). This monumental complex features a playful contrast between openings and solid walls on the facade, re-introducing the arched windows as an element of composition, as well as the use of brick as a cladding material.

The Jordanian architect Jaafar Tukan's SOS Children's Village in Aqaba, Jordan (1991) (fig.5.20) provides another example of a sensitive interpretation of traditional typologies. The complex of individual units was designed as a cluster of small houses, with a kindergarten, an administration building, staff housing, a sports hall, and auxiliary functions. The units were arranged to form shaded courtyards accessible through vaulted archways, and constructed of reinforced concrete structures with stone infill.

In many of the Gulf states that witnessed a surge in development after their independence in the 1970s, foreign architects who were commissioned to design major projects often resorted to a similar search for an architecture that would address the local traditions and the different climatic constraints, while also responding to new requirements. I.M. Pei's Museum of Islamic Art in Doha (2008) is exemplary, where the concept was inspired by the 13th-century ablution fountain of the Mosque of Ahmad Ibn Tulun in Cairo. The museum is composed of a five-storey main building and a two-storey education wing, which are connected across a central courtyard. The main building's angular volumes step back progressively as they rise around the high atrium. The dome covering the atrium is concealed from outside view by the walls of the central tower. The desert sun plays a fundamental role, transforming the architecture into a play of light and shadows.

The trio Saad el Kabbaj, Driss Kettani, and Mohamed Amine Siana collaborated on a series of exemplary projects in Morocco, combining the lessons of Modernism with the particularities of the North African context. Their projects for Taroudant University (2006–10) and the Technology School of Guelmim (2008–11) were exhibited and shortlisted for several awards. Their approach is based on the search for a contextual Modernism, inspired by the site, the local culture, and the geography. In Taroudant (fig.5.21), the architects developed the plan for a large university complex – including auditoria, classrooms, and laboratories – laid out in a geometrical order as a series of pavilions around

5.20   Jaafar Tukan, SOS Children's Village, Aqaba, Jordan, 1991

above and below

5.21   Saad el Kabbaj, Driss Kettani, and Mohamed Amine Siana, Taroudant University, Morocco, 2006–10

a central space, known as 'Riyad', which constitutes the green oasis at the centre of a town in traditional Arab architecture. The pavilions are uniformly rendered in the traditional brown-ochre stucco, with opaque facades to the exterior that open up selectively to the interior courts and other views.

The Technology School of Guelmim (fig.5.22), like its sibling in Taroudant, is characterised by the opaque and introverted arrangement of its elementary volumes, built of concrete and covered in stucco in typical ochre colours, assembled in a linear fashion along a main axis route. The

architecture appears as a monumental composition of elements, enclosing internal courtyards, with openings punctuating it in a rhythmic order that recalls, without overt imitation, the traditional architecture of the region.

This architectural language that Kabbaj, Kettani, and Siana adopted for their institutional projects in Morocco was also taken up by the Catalan architect Ricardo Bofill, in his project for the Mohammed VI Polytechnic University in Ben Guerir, Morocco (2016) (fig.5.23). Seeking to find the synthesis between Morocco's heritage and modern architecture, Bofill laid out the plan of this campus on a grid of different modules, each containing one of the main functions. Arcades, as well as semi-covered streets and alleys, duplicate the typologies of the traditional urban realm in the region and create a variety of spaces, with a central square as its nucleus, covered by a large undulating steel and glass canopy. The multiple volumes are all rendered in the typical ochre-colour stucco, creating a monumental composition.

In a similar vein to Studio Mumbai's work in India in its incorporation of local techniques and materials in the process of construction, is the work of Francis Kéré who returned to his native Burkina Faso to develop projects that serve the community and expand social services to the disadvantaged population. The primary school in Gando (2001) (fig.5.24) is a basic linear composition of three large classrooms connected by a covered patio, built

above and below

5.22   Saad el Kabbaj, Driss Kettani, and Mohamed Amine Siana, Technology School of Guelmim, Guelmim, Morocco, 2008–11

of local bricks. A rhythmic set of brick columns project from the wall and frame a colourful set of windows that give it a particular accent. The whole is covered by a vaulted brick roof that is overlaid by another metallic umbrella-roof, held by a truss system, serving to protect from rainfall while allowing natural ventilation through the openings of the brick vault. In his architectural approach, Kéré is not only inspired by the traditional architecture of the region, but also by 'natural' elements, searching for a synthesis between the natural and the artificial. One reads in Kéré's work a deep appreciation of the richness of nature and a search for the characteristics by which it can inform the architectural project. This is evident, for example, in the project for a National Assembly in Benin, which the architect explains as:

5.23   Ricardo Bofill, Mohammed VI Polytechnic University, Ben Guerir, Morocco, 2016

When built structures resemble patterns that occur in nature, they become capable of offering a sense of embrace and comfort, because one recognizes these elements from the outside world. Just as the enticing details of the Nando Mosque in Mali seem to have been honed by forces like wind, water, and organic growth, so has my team at the Kéré Architecture Studio taken cues from tree trunks and branches to design an assembly hall that conjures the protective cover of a magnificent kapok tree for the National Assembly of Benin. And just as with the inspiration, the seeming minimalism and simplicity belies the intricate complexity of such a structure.[10]

The Benin National Assembly (under construction) in Ouagadougou was conceived as a pyramidal structure enclosing a large, covered forum space, reflecting the ideals of democracy through openness and transparency, after a long dictatorial rule. Following traditional patterns of congregation in the villages, Kéré reinstated the *Arbre à palabres* [tree of discussion] in a private garden adjacent to the assembly hall where members of parliament could also convene. In the same spirit, the stepped pyramid offers a space for citizens to gather and ascend all the way to the top to view the city.

In an earlier work, the National Park of Mali (2010) – commissioned by the Aga Khan Trust for Culture – the architect resorted to different materials to create a series of pavilions, including a restaurant and a sports centre, in a natural setting. The buildings he inserted in the park

5.24   Francis Kéré, Primary School in Gando, Burkina Faso, 2001

5.25 Toshiko Mori, Thread Artists' Residences and Cultural Center, Sinthian, Senegal, 2015

setting all feature a series of enclosing walls, of brick and perforated concrete blocks, surmounted by a canopy that is lifted on a slender steel truss, evoking the traditional shelters of the region.

In Senegal, the Japanese-American architect Toshiko Mori designed the Thread Artists' Residences and Cultural Center (2015) (fig.5.25), a project funded by the Josef and Anni Albers Foundation to provide cultural facilities for this region. The project was designed on a rectangular grid, with two oval-shaped openings cutting through it, providing the space for internal courtyards. Supported on a structure of white-painted concrete columns and beams, and enclosed by brick walls, the roof creates the element of interest in this project, wedding traditional materials to modern ones. The project involved local craftsmen who shared their techniques and realised the undulating roof canopy that responds to the complex design, using bamboo and thatch. From a distance, the building appears like a traditional construction, blending naturally into the landscape.

Toshiko Mori's other project in Senegal, the Fass Elementary School (2019), appears like a vast canopy, a shading device also using bamboo and thatch for the roof, which takes the shape of a large saucer covering an elliptical space, while channelling rainwater to the underground. The elliptical-shaped ground floor is enclosed by mud-brick walls, supported by steel and bamboo elements, and compartmentalised into classrooms that are separated by open spaces, allowing natural ventilation. The open-air spaces are used for recreational activities, school gatherings, and celebrations. Instead of regular openings that bring direct sunlight and heat, Mori used perforated brick panels to bring filtered light into the classrooms. In the hot climate of the region, shade and shelter become the key factors, with the architect working closely in collaboration with the craftsmen and artisans.

6 The Technological Paradigm

There were many streams throughout history that inspired the development of a 'technological paradigm' within modern architecture. Some historians attribute this influence all the way back to the Gothic builders whose masterpieces were exemplary in their 'structural' sophistication. Yet the impetus towards adopting new materials, principally steel and glass, as construction materials goes back to the 19th century, and specifically to Joseph Paxton's Crystal Palace (1851), which was the first monument, albeit temporary, to incorporate standardisation and the use of these new materials. And despite the call for standardisation which was articulated at the Werkbund exhibition in Cologne in 1914, and later adopted by several architects, it was not until the second half of the 20th century that such calls began to be translated, first in fictional projects by Archigram and Superstudio, and later in the experimental work of Buckminster Fuller which was geared towards a more sustainable architecture. The new trend that developed out of these experiments, and which came into being in the 1970s, would be given the label of 'High-Tech', despite the reservations that some architects would have about this designation.

One of the major critics to voice his support for a futuristic direction in architecture was the critic and historian Reyner Banham. Banham's thesis on modern architecture took the symbolic title of *Theory and Design in the First Machine Age*, implying that the first phase of modern architecture, roughly running from 1910 to 1960, was only a prelude to the full realisation of a 'machine age', which should ultimately find its fulfilment in a complete technological revolution that would incorporate new scientific and ecological developments in architecture.[1] Banham faulted the early Modernists for having only flirted with technology, abandoning its potential and relapsing into an 'academic' tradition that favoured the adaptation of types. Between the revolutionary 'Dymaxion House' by Buckminster Fuller and a more symbolic 'Villa Savoye' by Le Corbusier, it was clear to Banham that, had the former been realised, it would have rendered the latter technically obsolete. He thus summarised this lapse into symbolic forms:

> In picking on the Phileban solids and mathematics, the creators of the International Style took a convenient short-cut to creating an ad-hoc language of symbolic forms, but it was a language that could only communicate under the special conditions of the Twenties, when automobiles were visibly comparable to the Parthenon, when aircraft structure really did resemble Elementarist space cages [. . .][2]

Banham's ideas were quite radical for the times, and intentionally polemical. Yet he maintained a certain momentum that inspired many others to think of an 'architecture autre' that would transcend the formal limits imposed on it. For Banham, even the work of Mies, celebrated for its technological sophistication, did not really fulfil the objectives of a second machine age; objectives that should not focus on scrupulous attention to detail, but rather on the incorporation of new technologies that would bring it nearer to becoming a disposable product. Projects that came close to reaching that level were, in addition to Fuller's Dymaxion House, CLASP's model school for the Milan Triennale of 1960 and the case study house of Charles Eames.[3] The mixture of ad-hocism, of experimental and innovative technological solutions, as well as adopting the lessons of consumer culture, would mark the approach of Banham which filtered through his numerous writings.

As the majority of historians agree, the general characteristics of this new style that would be labelled as High-Tech were its commitment to the implementation of the original agenda of modern architecture, through the expression of structural and mechanical components and their separate articulation from the building envelope, and use

6.1   Renzo Piano and Richard Rogers, Centre Georges Pompidou, Paris, France, 1971–7

of new technologies and materials in addition to adoption of industrialisation as an integral process in building construction. At a time when Post-Modernism was on the rise across much of the world, the continued commitment of these architects to this agenda was quite admirable. It is to be noted here that all of the major High-Tech projects would actually not have seen the light of day without the efforts of structural engineers, noteworthy among whom are Ove Arup, Peter Rice, and Anthony Hunt, whose collaboration with the architects from the early phases of the design process was instrumental in realising these works.

CENTRE POMPIDOU: A HIGH-TECH MANIFESTO IN BUILT FORM

If Paxton provided the first major industrial building of the 19th century, with the Crystal Palace, then Renzo Piano and Richard Rogers should be credited with the first High-Tech building of the 20th century, the Centre Georges Pompidou in Paris (1971-7) (fig.6.1). The team of Piano and Rogers, in close collaboration with Peter Rice of Ove Arup & Partners, won this competition in 1971, beating 680 other entrants. Their radical design proposed a steel skeletal structure that would free the interior spaces from any posts, allowing a flexible arrangement of spaces, and expressing all the structural and mechanical parts of the building. The building design went through a series of adjustments until it reached the final design stage. The escalators leading to the various floors were all relegated to one side of the building, suspended from the main facade and overlooking the great plaza, while colour-coded mechanical components were arranged on the opposite side, facing the street. Inside, large steel truss systems supported the different floors and were connected to the peripheral truss system carrying the whole building and its components. Working closely with the structural engineers, the architects devised new details, such as the famous 'gerberettes' (fig.6.2) which along with the wide-span trusses, were all cast in moulds in Essen, Germany and transported to be assembled on site. The Centre Pompidou took six years to complete and was inaugurated

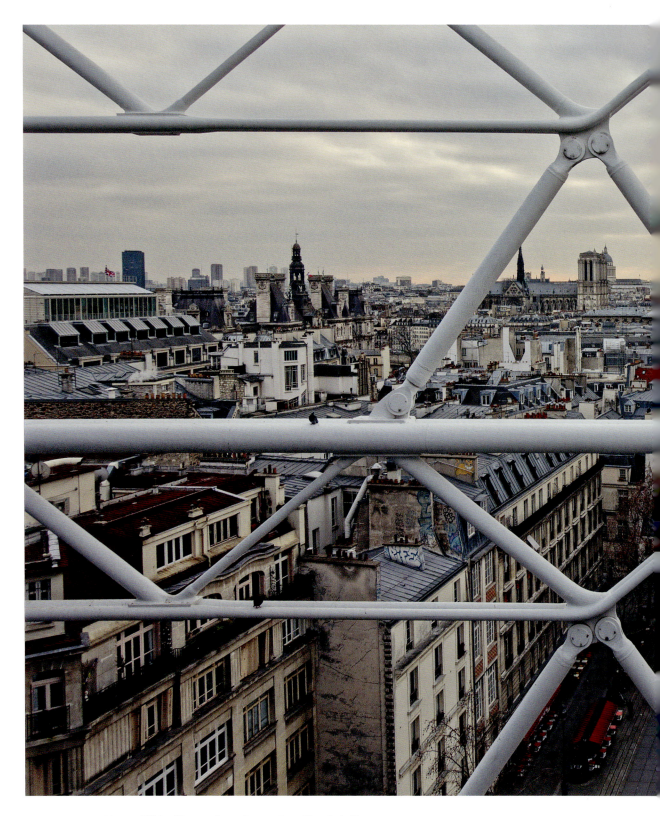

6.2   Renzo Piano and Richard Rogers, Centre Georges Pompidou, Paris, France, 1971–7

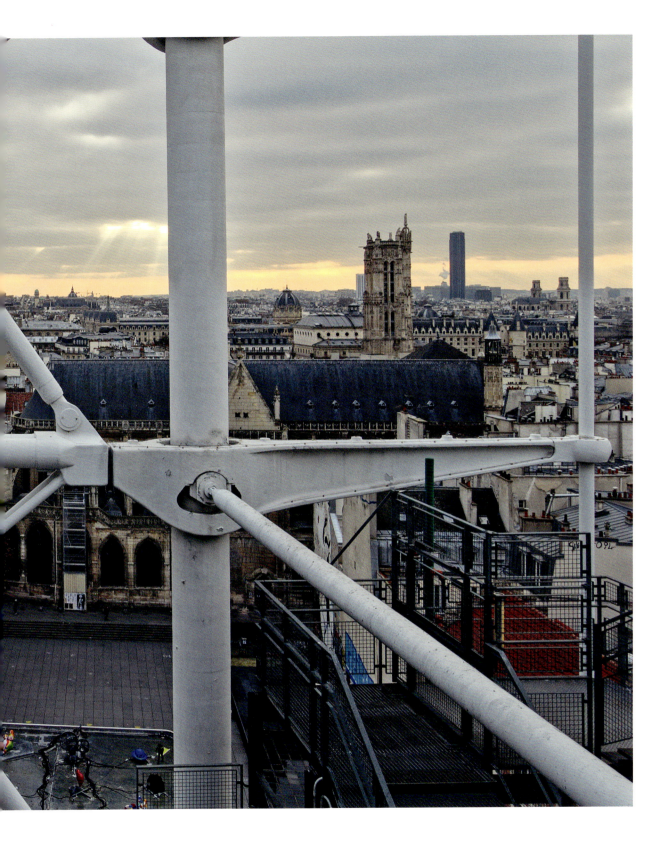

in 1977. The concept of the building as a machine, first evoked by Le Corbusier, appears to have been finally fulfilled here in Paris, in this large-scale project.[4]

Writing about the Centre Pompidou (or Beaubourg) years later, Renzo Piano actually dismissed its 'High-Tech' connotations. For him, it was a provocation, a counter-culture manifesto, not simply a technological machine:

> Beaubourg is a double provocation: a challenge to academicism, but also a parody of the technological imagery of our time. To see it as high-tech is a misunderstanding. The Centre Pompidou is a 'celibate machine', in which the flaunting of brightly coloured metal and transparent tubing serves an urban, symbolic, and expressive function, not a technical one.[5]

The partnership of Piano and Rogers dissolved after the Centre Pompidou, each one going his own way. Renzo Piano created his own 'workshop' where his interest in new materials and technologies did not overwhelm an innate penchant towards craft and fine detailing. His other projects continued to explore new techniques and materials, but were no longer obsessively concerned with a 'High-Tech' imagery as manifested in the Centre Pompidou. Later projects, such as the Menil Collection in Texas (1982–6), the Beyeler Foundation Museum in Riehen, near Basel (1991–7), the Morgan Library & Museum in New York (2003–6), and the Isabella Stewart Gardner Museum addition in Boston (2005–12), betrayed a continued attention to structural articulation, symbolic expression, and elaboration of new solutions to climate and energy. In all these projects, Piano displayed his versatility as a designer who carefully analyses the particularity of each problem and the different functional and climatic conditions related to it, in order to devise a solution that is characterised by a certain lightness and clarity of conception. If we take the Menil Collection (fig.6.3) as an example, the structure was designed as a simple rectangular frame, with an ingenious solution that allows natural

6.3 Renzo Piano, The Menil Collection, Houston, Texas, USA, 1982–6

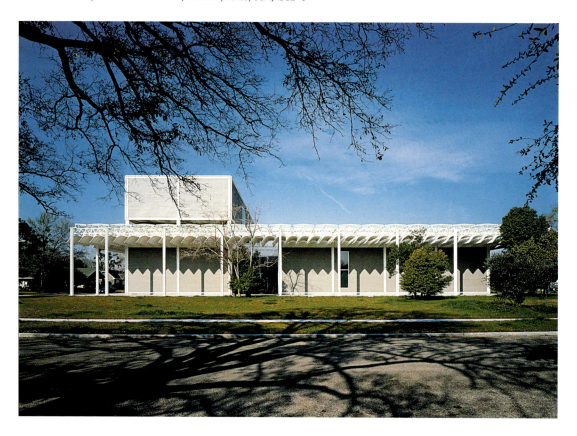

6.4 Renzo Piano, Beyeler Foundation Museum, Riehen, Switzerland, 1991–7

light to come indirectly through the ceiling, through a system of ferro-concrete 'leaves', designed to modulate light in a way so as not to damage the artworks. The schematics confirm to what extent light was the main generator of this project, with everything else following from this basic parameter. The building was thus conceived as an arrangement of repetitive modules on an orthogonal grid, with a steel frame structure in which wooden panels were incorporated as partitions. The interior space exudes a sense of calm and restraint, which allows for the contemplation of artworks in a rather neutral background.

The Beyeler Foundation Museum (fig.6.4) is not too different in conception from the Menil Collection. Here again the architect focused on creating the most favourable setting for the art collection of Ernst Beyeler. And as in the previous case, but deploying another set of tools, the architect designed a structure that allows light to filter through the roof, which cantilevers beyond the building footprint. A system of walls of different heights, built in a red stone that mimics the stone of Basel Cathedral, articulates the different spaces and creates an interesting dialogue with the ethereal roof.

In the Isabella Stewart Gardner Museum Extension (fig.6.5), Piano carefully inserted a new complex at the back of the original Neo-Renaissance palazzo, rendered in typical steel and glass. The addition, composed of four volumes clad in green pre-patinated copper and red brick, contains a large exhibition hall and an auditorium. The new wing was designed as a transparent box to provide uninterrupted views of the historic building and gardens. Somewhat controversial was the decision to move the entrance from the old museum to the new addition in order to accommodate a larger lobby space with cloakrooms and other amenities.

MODERN ARCHITECTURE IN A POST-MODERN ERA

6.5   Renzo Piano, Isabella Stewart Gardner Museum Extension, Boston, Massachusetts, USA, 2005–12

The new entrance thus opens to a glass and steel shed, appended to a 'greenhouse', leading to the new facilities. On the upper levels were located the two volumes containing the exhibition gallery, with an adjustable ceiling height and a large music hall.

Piano's workshop also tackled extra-large projects, such as the Kansai International Airport in Japan, which was built over an artificial island near Osaka (1990–94). Piano won this competition in 1988, and construction began in 1991. The design solution had to take into consideration the multiple factors of land settlement, earthquake resistance, and functional complexity resulting from a large-size structure stretching over almost two kilometres over a man-made island. Clad with 82,000 uniform stainless-steel panels, which makes the building appear to float over the island like a 'glider', the airport opens up at the central atrium, where it encompasses the large open space. The main form-

6.6   Jean Nouvel, Institut du Monde Arabe, Paris, France, 1981–7

120

6.7   Jean Nouvel, Fondation Cartier, Paris, France, 1991–4

giver of this complex structure is its roof, designed in such a way as to channel the air from the passenger to the runway side, while responding to structural criteria. Piano described it as a 'precision instrument', where every element was shaped and designed through a process of mathematical calculation.

Another architect who adapted the High-Tech aesthetic, especially in his early works, is Jean Nouvel. Nouvel's approach can be traced through three different projects: the seminal Institut du Monde Arabe in Paris, the Cartier Foundation, and the Lafayette Galleries in Berlin. Nouvel designed the Arab World Institute (1981–7) (fig.6.6) as a mediator between the West and the Arab world. A structure of steel and glass that could be considered as well among the masterpieces of High-Tech architecture, the building distinguished itself by incorporating the motif of the 'mashrabiyah', the traditional screen windows found in Arab architecture, interpreted here as repetitive apertures on the southern facade that respond like the lens of a camera to the different light conditions. The building was conceived as an L-shaped structure with the main vertical slab facing the urban square and a curvilinear slab facing the riverside, with an internal plaza forming the nexus between the two elements.

Along similar lines, but with a radically different effect, the Fondation Cartier (1991–4) (fig.6.7) is an example of the reinterpretation of the Miesian aesthetic, with a building that presents an imposing facade of glass to the street, behind which alternate views of the internal spaces and the natural landscape. Like a showcase displaying samples of natural vegetation, the facade, which extends to the edge of the site, at some point acts as a freestanding screen that blurs the boundaries between the real and the virtual. As Nouvel explained, the building is 'about lightness, with a refined framework of steel and glass'. It consists of 'blurring the tangible boundaries of the building and rendering superfluous the reading of a solid volume amid poetics of fuzziness and effervescence'.[6]

The Galleries Lafayette, designed on the major avenue of Friedrichstrasse after the fall of the Berlin Wall (1991–6), is a large department store that occupies a whole corner block, providing a homogenous surface of dark curtain glass, and marked by horizontal strips that incorporate the graphic displays and technical elements. The interior presents a spectacular composition with a large conical form originating at ground level, reaching up to the top, and bringing light to the interior, complemented by a smaller inverted cone that draws light all the way to the basement levels. Nouvel presented in this case a contemporary version of the department store type, which hints at the iconic buildings of 19th-century Paris, without imitating those historic landmarks.

THE BRITISH CRUSADE FOR A TECHNOLOGICAL ARCHITECTURE

There is no question that the epicentre of the High-Tech movement was in the United Kingdom, with many of its architects coming from this particular context, due to its historic affiliation to industrial centres of production. Before the Centre Pompidou episode, Norman Foster and Richard Rogers, who had met at Yale, formed a brief partnership known as Team 4 which included their spouses, respectively Wendy Cheesman and Su Brumwell. After a few experimental projects that were inspired by their former tutor Paul Rudolph, Team 4 received a commission to design a factory on the outskirts of Swindon for a manufacturing company. The constraints of the programme, which necessitated a fast construction, gave the architects the opportunity to propose one of the earliest High-Tech structures: the Reliance Controls factory. The design relied on standardised components that could be assembled on site, based on a standard

below and right
6.8   Richard Rogers, Lloyd's of London, London, UK, 1978–86

module of steel-frame square, on an open floor system that was quite innovative for the time. The factory featured a clear expression of the structural system, composed of steel posts and beams, with cross-bracing on the exterior, and a wall system of profiled metal panels, as well as glass.

At the completion of the Centre Pompidou, Richard Rogers landed a major commission to design the new headquarters for the Lloyd's of London insurance company (fig.6.8), which was completed in 1986. The company required a large expansion of its offices, as well as a fitting monument to its new, global presence. Rogers designed a landmark building featuring a large open atrium space surrounded by a cluster of towers that house the various offices, with all the mechanical systems relegated to the exterior of the building, located within separate vertical units. The resultant effect, with the stainless-steel cladding of the facades, is that of an aggregate of components, almost as intricate as a mechanical engine. On the interior, large concrete columns carry the structural load of floors and mitigate the steel and glass aesthetic, while the imposing atrium, with its barrel-vaulted skylight, extends to the full height of the building, giving it the appearance of a modern Gothic cathedral.

In post-reunification Berlin, following a master plan for the reconstruction of Potsdamer Platz, Rogers (now as Rogers, Stirk, Harbour + Partners) was commissioned to design three buildings on the Daimler Chrysler portion of the site (1993–9). Respecting the strict regulations regarding building height, but subverting other criteria related to typology under a 'Post-Modern' regime, Rogers proposed a set of buildings with a definite technological appearance, with the chief aim of reducing energy consumption, allowing daylight and ventilation to penetrate through the complex. The three blocks share the same overall configuration, based on a square plan with a central atrium covered by the last two floors, and open on one side through a diagonal cut that allows light into the atrium. Each block is a mixed-use unit, with retail on the ground level, offices and residential units above. The atrium space is naturally ventilated, with fresh air circulating through the plenum located between retail and office areas. Solar radiation reduces energy consumption in wintertime. The facades are faced with both clear and opaque glass panels, ceramic tiles, external and internal blinds, allowing adjustment of sunlight to internal needs. The prevailing metallic elements on the facades and the curtain glass wall, in addition to the cylindrical units acting like pivots at the corners, give this complex the appearance of a 'machine in the garden', carefully set within its landscaped urban context.

Another stimulating project by Richard Rogers and his team was the design for the Law Courts of the City of Bordeaux (1992–8) (fig.6.9). Won through a competition in 1992, this project aimed at offering an alternative vision for what a courthouse would look like, while employing all the tools at their disposal to reduce the energy consumption of such a large complex. The complex was transformed into a grand forum, accessible to the public, where the individual courtrooms take the form of cylindrical pods, like suspended 'eggs', covered in cedar-wood and elevated above the plinth, within a large rectangular space covered by an undulating copper roof. Administrative areas that include the judges' and lawyers' offices are all located within a five-storey block at the street side. The functions are articulated to ensure legibility while providing separate access routes for the judges and the public. As usual, the design was informed by environmental factors that

6.9 Richard Rogers, Law Courts of the City of Bordeaux, France, 1992–8

determined the overall layout and construction details. It incorporated measures to reduce energy consumption, relying on passive control systems that eliminated the need for air conditioning. Manually operated brise-soleils were located on the western side, thus reducing solar gain during the hot months. The atrium acts like a buffer-zone from the outside environment, providing a continuous supply of fresh air through a specially designed waterfall system that cools the air inside the building. The individual courts are ventilated naturally, drawing hot air upwards and out at roof level. Through this intelligent design system, Rogers not only succeeded in responding to the environmental challenges, but also in subverting traditional typologies related to important civic functions.

Norman Foster graduated from the University of Manchester, then went to Yale, where he met Richard Rogers. As previously mentioned, their collaboration lasted only from 1963 to 1967, and led to one of the earliest High-Tech structures, the Reliance Controls factory. Foster went on to found Foster + Partners, a firm that collaborated with Buckminster Fuller on a series of projects, where the passion for technological innovation was coupled with an increasing concern for environmental issues. Foster's first major work after the Team 4 collaboration was the Willis Faber & Dumas headquarters in Ipswich (1975). In addition to its unusual appearance – a curvilinear wall of dark glass that wraps around an irregular site – this building was far from the technological premises of the earlier Reliance Controls factory. In fact, it was conceived as a concrete structure, with a regular grid of columns supporting coffered slabs, and enclosed at the outer edges by a necklace of irregularly placed columns that delimit a free circulation space. The distinguishing aspect of this office building was the open space layout, spread over three storeys around an internal court, served by escalators. By following the contour of the site, the glass curtain-wall reflected the historic structures around the square.

A more significant commission, in terms of its response to the High-Tech agenda, was the Sainsbury Centre for the Visual Arts at the University of East Anglia (1974–8) (fig.6.10). As opposed to a typical academic building, and

6.10   Foster + Partners, Sainsbury Centre for the Visual Arts, University of East Anglia, Norwich, UK, 1974–8

in contrast to the Brutalist language of nearby structures, Foster proposed a large hangar with a free internal space to accommodate a variety of functions and exhibitions. The shiny metal enclosure was given ample thickness to integrate the mechanical systems, as well as other utilitarian functions, forming a continuous wrap-around envelope and eliminating any distinction between rooftop and sidewalls. At the two extremities of the form, large panes of glass constituted the main openings, framed by an imposing truss system.[7]

From these early works of somewhat modest scale, Foster's major breakthrough came with the design of the HSBC headquarters in Hong Kong (1979–86) (fig.6.11), a building that reveals some affinities with Rogers' Lloyd's of London building. Both buildings were completed around the same time, yet Foster's tower is an example of a sober monumentality, its structure designed as a system of trusses that span like bridges, articulated across the vertical tower and carrying the floors like suspended trays. The idea of the bridge structure originated with the design brief, which stipulated the preservation of the original HSBC building on site, prompting the architect to elevate the new tower above ground. The idea of preserving the original building was later dismissed, but the design

6.11 Foster + Partners, HSBC Headquarters, Hong Kong, China, 1979–86

building is an example of a 'Gesamtkunstwerk' with all the details, from door handles to washroom modules, industrially produced like a kit of parts, prefabricated by different industries across the globe and mounted on site.

Among the litany of projects that Foster + Partners completed over the years, two hold a special position for their symbolic functions. The Carré d'Art in Nîmes (fig.6.12), completed in 1993, is a distinctive project that occupies a highly strategic site, in close proximity to a well-preserved Roman temple. In the vicinity to an antique masterpiece, Foster designed a building that fulfils its functional requirements by locating half of the total area underground, thereby reducing its height and making it fit into the context. A skylight ceiling, in addition to the transparent walls, allows light to penetrate down to the lower levels through a generous atrium space. The building, which serves as a médiathèque, includes a library and a space for the visual arts, in addition to a roof garden with a view to the adjoining temple.

Another project of symbolic significance is the restoration of the Reichstag building in Berlin (1992–9) (fig.6.13), and the redesign of the cupola that would become the new symbol of a reunified city. Here, Foster proposed a glass skylight held together by a steel structure which would also carry a circulation ramp accessible to the public. From this platform, the visitor could not only have a panoramic view of the city landscape, but also of the chamber of deputies below, reflected in the mirror-glass element at its core. The cupola was only the crowning element of a complex restoration scheme which refurbished the building to become again the seat of the German parliament after reunification.

Nicholas Grimshaw's work is characterised by an obsession with structural perfection, as one can see in his designs for the British Pavilion for Seville's Expo '92 and one year later for the Waterloo International Terminal in London. The Seville Pavilion may be the first example of a 'High-Tech' structure that addresses questions of ecological sustainability, turning into a manifesto for environmental responsiveness. The challenge of designing a pavilion in a hot climate led Grimshaw to elaborate a design proposal that brings together multiple experimental approaches to sustainability. Harnessing the site's natural resources of sun,

remained as stipulated, keeping the ground floor free as an open plaza. Employees and customers of the bank access the building through an escalator that pierces through the glass canopy isolating the interior from the street. Once inside, they are greeted by a large atrium space around which are hung the slabs carrying the office areas. The whole

6.12   Foster + Partners, Carré d'Art, Nîmes, France, 1984–93

water, and wind, the pavilion was assembled from prefabricated elements, with distinct elevations, each one relating to the different orientation. The eastern facade is covered by a water-wall where water flows down, cooling the facade, into a pool, from where it is redirected back, powered by solar panels placed on the roof. The western wall, which in turn receives the greatest heat exposure in the afternoon, is buffered by a stack of water containers that create effective thermal insulation for the interior. The northern and southern walls are covered by PVC-coated fabric, stretched along steel masts, like boat sails. Within this structure, pods are suspended to contain the various exhibition spaces, comfortably cooled through this passive system of air conditioning.

The Waterloo International Terminal (1993) (fig.6.14), which was conceived as a new terminal for trains linking London to the Continent, was designed to accommodate a multiplicity of functions on a rather tight and irregular site. Working in close collaboration with the engineer Anthony Hunt, Grimshaw designed a curvilinear structure that covers the main platform, free of columns, while accommodating the auxiliary functions on three floors below. The main problem was to design a roof system to cover this sinuous structure, without resorting to any obstructing columns, while adjusting to a tapering site that varies from 50 to 35 metres in width. A triple-hinge steel truss was designed to span the platforms, with an off-centre hinge at the contra-flexure of the arch.

As the critic Angus Macdonald states:

The Waterloo Terminal may be considered to be an example of genuine high tech, as opposed to stylistic High Tech, because it is an extremely successful solution to a difficult

6.13　Foster + Partners, Reichstag, New German Parliament, Berlin, Germany, 1992–9

THE TECHNOLOGICAL PARADIGM

technical problem and contains no features that were introduced for purely visual reasons. The technical difficulties imposed by the hugely demanding design requirements were such that no compromises were made with what was technically necessary for purely visual reasons, and the level of complexity of the structure was fully justified given the spans and loads involved.[8]

The roof structure is covered in glass panels that are fixed by means of elaborate joints and custom-designed, stainless-steel brackets, which by themselves are elevated to the level of artworks through their ingenious detailing, approximating the details of elaborate machinery.

Michael Hopkins graduated from the Architectural Association, which at that time had among its faculty the Smithsons, Robert Maxwell, Alan Colquhoun, and Cedric Price. After stints at various practices, and following the breakup of Team 4, Hopkins joined Norman Foster's firm, where they collaborated on the projects for the IBM plant in Cosham (1971) and the Willis Faber & Dumas company in Ipswich (1975). Following that, Hopkins moved to establish his own practice.

Michael and Patty Hopkins' own house in Hampstead, London (1976) (fig.6.15) was the first fruit of their independent practice and constituted another experiment in lightweight, industrial construction, using a steel structural system. There, they set another example of the refinement of the 'Miesian' idiom, inspired as well by the Eames House (1949). The simple rectangular composition of a

left

6.14   Nicholas Grimshaw, Waterloo International Terminal, London, UK, 1993

below

6.15   Michael and Patty Hopkins, Hopkins House, London, UK, 1976

10 × 12-metre footprint, over two floors and based on a steel structure, frames this house and studio in suburban London. Full height, horizontally sliding glazed panels line the front and back elevations, while insulated metal sheeting walls constitute the side walls. The house is all built of industrial components, with few partitions on the interior, subdivided through venetian blinds. From the street level, the house is accessed through a metal bridge, and gives the impression that it is a single-storey shed, as the lower level, which includes the living area and bedrooms, is embedded in the ground, opening out to the garden at the back.

Following this early work, Hopkins turned his attention to designing an industrial 'building system', named Patera (1982), that would serve to assemble standardised building modules for warehouses, offices, or other functions. This project presented a rare opportunity to realise one of the ideals of modern architecture, that is, to produce

129

6.16 | Michael and Patty Hopkins, Schlumberger Cambridge Research Centre, Cambridge, UK, 1992

a building completely in a factory and re-assemble it on site. The prototype building was based on a rectangular format with a standard height of 3.5 metres, its structure made of a tubular steel lattice frame, external to the envelope, and glazed surfaces on the gable ends. On the other sides, panels of insulated ribbed steel form the facades and extend to the roof. The structure was designed to withstand wind loads through a sophisticated truss system and could be erected on a concrete ground slab in ten days.

The original structure for the Schlumberger Research Centre in Cambridge (1992) (fig.6.16) constituted another tour-de-force for Hopkins. Conceived as a research and experimental centre for oil drilling and exploration, the building gives the appearance of a temporary construction, a combination of a large tensile structure at the centre – which takes on an even more mysterious appearance when lit at night – framed by two horizontal slabs that contain the laboratories and researchers' offices. The two slabs are connected by the central tent-like space which houses the main experimental function, the testing station, in a winter-garden space. The Teflon-coated glass fibre covers this central space, suspended on a set of tilted posts, with tensile cables anchoring it to the ground and to the adjoining pavilions.

If these projects constituted the highlights of the High-Tech movement in architecture – which most historians attribute to the period of 1970 to 1990 – these experiments did not end there, and would morph later on into a more significant development, that is, the adaptation of High-Tech to the demands and challenges of sustainability. Many of these architects would continue their research into creating an architecture that would reduce the carbon footprint, rely on renewable energies, and adapt better to specific climates. This transformation will be addressed in the last chapter.

7 The Continuing Legacy of Modernism

The rise of Post-Modernism around the world and its consecration as the 'style' that would replace Modernism, through exhibitions and publications, and most importantly through major commissions in Europe and North America during the period spanning from the 1970s to the 1990s, somewhat eclipsed the discussion on the continuing evolution of modern architecture in its various strands, which continued unabated during that same period. Cities around the globe witnessed the continuous production of 'Modern' buildings, especially in the developing countries where the debate on Post-Modernism had not yet made its impact, and where the objective of assuming the mantle of 'progress' by adopting the language of the International Style was still desirable. This is especially the case of Latin America, where the work of several architects continued in an unapologetic, Modernist style, with some continuing to build structures in fair-faced concrete, as seen in a previous chapter. There were, as well, a number of variations within an overarching 'Modernism', which gave the movement a diverse output.

Thus, contrary to Charles Jencks' prognostics, modern architecture did not finally die on 15 July 1972, when the Pruitt-Igoe housing complex in St. Louis, Missouri was demolished. History actually showed that Modernism continued to evolve with variations sprouting up around the world, from America to Asia, without of course neglecting the surge of its radical offspring, that is, High-Tech, in the more advanced economies. Among these variations is 'critical regionalism', which was addressed in a previous chapter, characterised by more specific approaches to the question of context without breaking with the main principles of Modernism.

After the Second World War, an invigorated modern architecture emerged in Latin America, spearheaded by architects who had worked with, or been influenced by Le Corbusier, Mies van der Rohe, Walter Gropius, and others. In particular, the names of Oscar Niemeyer, Paulo Mendes de la Rocha, Lina Bo Bardi, and Clorindo Testa figure prominently. These architects continued to explore Modernist aesthetics in a new idiom which consisted of working with concrete in its raw matter. This became somewhat characteristic of the work of major Latin American architects, as mentioned in the earlier chapter on Brutalism.

However, the work of Oscar Niemeyer, in its distinctive style, went beyond the confines of Brutalism and continued to develop well into the new century in a 'hybrid' mode that many scholars attributed to the cultural characteristics of his native Brazil. His architecture succeeded in transcending the European models, imbued with a spirit associated with the distinctive elements of a tropical culture, presenting a variation on normative Modernism. This manifestation of a new spirit in architecture can be traced back to Niemeyer's early works such as the group of buildings on the artificial lake of Pampulha, which exhibit a certain sensuality, which, ironically, led to his marginalisation by American and European critics who relegated him to a fringe group that was capable of producing spectacular architecture, while going against the dictates of mainstream Modernism. Niemeyer never denied the decisive influence of Le Corbusier, while at the same time striving to create an architecture based on 'self-conscious shifts, distortions, and inversions of the canonical forms of the so-called Western architectural tradition'.[1]

THE REVIVAL OF A WHITE MODERNISM

Many architects continued working in the Modernist idiom in North America, even attempting to revive the principles of its early 'White Period' phase. Among those were Richard Meier, Peter Eisenman, Charles Gwathmey, John Hejduk, and

7.1 Richard Meier, Smith House, Darien, Connecticut, USA, 1965–7

Michael Graves, who figured in the exhibition on 'The New York Five'. Among this group, Meier would be the only one to hold on religiously to the Modernist line: Peter Eisenman would veer off towards a 'post-structural' direction in his work; Michael Graves would defect to the Post-Modernist camp; Charles Gwathmey would eventually develop a corporate practice more in tune with the demands of the market; while John Hejduk would dedicate himself to academia, realising a few projects that displayed an esoteric approach.

Meier continued to explore the linguistic variations of the 'White Period' of modern architecture, most noticeably building on the legacy of Le Corbusier, and turning it into a personal style. It is for this that he was called 'the most European of North American architects', receiving both acclaim and commissions in America as well as Europe.[2] One of his early projects, the Smith House in Darien, Connecticut (1965–7) (fig.7.1) laid down Meier's basic strategy: a clear expression of structure on a rectangular template, a contrast between transparent and solid surfaces, and a playful articulation of internal volumes that recalls the early work of Le Corbusier, from Villa Cook to Villa Stein. Meier adapted the Corbusian language to the American context, creating an engaging relationship between the building and its context, and in the case of the Smith House, using white-painted wood panelling as cladding material. The house is approached via a small bridge, leading directly to the double-height piano nobile, from where one would access the bedrooms above, or the studio below. The particular setting, overlooking the lake, amidst trees and greenery, lent this first project its iconic appeal, an example of an abstract piece of art set in the midst of nature.

The Atheneum in Indiana (1975–9) (fig.7.2) presented an opportunity to build a large 'machine in the garden', raised on pilotis above the ground to avoid regular flooding by the nearby river. Located at the edge of the utopian town of New Harmony, the building was designed as the starting point for the tour of the historic town and a venue for cultural events. It is configured around the notion of architectural promenade that starts from the long path leading to an internal circulation ramp which serves as the main pedestrian route through the building, and as a mediator between the exhibition spaces, auditoria, and the areas overlooking the landscape. The particularity of the Atheneum, while designed on a grid, is that it breaks with the simple geometrical organisation of the majority of Meier's work. This is a project that was designed as a collage of different elements, articulated around a central atrium. From afar, it appears as a ship that has landed on this plot of land. The nautical metaphors of railings and other details reaffirm

7.2   Richard Meier, The Atheneum, New Harmony, Indiana, USA, 1975–9

7.3 Richard Meier, Hague City Hall and Central Library, The Hague, the Netherlands, 1986–95

this interpretation, which may have been intended, perhaps, as an allusion to the Ark of Salvation.

Following these initial successes, a flurry of commissions followed for single residences as well as institutional buildings, both at home and abroad, among them the Museum for Decorative Arts, Frankfurt (1979–85), the High Museum of Art, Atlanta (1980–83), the Des Moines Art Center Addition, Iowa (1982–4), the City Hall in The Hague (1986–95), the Exhibition Center, Ulm (1986–93), the Barcelona Museum of Contemporary Art (1987–95), and the Getty Center, Los Angeles (1984–97).

The City Hall in The Hague, the Netherlands (fig.7.3) was the result of a competition, in which Rem Koolhaas/OMA also presented an ambitious scheme. However, the final commission went to Meier who proposed a composition of two L-shaped elements, defining a large, covered atrium space, reminiscent of such public spaces as the Galleria in Milan. The connecting bridges on all levels between the two slabs, in their transparency, add another element of interest to this majestic public interior. At the corner of the site, Meier attached to the main building a lower-height curvilinear element, to relate to the scale of the urban context. The whole complex is clad in what became a typical Meier material of choice —porcelain-enamelled metal panels, intended to better respond to weathering conditions.

The golden commission in Richard Meier's career was without doubt the project for the Getty Center in Los Angeles (fig.7.4), a commission he won against other prominent architects like Stirling and Maki, to build a large complex that brings together all the different functions of the Getty Trust Foundation. The large complex included, besides the art museum, separate clusters for the art trust, a centre for study of the history of art, a conservation institute, and other auxiliary functions. Given the code restrictions and the demands of the client, Meier had to moderate his white palette of ceramic tiles by cladding large sections of walls in travertine stone, to bestow a more monumental presence.

The mega-project, which extends over a whole hilltop site, was branded as a modern-day Hadrian's Villa by the architect himself, who stated:

> I see a classic structure, elegant and timeless, emerging, serene and ideal, from the rough hillside, a kind of Aristotelian structure within the landscape. [. . .] In my mind, I keep returning to the Romans – to Hadrian's Villa, to Caprarola – for their sequence of spaces, their thick-walled presence, their sense of order, the way in which building and landscape belong to each other.[3]

Yet despite his approach in creating a collage of elementary forms, the analogy does not quite hold, for against the overall sense of order that Hadrian's classic villa projects, the Getty Center fails in reality to reach that harmony and sense of order, which Meier had mastered in other projects. The central plaza appears like a lost centre amidst a cacophony of volumes, which turn their back to it, in favour of the vistas beyond. Against the claim that the architect had in fact been inspired by Italian urban types, the project appears like a collection of disjointed parts, without a central urban focus.[4]

THE QUEST FOR A NEW MONUMENTALITY

While many architects of the post-Second World War generation found a source of inspiration in the work produced by the Modernists in Latin America, others continued to explore the paradigmatic examples of mainstream Modernism, exemplified by the work of Walter Gropius, Mies van der Rohe, Marcel Breuer, and others of the first generation. An important figure in this group was the Chinese-born I.M. Pei, who graduated from MIT in 1940. Much of

7.4 Richard Meier, Getty Center, Los Angeles, California, USA, 1984–97

7.5   I.M. Pei, National Gallery of Art, East Wing, Washington, DC, USA, 1968–78

his work, such as the Dallas City Hall (1977), testifies to his straight-forward functionalist approach, which manifested a certain monumentality in projects such as the J.F.K. Library in Boston (1976–9) and the National Gallery East Wing in Washington, DC (1968–78).

For this major commission to build an addition to the National Gallery (fig.7.5), Pei addressed the design challenge of resolving the functional requirements on a difficult site, constrained by a diagonal street, by establishing a modern landmark that could engage in a dialogue with the historic, Neo-Classical structure. The site provided the opportunity for a geometrical composition of two triangles that combine to fit within the trapezoidal area. The larger isosceles triangle contains the exhibition space and a generous atrium, while the second one includes offices, as well as a library and research centre. Circulation is organised around the atrium space, which unifies the composition. The building was clad with Tennessee marble, the same material used in the old museum, as a way to establish a visual connection with its Neo-Classical neighbour.

In France, Christian de Portzamparc rose to prominence during the 1980s through his distinctive approach, in which the lessons of Modernism – in terms of emphasis on spatial articulation, plasticity, and abstract forms – found new expression in projects such as the Cité de la Musique complex at La Villette (1984–95) (fig.7.6). There, Portzamparc designed the two separate wings of the complex.

The Western Wing or Conservatoire, comprising the student housing, administrative offices, dance studios, in addition to rehearsal halls, is composed as a U-shaped agglomeration of slabs around an internal court, punctured by voids that open this modern 'monastery' to the outside world. The main facade to the avenue is punctuated by the rhythm of the four volumetric elements that face the street, joined by a curved line and capped by the roof. The large slab is also topped by an undulating roof, punctured at the middle by a large oculus that opens to the piazza below. A complex set of functions are thus brought together in a harmonic whole that offers stimulating spatial experiences.

For the Eastern wing, which comprises the public concert halls, the architect devised a strategy to occupy the triangular site, filling the contours with the required administrative and auxiliary functions, while at the centre lies an oval-shaped space containing the large concert hall. A spiralling pathway wraps around the concert hall to the foyer and separates it from the other functions, a separation that is further emphasised through skylights that wash the stone-clad surfaces of the concert hall in gentle light, while a diagonal axis cuts across the space, connecting the park side to the other side of the complex.

7.6   Christian de Portzamparc, Cité de la Musique, La Villette, Paris, France, 1984–95

Another monumental project by Portzamparc that shows greater affinity to the work of Oscar Niemeyer is the Cidade das Artes in Rio de Janeiro (2002–13) (fig.7.7). Conceived on a site on the

7.7   Christian de Portzamparc, Cidade das Artes, Rio de Janeiro, Brazil, 2002–13

outskirts of the city, on an island surrounded by a belt of highways, the architect chose to elevate the project on a podium, standing as a belvedere overlooking the city and the landscape. His early schematic encapsulates the concept for this project: two horizontal lines, elevated above the ground, would constitute the open frame that contains the various functions. It would become like a container of free-form objects that house the auditoria, concert hall, and rehearsal rooms. And in an effort to accentuate the free-form composition of this ensemble, the two slabs would be connected to the ground by a set of fan-shaped concrete walls, that touch the ground at select points, leaving much of the facade open to the elements. These are supplemented on the interior by a grid of columns that support the roof. In a sense, Portzamparc succeeded in reviving Niemeyer's legacy by creating a building of great sculptural presence, an artistic statement that complements its context.

Jean Nouvel's masterpiece, the Louvre Museum in Abu Dhabi (2006–17) (fig.7.8) takes its cues from the context in a composition that recalls traditional Arab villages. A series of cubical volumes, containing the different functions and exhibition halls, are clustered around an open space, the whole covered by a vast, elliptical dome. The dome, 180 metres in diameter, featuring an intricate web of steel and aluminium elements, appears to float over the ensemble, supported by four embedded piers, and providing a wide canopy over the outdoor space that opens onto the seaside.

Bernard Tschumi's New Acropolis Museum (2001–9) (fig.7.9) is another exercise in restrained monumentality. While attempting to relate to its paradigmatic model – the Temple of Athena on the acropolis which overlooks it – Tschumi's

137

left

7.8   Jean Nouvel, Louvre Museum, Abu Dhabi, UAE, 2006–17

below

7.9   Bernard Tschumi, New Acropolis Museum, Athens, Greece, 2001–9

to the 4th century. Inside, the museum displays a collection of artifacts, arranged in chronological sequence, taking the visitor from pre-history to the late-Roman period, and ending ceremoniously with the Parthenon Frieze, from where one could have a panoramic view of the Acropolis.

While distinct in terms of its form and function from Tschumi's museum, Emre Arolat's design for a new hotel in Turkey, the Museum Hotel Antakya (2010–19) (fig.7.10), shares the same problem of negotiating a difficult condition and adopts a similar strategy of lifting all the main functions above the archaeological level, while allowing visual access and protecting it in the process. Situated nearby Saint Peter's Church on Mount Starius in the historic city of Antioch, the large hotel integrates the ruins, including mosaics, discovered during the

intervention in this historic context adopted the rather modest strategy of two slabs sitting on top of each other, with the upper one slightly shifted to be parallel to the temple. The museum was thus composed as a set of concrete plates with a glass facade, floating above the ground on pilotis to avoid destroying the archaeological ruins dating back

7.10   Emre Arolat, Museum Hotel Antakya, Antakya, Turkey, 2010–19

7.11 Snøhetta, Bibliotheca Alexandrina, Alexandria, Egypt, 1989–2001

7.12 Snøhetta, Norwegian National Opera and Ballet, Oslo, Norway, 2000–2008

excavation. The hotel was designed as a set of four layers: the first one the open-air museum, with the main hotel foyer on the second level offering visual access to the ruins; the third level incorporating the hotel rooms conceived as a set of prefabricated modules, the whole culminating at the canopy which incorporates the entertainment functions. The steel structure, metal panelling of the exterior, cantilevering room units, and largely glass facade, give this complex a futuristic appearance, while the interior offers a generous atrium space overlooking the ruins.

Another direction in modern architecture emerged from Scandinavia with firms like Snøhetta, the winner of an international competition to design the Bibliotheca Alexandrina in Egypt in 1989 (fig.7.11). The library, a synthesis of monumentality and functionality, takes the form of a giant inclined disc that lifts itself slightly above the ground, tilting towards the Mediterranean. This geometrical element brings to mind the pure forms proposed by theoreticians like Boullée, in the 18th century. Partly as a response to the site and the harbour, partly as a design intention, the circular-shaped plan also provided the opportunity to create a wide-open interior space, covered by glass skylights that diffuse light into the interior. The interior space is organised around the grand reading room, surrounded by several platforms, with soaring columns supporting its roof. The exterior of this monolith is clad in granite, an homage to the building traditions of ancient Egypt, incised in various signs and letters that recall the manifold forms of writing around the world.

The Norwegian National Opera and Ballet (2000–2008) (fig.7.12) offers another example of Snøhetta's formal strategy. Taking advantage of its prime location at the edge of the harbour, the Opera House creates a relationship between the fjord and the Ekeberg hill to the east, emerging from the topography as a hybrid between architecture and landscape through its slanted roofscape and multiple ramps which double as broad public paths. This topographic articulation is punctured at its centre by the glass box of the opera house, which opens up like a shell, drawing light into the internal foyer. The building is divided in two by a corridor running north–south, dubbed the 'opera street'. To the west of this line are

7.13   Henning Larsen, The Royal Danish Opera, Copenhagen, Denmark, 2004

located all the public areas and stage areas, while the eastern part houses the production areas. The interior of the opera house is clad in oak, chosen for its acoustic and textural qualities, and also applied on the 'wave wall' in the foyer, as well as the floors and ceilings. As in other modern structures, there is a clear articulation between the horseshoe-shaped opera hall, and the structure that envelops it.

Henning Larsen's Royal Danish Opera (2004) (fig.7.13) gives another example of this contemporary approach to monumentality, featuring a transparent structure that hovers at the edge of the harbour, projecting a view of its internal foyer at night, with the horseshoe-shaped opera hall clad in maple wood, contrasting with the rectangular grid. A sweeping horizontal canopy floats above the rectangular volume, covering the external plaza and the steps that reach down to the water. The palette of colours and materials, from wood to stone to metal panels, gives the whole ensemble a rich texture that does not negate the overall lightness of the structure.

ÁLVARO SIZA, RAFAEL MONEO, AND THE IBERIAN DIRECTION

One can set the work of Álvaro Siza in a category apart. Yet it forms another variation on modern architecture, which led to his consecration as the father figure of the 'Porto School'. Siza's approach was inspired by the works of Adolf Loos and Alvar Aalto, yet tailored to the particular context of his region, later developing an idiosyncratic style that blended the principles of functionalism with a certain 'mannerism'. I use the term 'mannerism' here to describe his work which followed functionalist precepts yet always managed to distort them, creating certain ambiguities that gave it its peculiar character. In his essay on 'Mannerism and Modern Architecture' in the 1950s, Colin Rowe drew a parallel between some of the work of Le Corbusier and Mies, and the mannerist architects of the 16th century. One particular description by Rowe seems to fit very well the work of Siza:

> In this idea of disturbing, rather than providing immediate pleasure for the eye, the element of delight in modern architecture appears chiefly to lie. An intense precision or an exaggerated rusticity of detail is presented within the bounds of a strictly conceived complex of planned obscurity; and a labyrinthine scheme is offered which frustrates the eye by intensifying the visual pleasure of individual episodes, in themselves only to become coherent as the result of a mental act of reconstruction.[5]

This statement can be applied verbatim to explain the complex spatial sequences one may find, for instance, in the Serralves Museum in Porto (1991–9) (fig.7.14) or the Porto School of Architecture (1984–93) (fig.7.15). In the Porto School, an assembly of different volumes forms the backbone of the project, containing in a sequence the administrative functions and the auditorium, the exhibition hall, and culminating in the library. The irregular composition of two rectangular elements with the half-cylindrical exhibition hall acting as a pivot, leads to various 'individual episodes' which open up to different vistas, and result in provocative accidental compositions. In working out the details of these 'spatial accidents', Siza operates very much like a sculptor, without any a priori notions. Against the irregular arrangement at the back of the site, the other side is framed by a series of pavilions, four in total, housing the studios and faculty offices, with one missing element that bears witness to a 'poetic absence'. The individual pavilions act as belvederes, overlooking the city and the river below, and providing in their linear organisation a rhythmical datum to the ensemble.

right, top

7.14 Álvaro Siza, Serralves Museum of Contemporary Art, Porto, Portugal, 1991–9

right, bottom

7.15 Álvaro Siza, Porto School of Architecture, Porto, Portugal, 1984–93

Peter Testa's dissertation on Siza casts additional light on this enigmatic architect. While rejecting the claims made by Frampton, associating Siza to 'critical regionalism', Testa drew a connection between the architect's work and Cubism, based on his unorthodox approach. The intentional distortions that Siza employs, while potentially referring back to Baroque formal strategies, are seen as closer to a Cubist sensibility, starting with his design for his brother's house, the Antonio Carlos Siza House (1978), composed as an irregular arrangement of elements around a trapezoidal patio, within a tight site.[6] The 'Cubist' attributes of Siza's architecture can also be traced in later works, where this intentional distortion is applied with the objective of modulating the project to the particularities of the site, the programme, and other conditions. This is evident again in the Pinto and Sotto Mayor Bank (1974), in which the constraints of the site, as well as the intentions of the architect to explore complex geometrical interplays, result in a rather complex 'organism' with intriguing spatial qualities. The exterior, on the other hand, presents a somewhat plain, Modernist, facade. In the words of Moneo, this work demonstrates Siza's brilliant aptitude in geometrical manipulation, aimed to show 'architecture at its purest', that is, 'space at its purest, space without the limitations that use confines it to in buildings'.[7] A few years later, another bank commissioned him to design one of its facilities. The Borges and Irmão Bank (1978 and 1982–6) presented the challenge of inserting a modern structure in a small town. Featuring a sleek, curvilinear facade that opens up towards the street, reflected again at the back, the new building is rich in subtle details, with internal spaces that are sculpted sensitively to accommodate the movement through space, within tight spatial constraints.

Siza undertook early on the challenge of tackling social housing projects, where economic

7.16   Álvaro Siza, SAAL Bouça Social Housing Complex, Porto, Portugal, 1973–7

considerations often led to sub-standard architecture. Yet in his own sensitive way, he succeeded in creating urban projects that avoided some of the usual pitfalls of public housing. In the SAAL Bouça Social Housing Complex in Porto (1973–7) (fig.7.16), which was the second experiment in this type, Siza involved the inhabitants in the design process. The idea was to stack two-storey homes on top of one another, with the upper homes set back to provide outdoor space. The Modernist style is reminiscent of 1920s social housing in Germany and the Netherlands, where rows of housing are arranged around planted courtyards designed to provide community space. Some years later, he realised another major social housing project, the Malagueira Social Housing in Evora, an extensive project consisting of 1,200 units designed for low-income families, which evolved over two decades (1977–95). Each unit was designed as a two-storey house with its own private courtyard. The units were laid out in continuous rows, parallel to each other, forming narrow streets in-between and serviced by elevated aqueducts.

Among his institutional projects, another project merits attention: the Galician Centre for Contemporary Art in the town of Santiago de Compostela in Spain (1988–93) (fig.7.17). The museum is an intervention in a historic context, which reflects Siza's passion for geometrical play combined with his 'rationalist' approach: two overlapping L-planes define the museum which is scaled appropriately to the nearby convent. The use of granite stone as cladding on the facades is another gesture of respect to neighbouring historic buildings. The articulation of the solid masses that define the volumes does not hide the reality of the non-structural stone cladding, exposed at points by the steel lintels that carry the facade. Siza articulates this volumetric interplay in the interior, which results in various compositions of solids and voids. His use of the typical white plaster for interior walls contrasts, as usual, with stairs and other elements rendered in stone, with marble for select areas. The complexity of the building emerges out of these overlapping spaces, animated by a stimulating architectural promenade.

The small church of Santa Maria in Marco de Canaveses, Portugal (1990–96) (fig.7.18) also represents another fitting example of Siza's penchant for absolute simplicity, in line with the aesthetics of Loos, where an abstract cubical form defines the church on the exterior, while internally, the long nave is sculpted on both sides to modulate the sunlight and create an animated interior. The recessed entrance doorway is flanked on one side by a baptistery, and by a service space on the other. Throughout these diverse projects, Siza consistently demonstrated his understanding of the notion of type, without fully submitting to it. In fact, he resorts to certain typological tropes, which he then deforms, distorts, and subjects to a careful manipulation, bringing out the sculptural aspects of architecture. Siza manipulates the forms to suit his particular intentions, the site conditions, interior requirements, or simply the desired sculptural effects. He is first and foremost a plastic artist, who, in line with the precepts of Le Corbusier, succeeded in giving form to the idea of a 'plastic architecture'.

While he started his career as an assistant in Siza's practice, Eduardo Souto de Moura also rose to prominence through impressive projects which married architectural and artistic interests, producing a variety of buildings, some of which were fully integrated into the landscape – for example, the House in Moledo (1998) – while others veered towards Minimalism as in the House in Bom Jesus (1994); yet others took a more sculptural monumental form, as in the museum for the artist Paula Rego (2009).

The Casas das Historias Paula Rego was designed in a natural setting, surrounded by trees, to house the collection of the artist in the town of

7.17 Álvaro Siza, Galician Centre for Contemporary Art, Santiago de Compostela, Spain, 1988–93

Cascais in Portugal. Conjuring some of the aspects of a regional Modernism, the museum is composed of four wings of different lengths, arranged around a central atrium, reminiscent, in a way, of Aalto's Saynatsalo Town Hall, and rendered in red-painted concrete. As in Aalto's building, the horizontal composition is accentuated at one side by two

7.18 Álvaro Siza, Santa Maria Church, Marco de Canaveses, Portugal, 1990–96

7.19　Rafael Moneo, Kursaal Auditorium and Congress Centre, San Sebastián, Spain, 1990–99

pyramidal towers, evoking lanterns or chimneys, that affirm its presence in the landscape.

Rafael Moneo's work plays on different themes, with many of his projects responding in a sensitive way to contextual conditions, as examined in Chapter 5, 'Regional Modernisms'. Yet in some cases, Moneo also proposed buildings that stand out and affirm their presence in the landscape.

Before the famous intervention in Merida, Moneo's Bank Inter in Madrid (1976), in collaboration with Ramos Bescos, opted for a Modernist statement that contrasted with the adjacent historic palace of the Marquis de Mudela. The new building adopted the same type of brick used in the old palace, while articulating the facade in a planar, geometric way.

Another notable example is the Kursaal in San Sebastian (1990–99) (fig.7.19) which presented a radical manoeuvre in opposition to the man-made order of the city. There, on the banks of the Urumea river, Moneo projected two cubical elements wrapped in glass, standing precariously on a wide platform facing the ocean. The complex story of this project spanned three decades, with first, a competition won by Jan Lubicz-Nycz, Carlo Pellicia, and William Zuck in 1965, to replace a casino that had existed on the site since the 1920s. Their project, a rather absurd curvilinear volume elevated on pilotis, would have constituted an unusual intrusion on this site. A second competition, won in 1973 by F.J. Saenz de Oiza, presented a more conventional parti, occupying the triangular site and forming an extension to the city's grid. A third invited competition pitted Moneo against Baldeweg, Foster, and Isozaki, among others.[8] The two finalists, Moneo and Baldeweg, projected radically different solutions, with Baldeweg opting for a building that would extend the urban grid, while Moneo proposed a project composed of two gigantic crystalline rocks, standing in opposition to the urban order, and more in tune with the natural landscape. The complex appears therefore as an artificial extension of the promontories, a work of 'artifice' that offers a framed view of the sea. Wrapping the two cubical elements

146

that rise from the platform in a layered glass facade further gives the whole a surreal appearance, like a beacon at night.

A counter-example to the sculptural Kursaal is the Auditorium of Barcelona (1999), where the architect opted for a rectilinear volume that encloses the two concert halls, separated by an open atrium featuring a suspended glass structure, or 'lantern', which gives a distinctive character to this urban foyer. The building is clad on the outside by panels of Corten steel, giving it a rather industrial appearance, while the interiors of the concert halls are lined with rich maple wood. In a sense, following Loos' principles, the building projects a rather opaque, urban face, while reserving its special effects for the interior spaces.

Another great example of Modernist revival, inspired by the work of Mies, can be seen in the work of Gonzalo Moure. His Town Hall extension in Alicante, Spain (2005) is a masterpiece that occupies its rightful place next to the old Town Hall, built over a site composed of archaeological ruins which are integrated into the project, as part of a 'palimpsest'. The project consisted of restoring the old building and adding an extension, which appears like its dialectical opposite: in contrast to the classical and opaque old building, the extension is an exercise in transparency, composed of a steel structure and glass panels covering the facade, mounted over a solid stone base that attenuates the contrast with its neighbour. While the work conjures Miesian references, it also alludes to the serene monumentality of Terragni.

HYBRID MODERNISMS

In many parts of the world, various forms of modern architecture continued to evolve. These variations on the main theme were quite pronounced on the European Continent, and specifically in the Netherlands, where the important legacy of Modernism, followed by the reformist attempts of Aldo van Eyck and others, were still palpable. Yet a new wave of Dutch architecture, spearheaded by Rem Koolhaas – who will be covered more specifically in the next chapter – also took root. I borrow the term 'Hybrid Modernism' from Hans Ibelings, to designate these forms that impute to Modernism their articulation of volumes and functions, their use of materials and techniques, yet imbue it with a new and distinct flavour. Ibelings defined it as 'an architecture of crooked lines, contrasting materials, colours and structures, collage-like facades, and a mixture of various aesthetic forms', specifically referring to the architectural output of architects like Jo Coenen, Mecanoo, and MVRDV, which spread during the 1990s.[9] This new direction was disseminated around the world by a new generation of architects who built their practice on the principles of Modernism while also assimilating the lessons of Post-Modernism, such as attention to context, material pluralism, and the adoption of contemporary symbolism as a way to compensate for the semantic poverty of orthodox Modernism.

The architectural firm Mecanoo, led by Francine Houben, exemplifies the Dutch approach towards playful experimentation, on a Modernist platform that favours transparency, articulation of elements, and functional differentiation. The Faculty of Economics and Management in Utrecht (1991–5) (fig.7.20) expresses these principles, whereby the complex is divided into a main slab acting as a datum facing the campus, including the foyer on the ground floor and the auditoria projecting above it as distinct volumetric elements, while the classrooms are arranged into four perpendicular wings that abut the main datum creating a series of three courtyards in-between, each developed on a different theme. A few years after this project, Mecanoo proposed a structure that merges architecture with landscape: the Delft University Library (1997), a large space embedded under an artificial mound, interspersed by a large conical skylight that brings light into the interior, with the book stacks lined up on both sides of the trapezoidal space around the large atrium.

The experimental work of MVRDV – founded by Winy Maas, Jacob van Rijs and Nathalie de Vries – found many translations around the world, starting with innovative structures such as the WoZoCo Housing Complex in Osdorp (1997) (fig.7.21), designed for elderly people. This building was composed as a main slab with typical housing units overlooking one side of the site, with a series of cantilevered units suspended from the main structure on the other side. The cantilevered elements emerged out of a functional requirement,

7.20 Mecanoo, Faculty of Economics and Management, Utrecht, the Netherlands, 1991–5

7.21   MVRDV, WoZoCo Housing Complex, Osdorp, Amsterdam, the Netherlands, 1997

to accommodate additional units without increasing the footprint of the structure. The complex is clad in a variety of materials, from panel wood to glass and steel, thus breaking the typical image associated with housing projects. In the western part of Amsterdam harbour, another innovative project took shape, through an urban operation that transformed a former dam with its silo building into a contemporary 'Unité d'Habitation' that substitutes the language of shipping containers to that of raw concrete. The Silodam complex (2002) consists of a mix of social housing units of various sizes, built atop a secure foundation that contains the parking structure, drilled deep into the waters. The different housing units appear like shipping containers piled on top of each other, over a ten-storey structure, clad in different materials, creating a polychromatic ensemble that floats on piles above the water.

Neutelings Riedijk designed a modern landmark at the port of Antwerp, the MAS Museum (2006–10) (fig.7.22). The museum is an example of a playful articulation of elements, composed as a system of boxes piled on top of each other, with a variation in the height of the glass bays in-between. The boxes are clad in a textured pattern of red sandstone and separated by layers of corrugated glass curtain wall which extends in some areas to a double height, offering visitors a panoramic view of the port.

In a similar vein, one could read the work of RCR Arquitectes, founded by Rafael Aranda, Carme Pigem, and Ramon Vilalta. Their Casa Rural in Girona, Spain (2004–7) is a large country house that was articulated into a series of rhythmically disposed elements on a hilltop. Built on a steel structure and clad in panels of Corten steel, which give it the appearance of an artistic installation, the double height interiors faced by large panes of glass offer a captivating view of the landscape. The set of vertical elements thus appear like a series of periscopes, housing the various functions of bedrooms, living areas, and studios, and connected by the horizontal datum line, almost like a musical score.

right

7.22   Neutelings Riedijk, MAS Museum, Antwerp, Belgium, 2006–10

Another example of the work of RCR Arquitectes is the Library and Senior Citizen Centre in Barcelona (2002–7), an implant that responds adequately to the City Council plan of recovering and rehabilitating internal blocks within the city. The project is a combination of a library – a five-storey block hovering above the gateway to the internal courtyard – connected to a horizontal L-shaped plinth that accommodates the senior citizen centre. The library opens up to the street through large panes of glass, framed on both sides by vertical black steel fins that are repeated at ground level around the courtyard, giving the whole ensemble a sober character. Critics were keen to observe how the building related to the urban fabric, its distinct materiality standing out and contrasting noticeably with the surroundings.

STEVEN HOLL AND THE PHENOMENOLOGICAL APPROACH

Steven Holl is one of those maverick architects who advocated a phenomenological approach to architecture, which partly translates as a search for the sensorial qualities of space. In his focus on these aspects, Holl pays particular attention to light as a natural element that bears a major role in the definition of space. But in addition to these explicit qualities, Holl is also a 'sculptor' of form, whose projects sometimes take the shape of Cubist, free-standing sculptures. It is from this perspective that one can approach the work of this architect as a contemporary variation on Modernism, which is exemplified in many of his projects, from the Kiasma Museum of Contemporary Art in Helsinki, to the Chapel in Seattle, to the Knut Hamsun Centre in Norway.

The Kiasma Museum of Contemporary Art appears as a modern icon, a composition of two elements: a straight slab that runs into a curvilinear one, intersecting at the northern edge, where the curvilinear element is truncated to reveal a wide, sail-shaped facade of glass that opens towards the bay. Visitors enter the building through a spacious atrium, located in-between these two clashing slabs, revealing a certain 'plasticity' that is reminiscent of Siza's work, as well as Aalto's. A large ramp takes the visitors up through the

right, top

7.23 Steven Holl, Art Building West, University of Iowa, Iowa City, Iowa, USA, 2006

right, bottom

7.24 Steven Holl, Visual Arts Building, University of Iowa, Iowa City, Iowa, USA, 2016

different floors, where the main galleries are arranged in sequence, along the curvilinear wall, providing a variety of spatial experiences. Light plays an important role through a series of skylights that contrast the filtering light against the curved surfaces, diffusing it to the interior.

In contrast to the monumental Kiasma, the Knut Hamsun Centre in Norway (2006–9) is a more modest structure designed to serve as a cultural centre dedicated to the Norwegian writer. The building consists of a library, exhibition areas, reading rooms, and an auditorium for the projection of films. Inspired by the literary legacy of the novelist, Holl composed the building as a dialogue between two trapezoidal elements: one lies low on the ground, containing the auditorium, while the other stands up, like a figure dressed in black, displaying anthropomorphic features. The vertical element, housing the library and other functions, is slightly inclined and clad in black-painted wood, a nod to the wooden stave Norse churches, with a roof garden planted with reeds that also recalls the traditional sod roofs of Nordic farmhouses. The colourful and irregular balconies and window openings provide a counterpoint to the monotone exterior, and open up to the landscape at different points of view.

The Art Building West at the University of Iowa (2006) (fig.7.23) is an example of Holl's 'Cubist' approach, whereby the conceptual models show a project that owes a lot to the abstract compositions of the avant-garde artists of the 1920s, simulating a musical instrument. The architect himself defines it as a 'hybrid instrument' of open edges and spaces, clad in glass and Corten steel plates. While some sections of the building are laid on the ground, others float above ground. An internal pathway leads to a ramp that connects the different floors, with skylights drawing light into these public spaces.

The Visual Arts Building (2016) (fig.7.24) on the same campus, and adjacent to the Art Building,

was realised by Holl ten years later through a different approach. In this case, a square template was laid over the site, comprising multiple floors, and carved at various points along the edge and in the centre to denote 'porosity'. The idea of porosity was applied here as a means to encourage interconnection and crossover among the various disciplines within the building, from manual crafts to digital art. At the centre of the building, a stairway connects the multiple floors, circling around the open atrium space that extends the height of the building and turning it into a public forum. In contrast to its neighbour, this building presents a translucent/white facade, with a zinc-clad concrete structure.

VARIATIONS ON MODERN ARCHITECTURE

The British firm of Caruso St John displayed in their own work the different directions that a renewed Modernism was taking, responding to each project on its own terms while taking account of various contextual and programmatic conditions, but also experimenting with different materials. This is clearly expressed in the contrast between such projects as the Nottingham Contemporary and the Bremer Landesbank. The Nottingham Contemporary (2004–9) (fig.7.25) is a complex including visual and performance arts which occupies the triangular site of the Lace Market. The exhibition galleries were arranged on the upper level of the site, with skylights on the roof and a golden cladding covering the exterior, while performance spaces were composed on the lower level, with ornamented precast concrete facades that draw their inspiration from the context of the Market district. The complex appears like a Modernist collage of different fragments, with an interplay between the golden metallic and greenish surfaces giving the whole its distinctive character, and contrasting with the typical brick facades of nearby buildings, yet fitting in its own way within the urban context.

In a historicist approach, the headquarters for the Bremer Landesbank (2011–16) (fig.7.26), located on the main cathedral square in the medieval city centre, projected an articulate facade of dark brick, rhythmically arranged in slightly curved

7.25   Caruso St John, Nottingham Contemporary, Nottingham, UK, 2004–9

7.26 Caruso St John, Bremer Landesbank, Bremen, Germany, 2011–16

vertical columns, with expressionistic undertones that recall the work of Hans Poelzig. In the words of the architects, the building refers to the northern European traditions of brick construction which 'dress the building in a thick masonry skin'. This elegant facade is accentuated at the lower corner by a large arcuate entrance leading to the main building, while another entrance leads to the internal elliptical court of the building, dressed in white plaster, in contrast to the external envelope. The internal court, also respecting the traditions of large urban blocks, is open to the sky and consolidates around it the new structure as well as the older buildings that form part of the complex.

Grafton Architects, led by Yvonne Farrell and Shelley McNamara, developed a varied portfolio of projects that earned them worldwide recognition and the Pritzker Prize in 2020. Among their several educational projects the London School of Economics (2022) (fig.7.27) stands out as exemplary in its way of dealing with a historic urban context. The building offers a rational, rhythmically ordered facade of posts and beams, which meets the ground level in a more open, welcoming and

left

7.27 Grafton Architects, London School of Economics, London, UK, 2022

below

7.28 Grafton Architects, Luigi Bocconi University, Milan, Italy, 2008

irregular front that showcases the building interior. In their quest to position this new structure within its context and to find ways to articulate its various functions, which include an institute of philanthropy and social entrepreneurship, the architects were keen to create a building that represents 'a vision of diversity, openness and inclusivity', and one that would act as a gateway to the whole campus of the London School of Economics. In contrast with the more sober and 'rational' exterior, the interior of the building, in the main foyer and around the staircase, presents a dynamic and complex articulation of structural elements that give it an expressionistic character.

7.29 Sheila O'Donnell and John Tuomey, Glucksman Gallery, University College, Cork, Ireland, 2005

For the Luigi Bocconi University in Milan (2008) (fig.7.28), Farrell and McNamara devised a complex structure that provocatively addresses its urban context. A staccato of volumetric elements are extruded from the main base to articulate one of the public facades of the complex. On the opposite street front, a recessed and transparent volume invites people into the building. Internally, the building offers intricate spatial relationships, with high atrium spaces over the main vertical circulation that take the character of deep ravines, and a canopy of offices that are suspended at the top level, allowing light to filter in-between. The major room at ground level, the Aula Magna, extends in height to the top of the building and appears to project into the street, offering a public space for the city.

Sheila O'Donnell and John Tuomey established their practice at the end of the 1980s and developed a number of projects which display a characteristic interest in the craft of building attuned to the specificities of place. The Glucksman Gallery at University College Cork in Ireland (2005) (fig.7.29) is a case in point, where the building flexes and bends to adjust to its idyllic campus setting, surrounded by trees and greenery. The building occupies a small footprint and rises to the height of the old trees to avoid encroaching on the landscape, with a podium acting as a point of entry to the building. The structure was partially raised on pilotis, allowing a more symbiotic relation with the landscape. The 'vessel', as the architects label it, resonates with its environment, its wooden cladding ensuring a softer relation with the context.

Variations on modern architecture sprouted around the world, from Japan and China to Africa and the Middle East. The examples above centred

7.30   Toyo Ito, Tod's Building, Tokyo, Japan, 2002–4

mainly on the contexts where Modernism first developed, that is, Europe and the Americas, showing a renewed interest in it after the period of contestation of the 1960s and 1970s. In Japan, one could mention the work of Tadao Ando, which will be addressed in another chapter, in addition to a number of Japanese Modernists such as Shigeru Ban, Kengo Kuma, Toyo Ito, Waro Kishi, and others. As an example of these new variations on Japanese Modernism, one can take the example of Toyo Ito's Tod's Building in Tokyo (2002–4) (fig.7.30), where the architect reverses some of the long-held principles of modern architecture by reverting to a structural facade of irregularly patterned concrete mesh, which reflects the silhouettes of nearby trees, thus freeing the floor plans from any columns.

In China, a new generation of Modernists, such as Wang Shu and Vector Architects – who were discussed earlier – as well as Xu Tiantian, Zhou Wei, Zhang Bin, and Ma Yansong, formulated their own approach drawing on the lessons of modern architecture. Xu Tiantian's Erdos Gallery in Mongolia (2007), Wei and Bin's Sino French Centre at Tonji University in Shanghai (2006), Ma Yansong's Hongluo Lake Club in Beijing (2006), Wang Shu's Museum of Art in Ningbo (2006), and Standard Architecture's Wuhan French-Chinese Arts Centre (2005), constitute a sample of numerous examples of a revived Modernism in Asia.

Thus, modern architecture continued to thrive across various parts of the world, from the early attempts of the New York Five to reclaim an 'original Modernism', to more nuanced interpretations that sought to address particular contexts and programmes, which morphed into further variations that will be examined in the last chapter.

8 The Project of Deconstruction

Deconstruction emerged as a major movement in the 1980s, with a surge in interest in new forms and processes of design that overthrew previous practices by calling into question both the rational foundations of modern architecture as well as the historicist associations of its assumed successor, Post-Modernism. The major figure leading the way in this direction was Peter Eisenman, who had been engaged in structuralist exercises with a series of hypothetical 'houses', some of which found their way to realisation. This was paralleled by the emergence of a number of architectural practices which questioned the status quo, while rebelling against what they considered to be a naïve historicism and a regressive return to symbolism. While many of these practices did not really subscribe to the 'Deconstructive' agenda as promulgated within philosophical circles, they were somehow brought together under the umbrella of the new movement in architecture. A major venue for this was the Museum of Modern Art in New York, which organised an exhibition in 1988 on 'Deconstructivist Architecture', curated by Philip Johnson and Mark Wigley. This coincided with another major event, a symposium organised at the Tate Gallery in London by Andreas Papadakis, the editor of Academy Editions. These two events signalled the inauguration of 'Deconstruction' or 'Deconstructivism' in architecture.

Academy Editions later published a series of reviews, in addition to a concise introduction to Deconstruction featuring essays by Christopher Norris and Andrew Benjamin, the former an expert on Jacques Derrida, the philosopher who first coined the term 'Deconstruction'.[1] While Norris' essay attempted to give an overview of Derrida's theory within the context of philosophical developments from Plato to Heidegger, it was left to Benjamin to attempt an early translation of this philosophical approach into architecture. Benjamin saw signs of Deconstruction in the work of several architects who confronted the established practices in architecture, especially those founded on the concept of 'centrality of dwelling'.[2] His interpretation of Deconstruction was illustrated by several works, from Hiromi Fujii's Ushimado Art Festival Center and Frank Gehry's Winton House to Bernard Tschumi's Parc de la Villette and Daniel Libeskind's City Edge project for Berlin. While the work of Eisenman was also given its due share, it was not clear why the others were included under this rubric, except as manifestations of a rather eccentric approach in design. Benjamin's reading was also disputed by others, like Wigley, whose definition of 'Deconstructivism' referred it back to the Russian Constructivists, severing its connection to Derrida.[3]

THE PHILOSOPHICAL FOUNDATION OF DECONSTRUCTION

In 1967, the French philosopher Jacques Derrida published three key works: *L'Écriture et la différence*, *De la grammatologie*, and *La voix et le phénomène*, which ushered a new philosophical movement, initially under the label of post-structuralism and later taking the distinctive designation of 'Deconstruction'. The main task of Derrida was to dismantle the foundations of the Western philosophical tradition, namely the notion of 'logocentrism', that is, the referral and privileging of the *logos* – the spoken word – and through it, all logical structures, as well as the 'metaphysics of presence' epitomised in Heidegger's *Being and Time*. The main focus of Derrida's Deconstructive operations was language itself, used to uncover the hidden fault lines of certain seminal texts, from Plato to Rousseau, Freud, and Saussure. But for the French philosopher, the criticism of logocentrism itself was sustained by the very logocentrism it sought to unravel, rendering any attempt to develop a new science of meaning utterly impossible.[4]

Whereas the structuralists had limited themselves to analysing the structure of language and its operations, Derrida turned language against itself, to uncover its deficiencies and contradictions and thus, to dismantle the edifice itself on which the systems of religion, logos, and reason were founded. These Derridean operations were indebted somewhat to Nietzsche, although Derrida would use a different methodology in his work.

While putting into question the foundations of any systematic approach, Derrida remained vigilant and resistant to the substitution of his own concepts for those being questioned, in order to avoid lapsing into a new logocentrism. In *De la grammatologie*, he questioned the premises of the system elaborated by the structuralist Ferdinand de Saussure, based on the notion of 'sign', substituting for it that of 'trace', since concepts and words take on meaning only in relation to others, or as he put it, through a process of *différance*, a term that he concocted to signify simultaneously a process of deferral (in time) and difference from other signs.[5] In the same vein, Derrida launched an attack on the fundamental notion of the logos, which seemed to coincide, in the work of Levinas as well as Hegel, with divine substance, or the absolute. This metaphysical project was supported, in his opinion, by the oppositions of culture/nature, image/representation, sensible/intelligible; and above all, by a 'vulgar concept of time'.

As Derrida waged this attack on the metaphysical concept of time, it would not be too difficult to infer a similar critique of the concept of space, on which modern architecture had been similarly founded. And if all the foundational premises of Western thought were to be put under examination and deconstructed, then by inference, architecture as a discipline must also be subject to this same operation of radical dismantling. In *Margins of Philosophy*, Derrida explicitly questioned the notion of 'origin', on which many architectural treatises had been founded, and which appears throughout language in such prefixes as *archi*, *telos*, *eskhaton*, which all refer to 'presence'. Thus, the *archi* in architecture – the prefix that refers the *tekton* to its primary position as a foundational element – could not escape the Deconstructive operation. Derrida specifically spoke about architecture as an inhabited *constructum*, a totality that comprehends certain invariables, and thus would be amenable to a work of Deconstruction.[6]

For Derrida, architectural meaning directs the syntax of architecture according to four elements: the law of the *oikos* (dwelling), the law of commemoration, the teleology of dwelling, and the values of beauty, harmony, and totality (aesthetics). By operating in this manner, architecture not only affects itself, but also 'regulates all of what is called Western culture, far beyond its architecture' and stands as the 'last fortress of metaphysics'.[7]

PETER EISENMAN AND THE PROJECT OF DECONSTRUCTION

Peter Eisenman was one of the few architects who took the question seriously, seizing on the opportunity that Derrida had opened up, following its developments in philosophy and literary criticism as a prelude for the elaboration of a Deconstructive project in architecture. Unlike his peers, Peter Eisenman was directly influenced by the writings of Derrida, and before that, by the structuralist studies of Noam Chomsky. He explored the potential of this new criticism in architecture, despite the difficulty of translating this anti-structuring and anti-foundational critique into an architectural project. This can be seen in the gradual transformation of Eisenman from a 'structuralist' phase of experiments on the House series, to the House El-Even Odd, which, by its play on words as well as its play on the rules of syntax expressed a shift in Eisenman's work which continued in his later projects, animated by a continuous exchange and at one time, a collaboration with the philosopher of Deconstruction, Jacques Derrida.

The transformation in Eisenman's work also manifested itself in a series of writings that appeared after 1980. These writings moved from investigations of the architectural 'sign', as exemplified in his House studies,[8] to a study of Corbusier's Domino House,[9] to a formal study of Terragni's work,[10] to a post-structuralist phase which started around 1982 with 'The Representations of Doubt: At the Sign of the Sign',[11] and the seminal essay 'The End of the Classical, the End of the Beginning, the End of the End'.[12] The publications produced by Eisenman during this phase also reflected this radical shift, with *Fin d'Ou T Hou S*,[13] a collection of loose-plate drawings that document the last project of the House series,[14] elevating the architectural document to the level of a rare manuscript. A year later, another publication came out under the title *Moving Arrows, Eros, and Other Errors*, this time printed on transparent sheets, featuring the Romeo and Juliet project designed for Verona.[15]

Eisenman's major essay, 'The End of the Classical, the End of the Beginning, the End of the End', bears a striking resemblance to Derrida's title for a chapter in *De la grammatologie*,[16] although in this case, he confessed his debt to an article by Franco Rella which appeared in the same issue of *Casabella* in which his winning scheme for the Wexner Center for the Visual Arts in Ohio was featured.[17] In this essay, influenced by Foucault's concept of *epistemes*, Baudrillard's concept of *simulation*, and Derrida's notion of the *trace*, Eisenman set himself the task of critically exposing architecture as a humanist discipline, founded on the logocentric discourses of the Renaissance. Following Foucault, he defined the Classical as an *episteme*, a continuous period where a dominant form of knowledge reigned – since the Renaissance in this case – and was marked by the three 'fictions' of Representation, Reason, and History.

Eisenman later appropriated the notion of the trace from Derrida, in an attempt to overcome the predicament of architecture as an activity rooted in physical, functional, or representational purposes, in order to wage an attack on its foundational certainties: origin, function, and history. These 'certainties' constituted the foundations of a classical metaphysics of architecture, in which the representation of a fixed set of ideas edifies a complete 'body' of architecture, whether Classical or Modernist. Instead, he proposed an architecture which would negate these various 'fictions' through operations in which the architect would take the role of a decipherer, bringing to light hidden fragments, repressed meanings, or traces of other significations, transforming the site of each project into a palimpsest where architecture would be called upon to generate new fictions and multiple histories and narratives.[18] This transformation in Eisenman's work, from a practice focused on the study of 'syntax' to one which resorts to strategies of 'decomposition'[19] in the generation of architectural objects (that would then be read as 'texts'), began well before the attempted collaboration that brought Derrida and Eisenman together.[20]

Eisenman thus began to re-orient his work, after the series of experiments on the House series (1967–75), towards a practice of 'artificial excavation' which sought to uncover latent or hidden signs in the territory, to be subsequently subverted and turned against the original site of operation. These artificial excavations would take place in a number of 'charged' urban sites, from Canareggio (1978) to Berlin (1980), to other less historically laden sites such as Long Beach, California (1986).[21]

In Berlin, on a site marked by the tragic history of the city at the border of the divide between East and West, in proximity to the Checkpoint Charlie crossing point, Eisenman proposed a project (1981–5) (fig.8.1) that developed in response to two conflicting grids: one virtual – the Mercator Grid; the other real – the grid of the city blocks, bearing the trace of the city's past. This translation was realised partially as a single building at the corner of Friedrichstrasse and Kochstrasse. It did not fully express the initial proposal to radically transform the city block at the boundary between two worlds at that time. Here, Eisenman, for the first time, moved from exclusively syntactic operations to a more dissective practice, relying specifically on a horizontal layering of traces. Jean-François Bedard explained this operation as a form of archaeology that does not seek to recover or illuminate the history of the site, but rather, as in the case of Canareggio in Venice, expresses 'the meaninglessness of Modernist rationality'.[22] In other words, it appears as an operation with a clear objective of uncovering the fault lines of the Modernist edifice by subverting it and re-inscribing other formal operations over it.

This type of operation continued later in the Wexner Center for the Arts in Ohio (1983–9) (fig.8.2), a project that effectively signalled a change in direction in the architect's work, as well as in the architectural tendencies of the time. The Wexner Center attempted to resolve the opposition of two grids, that of the university campus and that of the city. In addition to this, the architect added the 'recovery' of fragments referring to the site's history, where an armoury once stood. This

MODERN ARCHITECTURE IN A POST-MODERN ERA

left

8.1   Peter Eisenman, IBA Social Housing, Berlin, Germany, 1981–5

below

8.2   Peter Eisenman, Wexner Center for the Arts, Columbus, Ohio, USA, 1983–9

operation not only opened new possibilities of 'reading' the project as a text, but also offered a new approach to the problem of history, different from the Post-Modernist approach. And it is this difference that gave the project its winning edge, against four other competing designs, most prominent among which were the projects of Michael Graves and César Pelli, which followed a typical, monumental Neo-Classicism. This appeared to be a turning point, as the completion of the Wexner Center in 1989 roughly coincided with the first public exhibitions on Deconstruction, mentioned earlier.

The Wexner Center seemed, to some critics, to resuscitate undesirable elements in the site's history, namely the towers symbolising the armoury which had been located there up until 1959.[23] Yet Eisenman resurrected these symbolic fragments intentionally to uncover repressed memories of the site, not in glorification of its military history, but merely to serve as a reminder. Again, Eisenman emphasised the opposition between the grid of the campus and that of the city in order to develop

left

8.3   Peter Eisenman, Aronoff Center for Design and Art, University of Cincinnati, Ohio, USA, 1988–96

below

8.4   Peter Eisenman, The City of Culture of Galicia, Santiago de Compostela, Spain, 1999–2011

the intervention, supplemented with historical elements, revived as fragments. The fragments of the armoury were thus sliced by the extension of the city grid, a steel structure canopy running as a spine across the site. The main entry to the building was camouflaged by this collage, leading the visitor to an underground sequence of rooms which house the various functions.

This phase in Eisenman's Deconstructionist work was marked by a challenging collaboration with Jacques Derrida, at the suggestion of Bernard Tschumi, on a section of the Parc de la Villette in Paris. This unrealised project was documented in a series of transcripts that appeared in book form as *Chora L Works*, idiosyncratic in its title as well as in its form,[24] as the grid of the proposal actually punctures the written text and renders the operation of reading a difficult exercise, in addition to the reversal of the traditional book organisation, by relegating the introduction to the centre of the book, among other things.[25] This work also revealed the limits of translating philosophical concepts into architecture, as the architect struggled to give forms to a discourse that does not always lend itself to formal translation. Derrida warned at the beginning of this exchange with Eisenman:

> I read your texts and examined Fin D'ou T Hou S, I recognized many things: your critique of origin, anthropocentrism and aesthetics is consistent with a general deconstruction of architecture

itself. Your work seems to propose an anti-architecture, or rather an anarchitecture, but of course this is not so simple, as what I do is antiarchitectural in the traditional sense of 'anti'.[26]

This exchange continued over two years, through several documented dialogues,[27] in addition to a set of generated drawings, culminating in a final exchange between Derrida and Eisenman, in which the philosopher posed a series of unsettling questions to the architect, putting into question his whole Deconstructionist experiment.[28] Yet Eisenman's practice continued to evolve with a number of projects which shared the generative approach of the early projects of 'artificial excavation', such as the Koizumi Sangyo office building in Tokyo (1990), the Greater Columbus Convention Center in Ohio (1993), the Aronoff Center for Design and Art at the University of Cincinnati (1988–96), and the Church of the Year 2000 in Rome (1996), all of which adopted the strategy of subjecting the site to a process of computer-generated transformations of its 'original' primary elements.[29]

The Aronoff Center for Design and Art at the University of Cincinnati (fig.8.3) presents an interesting evolution of the structuralist-inspired process with which Eisenman initiated his architectural investigations, whereby the idea of an author (the architect) determining the whole process and outcome of the design is put into question, making way for an alternative, self-generating process. Eisenman proposed here a new approach, whereby the site constraints and topography, as well as the footprint of the existing school building, were brought into play to generate the outlines of the new structure. This addition takes shape as a computer-generated form that bends and flexes to adapt to the site, and in the process deviates from normative types. Its floors appear like tectonic plates that have been destabilised by external factors, its openings follow the lines of these traces on the building and do not appear like regular windows, while one of its access points takes the form of a cavernous opening in-between clashing volumes, leading to a large processional passageway and to the large atrium space that separates the existing building and the new structure.

The City of Culture of Galicia (1999–2011) (fig.8.4) ushered in yet another direction in Eisenman's theoretical experimentation. In tune with the rise of a new philosophical tendency, drawing on the ideas of Gilles Deleuze, a number

of architects adopted the 'pli' metaphor in an attempt to overcome the limitations of a rational architecture, avoiding the idiosyncrasies of Derrida's complex theories. Deleuze seemed to imply, although this remains a contested issue, a way out of these Derridean peregrinations towards a contemporary 'Baroque', advocated by the likes of Greg Lynn, and later by Patrik Schumacher. In this project, Eisenman made a clear shift towards adopting some of the figural aspects of this new direction, in a complex that features a folding tapestry over the site. According to Eisenman, the City of Culture was inspired by the old city of Santiago and the pilgrim routes that led to it. The design emerged as an overlay of a Cartesian grid on the historic medieval grid of the city, transposed into this 'terrain vague' on the outskirts of the old town, and further infused by deformations that result from the imposition of a topological grid on the whole. The project consisted of six major functions, arranged within three pairs of units: a museum and international art centre, a centre for music and performance arts, a library, archives, and an administrative centre. All these functions were wrapped under the folding surfaces that cover the site, cut through by pedestrian paths and public spaces, somewhat recalling the organic structure of the old town. The conceptual schematics betray the typical Eisenman methodology of overlays, yet this time further accentuated by the topological dimension that turns the complex into a gigantic artificial landscape of swirling hills and excavated ravines, partially covered in stone. This complex which was planned to revitalise the city – much like its sister city Bilbao – ran into major hurdles resulting from excessive costs and an economic crisis that put an end to its construction by 2013, leaving it like an abandoned quarry amidst a desolate landscape.

BERNARD TSCHUMI: ANOTHER APPROACH TO DECONSTRUCTION

Another major figure associated with 'Deconstruction' is Bernard Tschumi. Tschumi started his career with a contestation of the established order in architecture, following civil unrest during May 1968. He first advocated an interactive architecture based on communication technology, in the form of a project titled 'Do-It-Yourself-City'. Seeking an alternative to the functional and formal paradigms in design, Tschumi incorporated lessons drawn from the writings of Bataille, Barthes, and Sollers, before turning to Derrida. He drew concepts derived from philosophy and literary criticism into architecture, including such notions as the 'erotic', 'violence, and 'pleasure'. In his approach to establishing a theoretical framework, Tschumi appeared closer to Rem Koolhaas than to Peter Eisenman, with his interest in cross-disciplinary ideas, specifically exploring the relations between film, literature, and architecture. Tschumi attempted to draw on these relationships in juxtapositions or what he called 'disjunctions', setting the stage for an opposition between the rational and the irrational.[30] One of his strategies, defined as 'cross-programming', juxtaposed programmatic uses in order to create unexpected activities, termed 'events'. For this, he relied on the cinematographic technique of montage as a tool for the generation of spaces that resist conventional 'reading' or interpretation.

Tschumi's friendship with Derrida had probably much to do with the interpretation of his first major work – the Parc de la Villette (1982–98) (fig.8.5) – as a Deconstructionist project, by the philosopher of Deconstruction himself.[31] The design overlaid three organising systems, with

8.5   Bernard Tschumi, Parc de la Villette, Paris, France, 1982–98

the intent of avoiding endowing any of them with hierarchical importance. One of these layers is a Cartesian grid, punctuated by a series of red pavilions, designated as 'follies', stripped of any functional role. The playful relationship between these follies, the formal language of which refers to the early Constructivists' works like Iakov Chernikov's, played on the Barthesian notion of the sign, showing that these 'recycled' signs could be reinterpreted in a new context where their semantic dimension becomes open to different readings. Tschumi referred the Parc de la Villette to his earlier experiments, specifically the 'Manhattan Transcripts' project of 1976–81, which ushered, in his own words, his Deconstructionist experiments. The Manhattan Transcripts – a collection of drawings and photographs arranged as a cinematographic script – aimed to transcribe events and spatial relationships that are normally excluded from architectural representation. These were associated with his theory of 'disjunction', a term he used to signify an architectural direction that rejects the notions of synthesis, the traditional opposition between form and function, and that 'implies constant mechanical operations that systematically produce dissociation'. He further posited a correspondence between 'dissociation' and '*différance*', the term used by Derrida to indicate a double-operation within language.[32]

In this sense, Tschumi interpreted his own work at La Villette as inscribed within the Deconstructionist project, while taking a very different approach from Eisenman. Through this, he attempted to dislocate meaning, rejecting the symbolic repertoire, and contesting the historical typologies of architecture, as well as the fundamental signified of functionality:

> La Villette, then, aims at an architecture that means nothing, an architecture of the signifier rather than the signified – one that is pure trace or play of language. In a Nietzschean manner, la Villette moves towards interpretative infinity, for the effect of refusing fixity is not insignificance, but semantic plurality.[33]

Despite his expressed intentions, La Villette seems more of a revival of a Constructivist approach to form-making on a Cartesian system of organisation, than a clear and incisive Deconstructionist work. Still, its subversion of normative typologies of architecture and landscape design earned it a distinctive place within that movement. However, the later development of Tschumi's architectural work, from Le Fresnoy School of Art in France (1991–7) and Lerner Hall at Columbia (1999), to his more recent Acropolis Museum in Athens (2008), showed a growing distance from his earlier agenda, as these projects no longer proposed a 'radical' revision of the discipline, but rather sought to explore new ways of subverting traditional typologies to generate an engaging experience of space, which returns, in the end, to some of the main principles of the Modernist project.

DANIEL LIBESKIND: TOWARDS A DECONSTRUCTION OF HISTORY

Daniel Libeskind was associated with Deconstruction, especially after the Derrida–Eisenman debate, in which the philosopher alluded to the Jewish Museum addition to the Berlin Museum (1989–2001) (fig.8.6) by Libeskind as the one that most appropriately reflected on the notions of absence, negativity, and the void, all of which refer to the trace, to writing and the 'place of deconstruction'. In his letter to Eisenman, Derrida approvingly quoted at length from Libeskind's statement on the project for the Jewish Museum.[34]

In his masterpiece, Libeskind was preoccupied with issues of memory, site, and narrative. And here, the weight of history in its tragic dimension added further impetus to the task of critical interpretation. Libeskind masterfully exploited the potentials of this difficult project to create a work that defied normal conventions, while effectively deconstructing the meanings associated with the museum as a type, through the problematic of commemorating Jewish presence/absence in this critical site. The work drew on three separate themes: the map of Jewish presence in the city as represented through its most illustrious names; Arnold Schoenberg's incomplete opera *Moses and Aaron*; and Walter Benjamin's essay, *One*

8.6 Daniel Libeskind, Jewish Museum, Berlin, Germany, 1989–2001

Way Street. Inspired by these three different references, respectively geographical, musical, and literary, Libeskind conceived the project as a separate volume, composed of two clashing elements: one straight and one broken line that cross at several intervals, creating different voids. The building's solid appearance, clad in zinc panels with diagonal slits of openings that do not allow any views of the interior, further accentuates its idiosyncratic nature in the urban landscape. Its entry point, through a basement passage that originates in the lobby of the original museum, made it possible to further deny any normative physical relation to the 'original' building. Outside, a slanted square garden planted with concrete pillars from which sprout olive trees, symbols of hope, further accentuates the symbolic dimension of the project.

In a long letter to the architect, the philosopher David Farrell Krell pointed out this inherent play on memory that the building represents, and the significance of its opacity to the external world, from which it demarcates itself:

> Your museum, dedicated to an avant-garde of humanity, a humanity 'incinerated in its own history,' will not be in service to any ethico-political teleology or kingdom of ends. 'Organized around a void,' neither collage nor collision nor dialectical synthesis, its lines will be jagged and truncated, resisting for ages to come the amnesia of commemoration. Precisely because it is all about not forgetting, your museum eschews anamnesis and spurns the allure of hieratic origins. No one will dwell in these 'fragments' or shards that have no access from the public level, but are accessible only underground and in very special ways.[35]

The success of the Jewish Museum led to other commissions, and to the establishment of a practice which nevertheless veered towards the repetition of the Jewish Museum topos on other sites and programmes, which presented a similar problematic in some cases, like the Felix Nussbaum Museum in Osnabrück, while in others had nothing in common with it, like the Denver Art Museum or the addition to the V&A Museum in London.[36] What began as a potentially significant 'Deconstructionist' project by Libeskind eventually fizzled down to a formal recipe that was indiscriminately applied to different projects around the world, none of which posed the same problematic as the Jewish Museum in Berlin.

MARK WIGLEY ON DECONSTRUCTION

One of the first critics to address the problematic topic of Deconstruction was the theoretician Mark Wigley. In his introduction to the exhibition catalogue on 'Deconstructivist Architecture' at the MoMA, Wigley postulated the connection between some of the architects who were labelled as 'Deconstructivist', and the Russian Constructivists, whose project did not fully materialise in the 1920s, replaced on the one hand by the ascetic purity of the Modern Movement, and on the other by the revival of Neo-Classicism in Russia and Germany. Wigley saw the new architecture as negotiating the 'relationship between the instability of the early Russian avant-garde and the stability of high modernism'. He further defined it as an 'architecture of disruption, deflection, deviation, and distortion, rather than one of demolition, dismantling, decay, decomposition, or disintegration. It displaces structure instead of destroying it.'[37] Among the seven projects displayed, Wigley singled out Coop Himmelb(l)au's office penthouse in Vienna as exemplary of this new approach.

In a slightly revised version of the same article, Wigley was even more critical of some works placed under this label:

> Deconstruction is often misunderstood as the taking apart of constructions. Consequently, any provocative architectural design which appears to take a structure apart by the simple breaking of an object – as in James Wines or the complex dissimulation of an object into a collage of traces, as in Eisenman and Fujii – has been called Deconstructive. These strategies have produced perhaps the most formidable projects of recent years, but remain simulations of Deconstructive work in other disciplines because they do not exploit the unique condition of the architectural object.[38]

It was not until *Deconstruction III*, published by *Architectural Design* in 1990, that Wigley finally came to acknowledge the impact of Derrida on this new movement. In this essay, Wigley explored in depth the philosophical background of Deconstruction, from Kant to Heidegger, culminating with Derrida. And in parallel, he elaborated on the difficult task of translation from philosophy to architecture, and vice versa, without mentioning any specific architectural projects, simply concluding that the effort of translating Deconstruction in architecture:

> [. . .] does not lead simply to a formal reconfiguration of the object. Rather, it calls into question the condition of the object, its 'objecthood'. It 'problematises' the condition of the object without simply abandoning it. [. . .] Consequently, the status of the translation of deconstruction in architecture needs to be rethought. A more aggressive reading is required, an architectural transformation of deconstruction that draws on the gaps in deconstruction that demand such an abuse, sites that already operate with a kind of architectural violence.[39]

In this essay, Wigley did not give hints about projects that may have explored the boundaries between philosophy and architecture, simply leaving the question suspended. Also, he did not revisit the earlier opposition between 'Deconstruction' and 'Deconstructivism', two terms that came to mean the same thing in the end, and which were being applied uncritically to designate projects that displayed 'fragmentation' and irregular compositions, superficially challenging the formal aspects of both 'Modern' and 'Post-Modern' languages.

9 Neo-Constructivism, Neo-Suprematism and the Return of the Avant-Garde

Modern architecture witnessed a major contestation with the rise of Post-Modernism, to which few strands, like High Tech, remained immune. Yet in the face of this attack, one architect, Rem Koolhaas, can be credited with launching a major counter-attack which nevertheless included a revision of the Modernist agenda. This revisionary movement did not seek to resurrect a bygone past, but rather to assimilate the lessons of history while addressing contemporary issues, and specifically, the challenge of communication. Before examining the legacy of Koolhaas, it is important to differentiate again what he and other architects of his generation were involved in – as a project of revival of the Modernist avant-garde, specifically the Russian architects' work of the 1920s – from other trends and movements, specifically 'Deconstruction'. As Catherine Cooke clearly articulated in an essay in the first volume on Deconstruction, many of the architects featured in that review used the work of the Russian avant-garde as their point of departure in developing a new formal language. Cooke was the first to designate this new architectural tendency that swept architectural circles and schools by the end of the 1980s, by the term 'Neo-Constructivism'.[1] It is on the basis of their distinct approach and different agenda that we will examine the work of Koolhaas, Hadid, and others separately from the 'Deconstructionist' camp under which they have all been lumped together. And while these architects were inspired by the formal language of the Russian avant-garde, excluding its socio-political dimension, their programme may still be considered as a revival of the avant-garde, in its various formal manifestations.

REM KOOLHAAS AND THE REVIVAL OF CONSTRUCTIVISM

Rem Koolhaas came to architecture after studies in film and journalism, which gave him a special viewpoint from which to examine architecture as part of a more inclusive cultural condition, and to revisit Modernism as an 'incomplete project' that needed to be reformulated in light of changing cultural, economic, and social parameters. The influence of his background in film and journalism was noted by several critics, which resulted in a new approach that incorporated 'script writing' in architecture, linking disparate episodes to generate a narrative in which suspense and the juxtaposition of unexpected events and elements would play an important part.[2]

Koolhaas emerged as one of the major figures of the informal group studying, and then teaching at the Architectural Association in London, at the beginning of the 1970s. His colleagues – among whom figured Elia and Zoe Zenghelis, Zaha Hadid, and others – formed the nucleus of his Office for Metropolitan Architecture (OMA). As a student, Koolhaas was very much interested in the legacy of the Russian avant-garde, specifically Ivan Leonidov, revealed to him by Gerrit Oorthuys, a professor of architectural history at Delft. This was compounded later by his interest in the Surrealist work of Superstudio and Archizoom. In his comprehensive study on Koolhaas, Roberto Gargiani drew the connections between these various sources and their impact on the young Koolhaas, whose work would later take a hybrid form, manifested in the juxtaposition of diverse elements, the reversal of traditional typologies, and the projection of illusory spaces. The surreal dimension in Koolhaas' work appeared with his first project, in which he collaborated with Elia Zenghelis, for a competition in Milan titled 'Exodus, or the Voluntary Prisoners of Architecture' (1971). Conceived as a continuous strip of different spaces contained within a set of two parallel walls overlaid on the city of London, this composition was intended as a provocation, where the real (the city as it is) faces its 'other', an idealised set of spaces intended as some sort of purifying zone for these 'voluntary prisoners'.

As Gargiani explains:

> In this 'Strip' vital activities take place, marked by an 'intense metropolitan desirability' and therefore capable, in the aims of the authors, of generating an exodus away from the historical city, which would thus be progressively reduced to a 'pack of ruins'. The 'Strip' is divided into eight Squares, each set aside for one activity. This form bears a certain similarity to the project by Leonidov for an ideal linear urban structure – the Palace of Culture – to be inserted in Moscow and subdivided into four square vectors devoted to scientific research, physical culture, mass demonstrations and expositions.[3]

Koolhaas' major study of New York, as a fellow at the Institute of Architecture and Urban Studies, already indicated his particular approach towards the interpretation of the modern city. In that study, he focused on the unusual events which affected the growth of the city as a metropolis, offering a new history that is neither centred around individual monuments and styles, nor on the grand schemes of urban planning, but around particular moments, and special technical developments – such as the invention of the elevator – revealing in the process certain subconscious elements in the history of this 'urban phenomenon'. The chapter on Long Island, for instance, carefully traced and interpreted the architectural development of this 'leisure park' and its impact on the physical as well as the psychological landscape of the city. Long Island would come to symbolise the 'alter ego' of the metropolis, its 'security valve' which allows the urban citizen to give free rein to their repressed desires.

It is not difficult to trace this alternative way of looking at things in the later works that Koolhaas would project and realise, which show his approach to re-formulating given programmes and re-packaging functional requirements within an envelope that would be at once formally and technologically innovative. Most of the projects realised by OMA do, in fact, appear to be different yet familiar, modern yet contemporary. Their avant-garde aspect translates into an experimental approach with materials and space, so that we are drawn into a building that appears to be familiar, only to be de-familiarised by its organisation, its materiality, and sequence of spaces.

One of the first attempts by Koolhaas to put into practice the Surrealist-inspired notion of *cadavre exquis* [exquisite corpse], which consists of assembling in a non-rational manner pieces from different sources into a provocative 'text', came in the form of the competition for the expansion of the Dutch parliament quarters in the old Binnenhof in The Hague (1978) (fig.9.1). Koolhaas and Zenghelis, with Zaha Hadid who had recently joined the practice, collaborated to compose an assembly of many parts, each one of them designing one segment, and then bringing the pieces together. While Zenghelis projected the low-lying slab containing the main public functions, incorporating a 'floating pool' which became a recurrent motif in OMA's works symbolising freedom and bodily pleasures, Hadid added a parallel slab of multiple storeys to house the offices of parliament, connected to the other slab through a cantilevering volume housing the assembly hall. Koolhaas added his part, an extruded tower of glass following the irregular shape of the plot, and connected to Zenghelis's wing via flying bridges that recall the Van Nelle factory in Rotterdam. The whole complex presented a rather playful contrast to the historic setting, while blending with it in a much more 'contextual' way than would have been the case with a purely modern structure.

The Villa Dall'Ava at Saint Cloud (1984–91) provided Koolhaas with one of the first opportunities to translate these ideas, a combination of Surrealism and Constructivism, into a project of 'small' size, as categorised later in his famous S, M, L, XL compendium. The Villa Dall'Ava, in a suburb of Paris with a view of the city, was conceived as an assembly of three main elements: two parallel blocks, connected by a trapezoidal element, the whole merging together at the ground level into

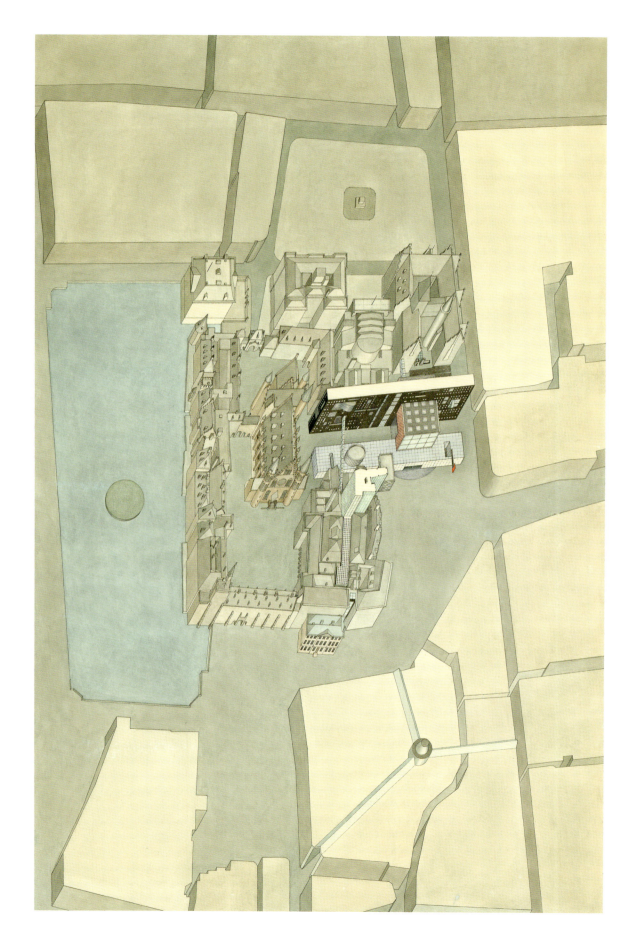

left

9.1   OMA, Dutch Parliament Extension (Project), The Hague, the Netherlands, 1978

below

9.2   OMA, Kunsthal, Rotterdam, the Netherlands, 1987–92

one continuous living space punctuated by certain markers, while acting as a divider at the upper level between the parents' bedroom on one side, and the child's bedroom on the other. This connecting/dividing element transforms into a 'floating pool' at the roof. Taking some cues from Villa Savoye, but in a more 'Constructivist' spirit, it reinterprets the Corbusian principles of the free plan, free elevation, pilotis, horizontal window, and roof garden in a novel way, while assembling the whole out of discrete units and diverse materials. The 'purism' of Villa Savoye is replaced here by a controlled promiscuity of materials, some noble, others very mundane. The bedroom at the front of the site floats over a forest of steel columns, irregularly distributed over the garden, which extends to the ground level space through the transparent glass walls.

The Kunsthal in Rotterdam (1987–92) (fig.9.2), a project of 'medium' size, employed a similar compositional strategy to Villa Dall'Ava, relying on the assembly of distinct elements composed within one overall rectangular diagram, sitting on the edge of a dyke which constitutes the main boulevard. The front elevation of this multi-layered complex projects a rather 'simple yet complex' facade, split into two by the entrance passageway: on the left side is a solid, stone-clad wall at the base, behind which are located the offices and the auditorium, while on the right side, a recessed glass facade recalling Berlin's New National Gallery provides a view towards the exhibition space. This frontal view is crowned by a thick steel beam, a nod to Mies, and topped by a steel-frame box containing the mechanical systems, and doubling as a billboard. The main exhibition space is accessed through the passageway, at the beginning of a ramp that goes down gently to meet the garden at the back. The rectangular volume is intersected longitudinally by this pedestrian ramp going down to the garden, and laterally by a service road running parallel to the main road, at the basement level, below the dyke. Going through the exhibition space, the visitor is led through a continuous ramp to a bridge crossing over the passageway to the garden, offering a sequence of different views – as in a filmic sequence – before reaching the back of the auditorium, and slowly descending back towards the point of entry. The auditorium is furnished in multi-coloured Tolleson chairs, its wall to the exterior glazed to offer a view of the garden, while the opposite one is clad in translucent polycarbonate panels that incorporate the lighting system. The Koolhaas approach of bringing together disparate elements and materials in a multi-faceted composition that offers intriguing

spatial experiences, inspired by a cinematographic culture, is brilliantly manifested in this project which acts as a 'processor' of images and spatial experiences. As Gargiani noted, Koolhaas succeeds in creating a work from 'discarded, untimely ideas', bringing them together in unexpected configurations.

The experimental approach of OMA continued with each new opportunity. In the design of a multi-functional educational facility at the University of Utrecht, Koolhaas applied a new principle that he started exploring with the project for a library at Jussieu (1992). At Utrecht, this plastic modelling of form resulted in a building that incorporated a 'pliable surface', a continuous concrete slab that curves at one end of the building, like a piece of paper, folding on itself. The large structure incorporates two large auditoria on the upper level, reached through continuous stairways, evoking urban streets, along the glazed, lateral facade. Underneath the curved slab, which continues as a ramp leading to the main entrance, a large cafeteria is located. At the main entrance, under the portico of the concrete slab, a large floor section serves as a cover to the bike parking below, lit by a collection of egg-shaped skylights, irregularly scattered over the space.

Another example of Koolhaas' quest for complex forms that contain a multiplicity of different functions, yet avoid the typical Modernist approach of systematic assembly, can be seen in the Zeebrugge Terminal Building (1988), which was projected to mitigate the effects of the new channel tunnel on maritime travel between the Continent and the UK. Here, OMA projected a capsule that appears like a spaceship which landed on the edge of the water, incorporating all the different functions that a terminal building should have, but condensing them in what appears to be a haphazard manner, from the access of the cars, to service functions like restaurants, hotels, and offices that are contained within the upper sections of the capsule. Koolhaas made use here of another 'topos' from his Surrealist kit of parts – the egg, which becomes the form-giver to the envelope – while internally the building translates the idea of a 'free section', as a follow-up to Le Corbusier's free plan and free facade.

Gargiani gave this perceptive description of this project which, unfortunately, was not realised:

From the hall of the Terminal a traveler who looks upwards sees the accumulation of platforms, balanced volumes, staircases and walkways, against the backdrop of a grand glass roof similar to the geodesic dome designed by Buckminster Fuller over Manhattan, a parody of Hood's City under a Single Roof. Inside the metaphorical egg of Zeebrugge the traveler re-encounters the image and the life of a metropolis, a place to dine outdoors or watch performances. Waiting for his ferry, he is accompanied in an ideal journey through the intense, pulsating Culture of Congestion. At the top of the office tower, he can even take a dip in Koolhaas's pool, taking part in an initiatic odyssey of the Floating Swimming Pool.[4]

In this project, which fits the 'Large' category, Koolhaas effectively proposed a new type of 'social condenser' which, unlike Moisei Ginzburg's horizontal slab for the Narkomfin building in Moscow (1928–32), takes a spherical form, and in which the mechanical world is forcefully brought into the picture, alongside traditional human activities. It is noteworthy here that Koolhaas, a few years later, would seek to patent the idea of 'social condenser' as his own invention.

Among the 'Extra Large' projects, the Euralille Master Plan (1989–94) (fig.9.3) was OMA's first largest project to be realised. Here, the architect's appetite for planning a new metropolis came to bear fruit, with a project that aimed to transform the old city centre of Lille into a modern metropolis, with the arrival of the new TGV station and all the associated infrastructural developments. Within this master plan, with several structures assigned to different architects, OMA designed the iconic project of the Grand Palais, known also as Congrexpo (1990–94) (fig.9.4). Designed to an egg-shaped plan – a recurrent motif – the egg is actually sliced off into three main zones, each dedicated to a particular public function or set of functions. At one edge lies the Zenith Hall, a large space for concerts, with an opaque, curved facade that is cut off at the base to exhibit the structural system and stairways. In the intermediate zone, within a rectangular section, three different lecture halls are located, each given its particular interior design. The Pasteur Hall, for instance, exhibits a slanted

above

9.3   OMA, Euralille Aerial, Lille, France, 1989–94

right

9.4   OMA, Congrexpo, Lille, France, 1990–94

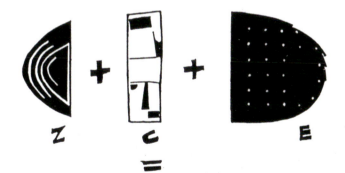

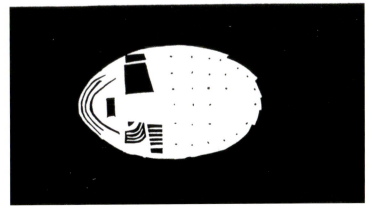

wall on one side, covered by light blue acoustic panels evoking a large-scale furniture fabric – like a *capitonne* – while other halls discretely uncover the structural and mechanical systems, offering a voyeuristic look into the inner parts of the architectural space. The large staircase serving these halls offers another 'surreal' dimension to this work, with its slanted walls covered by sheets of stainless steel that reflect a distorted image of the space and the visitors. A similar distorting effect is produced on the external facade, where irregular panes of glass, assembled at an angle to each other, produce the effect of a shattered curtain wall. The larger section of the egg is dedicated to exhibition spaces that can be configured according to need, through dividing panels.[5]

There are multiple ways to read the work of a complex and prolific character such as Rem Koolhaas. Some critics have assigned him a leading role in what became known as the 'new pragmatism' that would take over architectural practice at the turn of the century.[6] While his early works were clearly informed by a streak of avant-garde idealism inspired by a desire to resurrect the language of Russian Constructivism, his later works – such as the Seattle Library or the CCTV in Beijing – took on a more instrumental approach, influenced by information technology and a managerial approach towards the generation of form. Koolhaas's influence on contemporary architecture was not limited to the actual projects he developed and realised, but extended to his manifestoes disseminated through a number of publications, most notably *S, M, L, XL* and *Mutations*, in addition to the earlier *Delirious New York*. His influence was further expanded through his teaching, first at the Architectural Association in London, and later at Harvard, where his pedagogical framework took a new form of research on global cities. As Bart Lootsma indicated in *Super Dutch*, the influence of Koolhaas on a generation of young architects in the Netherlands cannot be overestimated. Koolhaas became not only the conscience of the new Dutch architecture, but also its catalyst.[7] In addition, several of the prominent figures of the new Dutch architectural scene graduated out of OMA's office to establish their own practices. Yet, the direction of this new generation of architects cannot be simply associated with Koolhaas and his idiosyncratic approach. They were not, so to speak, interested in his 'Constructivist' agenda, but more inclined towards a revisionary Modernism that attempts to chart its own course, seeking a synthesis between the 'structuralist' aesthetics of the 1960s and a new 'monumentality' that defies traditional typologies.

ZAHA HADID AND THE SUPREMATIST TENDENCY

It was at the Architectural Association where a young Zaha Hadid met Rem Koolhaas, studied under him and later worked, albeit briefly, in his Office of Metropolitan Architecture. Hadid's compositional and representational skills placed her above the others, and she was drafted to collaborate on the Binnenhof expansion project in The Hague. The first phase of her practice, from the period of her first independent project for a Prime Minister Residence in Dublin (1979), to the Rosenthal Center in Cincinnati (1997–2003), remained under the spell of the Russian avant-garde, which she had explored under Koolhaas. It is obvious that her later work, following Patrik Schumacher's active engagement as an associate in her firm, took a completely different direction.

At the Architectural Association, Hadid had explored the idea of implementing Malevich's *Tektonik* in the local context of London, as her final thesis.[8] Her design for a hotel on Hungerford Bridge took the form of an assembly of colour-coded rectangular blocks, in homage to Malevich's Suprematist compositions. Thus evolved a formal tendency that Hadid masterfully translated into her first major work which launched her on the international scene: the winning proposal for the Hong Kong Peak (1982–3) (fig.9.5), which was not realised. In this project, slabs of different sizes superpose and extend over the mountain edges in a gravity-defying mode, something clearly indebted to the formal language of Malevich, but also to Melnikov, the Vesnin brothers, and Leonidov. The definition given by Cooke about Suprematism may well apply to Hadid's vision of architecture at that point, treating the field or terrain as a 'space of collisions and events rather than objects with precise measure'. According to Cooke, the

9.5 Zaha Hadid, The Hong Kong Peak, Hong Kong, China, 1982–3

Suprematist work is manifestly 'scaleless and measureless'.[9] Unlike the restrained character of the London project, here the proposed resort defied the normative rules of composition, slicing through the site, unravelling layers, and recomposing them in a way that exacerbates the tension between them. Hadid explained her intervention on the Hong Kong hills in these terms:

> I felt from the beginning that any intervention upon this condition could not be vertical, but had to be horizontal. It also had to have a degree of sharpness – like a blade cutting through the mountain. When you ascend the mountain away from the city the congestion lessens and the towers of the city begin to fragment across what is called the Mid-levels. The top is almost isolated – that is where the project slides in. As the object is placed on Hong Kong it begins to violate and change the city.[10]

Zaha Hadid's first major work came in 1990, with a commission from the Vitra company to build a fire station on the grounds of the factory site (1990–93) (fig.9.6). A series of walls, freestanding, define the spatial composition and enclose the zone of the fire trucks, which opens through a large bay onto the exterior, covered by a flying canopy. The whole structure is of cast in-situ concrete, without any details to distract from the purity of the formal elements. The composition emerged as a manipulation of the field of forces, a vectorial composition in response to the site. While the ground floor was occupied by the main functions of the fire station, the upper level was dedicated to meeting areas with a panoramic view of the site. Following its decommission as a fire station the building was converted into a museum for Vitra's furniture collection.

Hadid's fourth built project – after the Spittelau Viaducts housing project in Vienna (1994–2005)

MODERN ARCHITECTURE IN A POST-MODERN ERA

9.6   Zaha Hadid, Vitra Fire Station, Weil am Rhein, Germany, 1990–93

and the Landesgartenschau exhibition space in Weil am Rhein (1996–9) – was the Rosenthal Center for Contemporary Art in Cincinnati, Ohio (1997–2003) (fig.9.7). This project effectively concluded Hadid's 'Suprematist-Constructivist' phase. Already, and around the same time, the Landesgartenschau indicated a different direction with the hard-edge elements giving way to sinuous forms. The Rosenthal Center occupied a corner site in the downtown area of the city, breaking down the programme into a series of tectonic rectangular blocks – some transparent, others solid – in concrete or even stone-clad, that appear to be piled on top of each other, as blocks in a quarry, hanging in a precarious condition. The ground floor lobby offers a transparent facade to the street, inviting visitors to take the escalator at the back of the site, which continuously wraps around the different floors, suspended within the tall atrium space. The internal disposition of exhibition spaces follows a more conventional approach, with the galleries lined along the external street side, their walls slightly shifted to express the dynamic play of internal forces.

Hadid's work at this stage, along with Gehry and others, was simply thrown into the 'Deconstruction' basket, as it showed similar 'stylistic' tendencies to Eisenman's 'post-structuralist' experiments, but without actually pursuing the same agenda. Her strategies emerged rather, from a provocative relation to the site and the landscape, attempting to literally scrape it or

9.7   Zaha Hadid, Rosenthal Center for Contemporary Art, Cincinnati, Ohio, USA, 1997–2003

slice it, producing not objects, but an assembly of planar elements held together in anti-gravitational mode. In her later projects, where the imprint of Patrik Schumacher becomes more evident,[11] Hadid gradually abandoned the earlier fascination with Malevich and his hard-edge tectonics, moving towards smooth forms that emerge from a plastic modelling, somewhat reminiscent of the work of Erich Mendelsohn and Eero Saarinen, but taken to a different level thanks to the new technological possibilities.

Despite these formal affinities to the Russian Constructivists' work, the relationship of Koolhaas and Hadid to Constructivism must be carefully evaluated given the scientific, systematic, and economic approach that the Constructivists took towards the problem of form, which distinguishes their work from these latter-day 'Neo-Constructivists'.[12] Moisei Ginzburg, one of the leaders of that movement, clearly expressed the priorities and design philosophy of Constructivism in this statement:

> There can be no question of any sort of artist losing creativity just because he knows clearly what he wants, what he is aiming for, and in what consists the meaning of his work. But subconscious, impulsive creativity must be replaced by a clear and distinctly organised method, which is economical of the architect's energy and transfers the freed surplus of it into inventiveness and the force of the creative impulse.[13]

So clearly, the agenda of the latter-day Neo-Constructivists differed substantially from the more 'objective', economically driven agenda of the Russians. Still, the formal similarities suggest a certain relationship that left its imprint on contemporary architecture.

VARIATIONS ON NEO-CONSTRUCTIVISM

Many architects working in the 1990s and early in the new millennium, though not as directly influenced as Koolhaas and Hadid were by the Russian avant-garde, appropriated a Neo-Constructivist language, which may be defined as the elaboration of new forms that defy traditional (and by now Modernist) types and norms, and which reaffirm the aims of the early avant-garde in their quest for a non-normative architecture. Yet unlike the other direction, exemplified by High Tech, the Neo-Constructivists did not seek to achieve standardised, economical, or 'objective' solutions, but rather revelled in the process itself which leads to provocative forms and configurations. It is under this umbrella that we can read the work of Coop Himmelb(l)au, Thom Mayne and Michael Rotondi (Morphosis), Eric Owen Moss, and others.

Coop Himmelb(l)au – a practice originally founded by Wolf Prix, Helmut Swiczinsky, and Michael Holzer in Vienna in 1968 – made its international impact with its seminal project for a penthouse in Vienna in 1989. This original artifact, which broke all the typological constraints of a normative penthouse, recalls metaphorically the tale of Kafka's *Metamorphosis*. It is as if the old roof broke out of its envelope, metamorphosing into a new spatial form. The rooftop explodes in multiple directions, and becomes a composition of different panels of glass, creating an unusual office space. The architects described it as the effect of a flashlight coming from the street, crossing the space, and breaking up the old rooftop.[14]

Coop Himmelb(l)au started off by experimenting with different concepts, from the 'Open Structures' that proposed aggressive interventions, to experiments such as the 'Blazing Wing' (1980), a 'happening' that set fire to a steel structure in the middle of a courtyard space in Vienna. One example of their 'Open Structures' is the Open House project designed for Malibu in California (1983–9) (fig.9.8). The architects defined their concept as a means to break from traditional forms, drawing specifically on the Surrealists and their method of 'automatic writing'. Thus, the house emerged from a sketch done with eyes shut, allowing for a spontaneous process 'in which the hand, functioning like a seismograph, records and transcribes the strong feelings and emotions that the future building must rekindle'.[15] While the Open House was inspired by the Surrealists, the Blazing Wing event was more 'Dadaist' in spirit, and was accompanied by a manifesto that expresses well this rebellious mood of the time:

> We have no desire to build Biedermeier. Not now or no other time. We are tired of seeing Palladio and other historical masks. Because with architecture, we don't want to exclude everything that is disquieting.
>
> We want architecture that has more. Architecture that bleeds, that exhausts, that whirls, and even breaks. Architecture that lights up, stings, rips, and tears under stress.
>
> Architecture has to be cavernous, fiery, smooth, hard, angular, brutal, round, delicate, colourful, obscene, lustful, dreamy, attracting, repelling, wet, dry, and throbbing. Alive or dead.
>
> If cold, then cold as a block of ice.
>
> If hot, then hot as a blazing wing.
>
> Architecture must blaze.[16]

right, top

9.8   Coop Himmelb(l)au, Open House for Malibu (Project), California, USA, 1983–9

right, bottom

9.9   Coop Himmelb(l)au, UFA Cinema Multiplex, Dresden, Germany, 1993–8

Coop Himmelb(l)au's later work had to accommodate different conditions and constraints, and adapt more to definite programmes. Their intervention in Dresden, after the fall of the Berlin Wall, was a cinema multiplex (1993–8) (fig.9.9), composed of several theatres, with all the associated functions. The building was conceived to respond in a proper manner to the street alignment on the side of the highway, while decomposing into a 'crystal' tower on the side of the pedestrian plaza, in a way, reminiscent of Paul Sheerbart and Bruno Taut's celebration of glass structures. The great polyhedral skylight wraps around the main foyer where the ticket sales counters are located and accommodates the escalators that lead the visitors to the upper-level theatres.

Their later work continued on this path of 'constructive' manipulation of High-Tech elements (steel, glass, composite materials), resulting in unusual configurations that at once respond to complex functional requirements while pushing the boundaries of formal composition in a provocative manner. Such is the case with their Akron Art Museum in Ohio (2001–7) (fig.9.10), an addition to a traditional Neo-Classical red-brick structure. Contrasting with its older neighbour, the new building projects a futuristic pavilion composed of what they called the 'Crystal', the Gallery Box, and the Roof Cloud. While the Crystal provides the enclosure for the main foyer, as in the Dresden multiplex, the Gallery Box is an opaque cube floating above ground that contains the galleries; the Roof Cloud acts as a semantic supplement, a symbolic gesture that contains some spaces while accentuating the landmark character of the building.

Concurrent with their work on the Akron Museum, the architects also completed the impressive BMW Welt in Munich, Germany (2001–7) (fig.9.11), a complex that groups together a large automotive museum, a car delivery centre, an exhibition space, and a number of

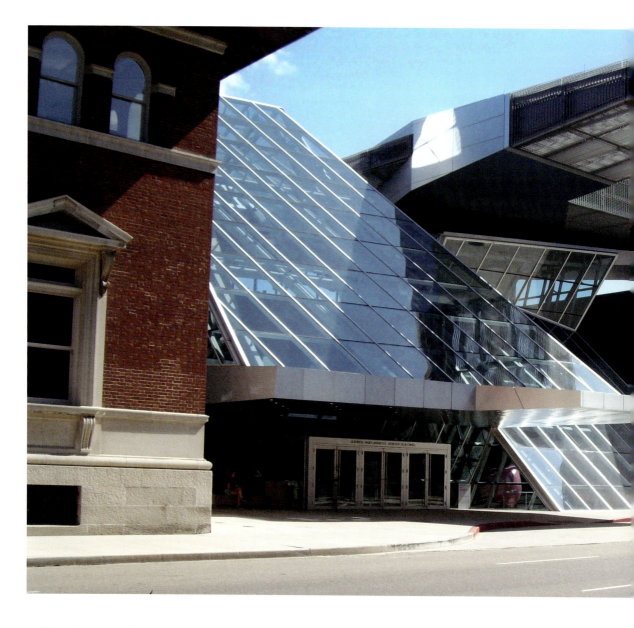

ancillary functions, all composed into a hybrid, organic arrangement of elements. The floor plan is an irregular composition of a large oval space, accommodating the car museum, a rectangular block housing an auditorium, a triangular section containing administrative offices, and a 'double-cone' at the corner end of the composition, used for exhibitions. All these functions are spread around a covered, meandering public space that takes the visitors on a journey through the multiple layers of this complex. Large concrete pilotis are spread around the structure, supporting the building, which is covered in glass and metallic panels, projecting a futuristic character that also recalls gigantic industrial complexes. Among their recent work, the Musée des Confluences in Lyon

NEO-CONSTRUCTIVISM, NEO-SUPREMATISM AND THE RETURN OF THE AVANT-GARDE

9.10 Coop Himmelb(l)au, Akron Art Museum, Akron, Ohio, USA, 2001–7

(2001–14) (fig.9.12) provides another example of this continuous search for unsettling compositions. The interface situation of the site at the confluence of the Rhône and the Saône rivers inspired the superposition of two metaphors: the crystal and the cloud. The cloud structure, floating on pillars, contains a spatial sequence of black boxes, admitting no daylight, so as to achieve maximum flexibility for exhibition design. By contrast, the crystal, rising towards the city, functions as a transparent urban forum and faces the city.

The early work of Morphosis, formed by the partnership of Thom Mayne and Michael Rotondi, did not allude to the idiosyncratic direction towards Neo-Constructivism that their later work would take. The 2-4-6-8 House (1978), for instance, appears like a modest essay in Post-Modernism, with its quaint, yellow-frame square windows and its symmetrical organisation. Designed as a studio addition to a typical beach bungalow in Venice, California, it was conceived as a miniature wood-frame house covered in asphalt shingles, elevated above the ground and resting on a garage behind the existing house. Its main distinguishing features, besides its simple cubical volume and pitched roof, are the window frames which take on the double function of window-cum-entrance portico, reminiscent of Venturi's double-coded elements. The renderings of the elevations also remind us of the colourful drawings of Michael Graves in his Post-Modernist phase. Yet it was not long before their language started to evolve into a Neo-Constructivist approach, which conceived the architectural project as an assembly of heterogeneous elements, where floors, walls, and supports are treated as independent components, subject to a playful combination that defies normative types. This is evident in their Venice III House in Los Angeles (1982–6) (fig.9.13), which was also an addition to an existing building, constructed on the typical wood-frame structure, but clad alternately in asphalt shingles and metallic panels. In addition to its metallic walls, the house featured a tensile structure on the roof, connected by pulleys to the external walls, which hinted at the later incorporation of mechanical elements in their buildings. This was more evident in their 72 Market Street Restaurant (1983), which is an early manifesto of sorts. Located in an old building in this coastal town, the restoration introduced an intricate structure of concrete walls within a rectangular space that was subdivided into three zones. The main area at the entrance, square in shape, is marked by a short central steel column connected by tensile

183

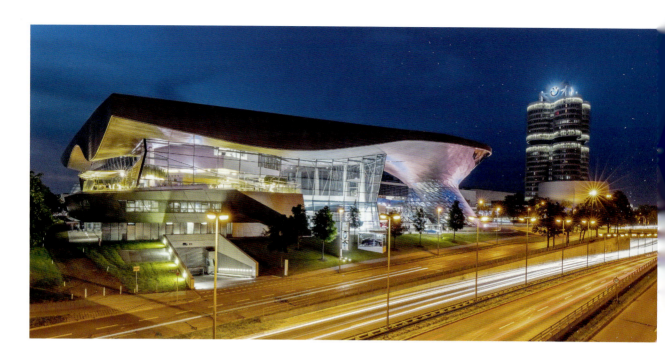

9.11　Coop Himmelb(l)au, BMW Welt, Munich, Germany, 2001–7

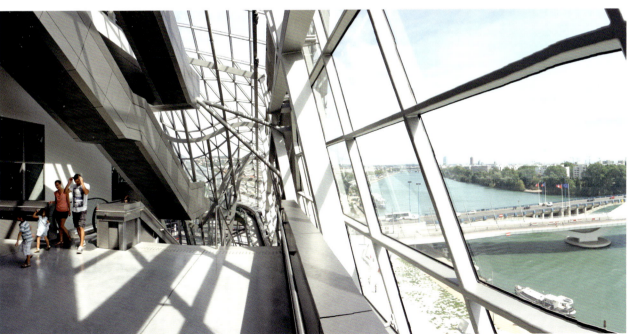

9.12   Coop Himmelb(l)au, Musée des Confluences, Lyon, France, 2001–14

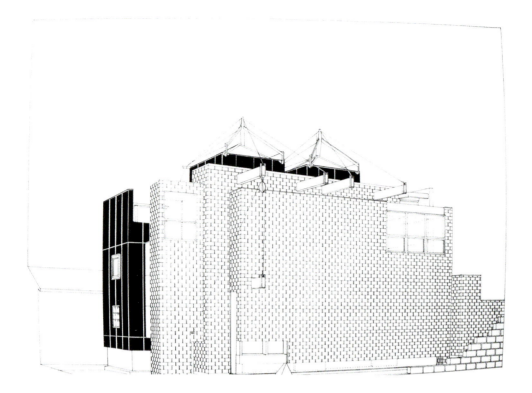

rods to the walls, which helps in supporting the latter, while a large skylight covers the space. The main space opens up to the colonnaded walkway through a large square glass pane, held by a steel frame that can be activated by a pulley. The contrast between concrete, brick walls, steel column, metallic elements, and skylight makes for a rich synthesis of elements.

A number of projects by Morphosis were never realised, yet they constituted important manifestoes that transformed architecture into complex apparatuses. Among these worth noting are the Yuzen Car Museum in Los Angeles (1991) (fig.9.14), which would incorporate the car movement as a generating factor, in a structure that would have contained three floors underground for parking and other facilities; and the Los Angeles Artspark Performing Arts Pavilion (1989) (fig.9.15), a work of great complexity designed as a cluster of facilities set in a suburban park, mostly underground, with various components projecting above ground, inviting people to discover the

above

9.13   Morphosis, Venice III House, Los Angeles, California, USA, 1982–6

below

9.14   Morphosis, Yuzen Car Museum (Project), Los Angeles, California, USA, 1991

9.15 Morphosis, Artspark Performing Arts Pavilion (Project), Los Angeles, California, USA, 1989

spaces underneath. The site is transformed into a 'palimpsest' of traces, a 'mechanical-archaeological' template of various components. As Anthony Vidler observed, Morphosis's approach to form-making was based on a process of investigation relying on experimental iterations in an almost filmic sequence of models and drawings, 'elevating the metamorphosis of form to a fine art, as a means of production rather than a system of representation'.[17] Yet Vidler drew a connection between Morphosis' work and early Modernism, specifically referring them to the experiments of the Dadaist avant-garde, rather than to the Russian Constructivists.

Morphosis, later under the sole direction of Thom Mayne, continued to develop innovative projects such as the Diamond Ranch High School in Pomona, California (1994–9) (fig.9.16), a project that evolved along the same experimental line of the Los Angeles Performing Arts Pavilion competition, treating the programme as an archaeological transformation of the landscape. The project translates into an urban complex, with a pathway that negotiates the topography, segregating the different components of this educational campus. The aim of the architect was to avoid the traditional campus typology, engaging the students in a 'kinetic experience', where the jagged forms of the land 'inform the language of the buildings as the scheme takes its organisational cues from the natural topography'. In their design for the Cooper Union Academic Center (2006–9), the architects again avoided the traditional typology of an urban institutional building, opting instead to create a structure that turns the interior space into a vertical piazza, through a large internal stairway that meanders through the multiple levels. On the exterior, the building conforms to the street alignment, yet projects a dynamic facade of perforated steel plates sliced through from top down, to allow for larger areas of glazing and panoramic views. The facade becomes a sculptural installation, lifted above the ground level, which is continuously glazed for better connection with the street.

9.16   Morphosis, Diamond Ranch High School, Pomona, California, USA, 1994–9

A close 'relative' of Morphosis, also operating in southern California, is the architect Eric Owen Moss. Moss's work takes geometry as its starting point, avoiding the rationalism of the Neo-Rationalists as well as the pastiche of the Post Modernists, and forging for himself another direction, of an 'alternative Modernism'.[18] Yet beyond what some critics identified as an affinity to the Baroque, Moss's architecture appears to express a Constructivist spirit, not only in terms of its formal manipulations, but in its attempt to carry a message of social reform, or as the architect himself states: a search for a 'redemptive' architecture that manifests a 'will to power' through dichotomies, oppositions, and contradictions. It is at this point that 'the emotive power of the space lifts you over the differences, resolves the contradictions at the next level'.[19] Many of the projects by Moss were designed for the industrial area of Culver City in Los Angeles, as restorations of, or additions to existing structures, which prompted the architect to think of creative ways to transform the normative into complex and provocative structures. Rather than thinking in a traditional way, Moss's restoration turns into a surgical operation, removing and adding pieces with a scalpel, intervening in specific areas, and turning the building into a 'body' that bears the traces of these operations. One early example of this procedure is the Kodak company headquarters, baptised 'Samitaur' (1996). This consisted of a long rectangular slab, projecting above a typical, saw-tooth roof of an existing warehouse, and utilising the air rights over a private road. The building is supported on a steel skeleton of post and beams, with a system of girders of different sizes creating an impressive, rhythmical arrangement of structural elements. The building is anchored at one end by an irregular double-cone containing the stairwell and carved in an expressive fashion like a modern sculpture, with the whole building taking on a green patina that contrasts with the existing brick buildings.

Among the several unrealised projects by Moss, the Aronoff House (1991) is quite exemplary in its provocative geometric transformation. Taking the sphere as its point of departure, the form is carved out, sliced, and transformed into an open vessel, reminiscent of Cubist sculptures. The architect conceived it as a 'pleasurable toy', that offers viewing platforms in different directions, culminating into a rooftop deck. The project was a combination of studio, office, and private apartment, all contained within this spherical form, with multiple exposed stairways that bring to mind the drawings of Escher. While the Aronoff House was not realised, the Lawson/Westen House (1993) did materialise and presented a complex interpretation of the domestic space. In plan, the composition of a long slab, intersecting with a cylindrical element at one end, generates a dynamic form. The cylindrical volume is the pièce-de-résistance of the complex: carved, sliced, and cut-out on one of its sides, it contains a kitchen space split over different levels, to serve each floor. Bridges connect the bedrooms on either side of the cylinder, adding to the spatial complexity of the interior. The building is a hybrid composition of concrete walls and surfaces, with wooden beams, steel girders, and trusses on the interior. The truncated cone, in its complex geometry, turns the house into an apparatus of sorts, as it extends to the roof. The twisted composition of the facade at the street level, with its shifted window, appears like a consequence of arbitrary collisions, adding to the uncanny sense of dislocation that the house expresses.

The Spanish architects Enric Miralles and Carme Pinós' Community Centre and Assembly Hall in Hostalets de Balenyà, Barcelona (1986–92) is another example of a Neo-Constructivist approach, generating a complex structure from an arrangement of straight lines, curvilinear shapes, and different materials. This Constructivist spirit also appears through the sophisticated juxtaposition of different planes, the development of new solutions for shading glazed surfaces, and the clear articulation of different building components: from passageways and stairs to ceilings and walls, all appearing to be suspended in a careful balancing act. The masterpiece of the Miralles–Pinos partnership was without question the Olympic Archery Range in Barcelona (1991) designed for the Olympic Games of 1992. This composition of massive, pre-fabricated concrete wall units, composed to house the training and competition areas, takes the form of an organic arrangement of curvilinear elements. Located on a flat site, the complex included two new facilities separated by the archery range. The whole complex was designed in response to the site, the requirements of the programme, but most importantly, generated by a conceptual approach that looks at architecture as the means to explore new formal configurations.

The Scottish Parliament in Edinburgh (1998–2004) (fig.9.17) by Enric Miralles and his second partner Benedetta Tagliabue, blended a sophisticated palette of forms, colours, and materials to create a complete work of art. Despite its initial negative reception due to political and economic reasons, the building was gradually appreciated as a contemporary feature of the Scottish urban landscape. Inspired by several sources, among them the paintings of Charles Rennie Mackintosh and fishermen boats, the complex was conceived as an irregular composition of various elements: on one side a long slab that aligns with the urban street, housing the deputies' offices and separated from the main chamber of parliament by skylights that take the form of reversed boats, or flower petals. This irregular composition, in its complexity and obsession with details, brings to mind another great Catalan master of improvisation, Antonio Gaudí.

On the other hand, recent work by Carme Pinós has taken a more 'domesticated' character. Despite

9.17 Enric Miralles and Benedetta Tagliabue, Scottish Parliament, Edinburgh, Scotland, 1998–2004

some dynamic gestures like inclined walls and the cantilevering volumes, the Headquarters for the Delegations of 'Les Terres de l'Elbe' in Tortosa, Spain (2017) presents a more balanced composition that fits well into its delicate medieval townscape. The programme was broken up into two main elements, a rectangular slab and a trapezoidal one, joined by the main foyer and articulating among them the public spaces. The volumetric aspect of the whole complex is accentuated by the irregular strips of windows, leaving the larger parts of the building in a neutral white finish. The building thus clearly demarcates itself from its surroundings, while engaging the positive public spaces and landscaped areas.

In another context, the work of the architect Bernard Khoury also attracted international attention, starting with his B-018 Nightclub in Beirut, Lebanon (1998), which consisted of an underground entertainment space designed as a circumference with a sombre decor and featuring a mechanically-operated roof that opens up to the sky. When closed, the structure takes the form of a mechanical apparatus, closed to the outside world, except for the ramp that leads down to the space. Khoury's work extended to other projects that explored the transformation of architecture into various constructions that reflect or confront their conditions. Khoury's interest in generating architectural projects that incorporate moveable parts, or that express a dynamism that also recalls avant-garde tendencies, is quite evident across his oeuvre. His design for the restaurant-cum-bar lounge Centrale (2001) (fig.9.18), also in Beirut, constituted a tactful and provocative approach to the question of restoration, rigging the dilapidated structure of a traditional mansion with a steel framework, turning it into a prosthetic apparatus, and replacing the traditional roof with a cylindrical implant that contains the bar, with a moveable section that opens the view at night towards the city.

Another project that demonstrates the architect's penchant for creatively reinterpreting traditional typologies is his design for a tower in downtown Beirut, the Plot 450 project (2020) (fig.9.19). Taking its cues from the imposed site constraints, the tower

right
9.18   Bernard Khoury, Centrale, Beirut, Lebanon, 2001

below
9.19   Bernard Khoury, Plot 450, Beirut, Lebanon, 2020

was broken down into three sections of different heights overlooking the port area, which informed the introduction of such components as cranes and cantilevers. The steel construction, expressed on the outside in a regimented order, gives the project an industrial look, while allowing a great degree of transparency modulated by the sun-breakers. The architect clearly expresses through such projects his desire to counter traditional conventions and to seek radical ways of reconfiguring normative programmes, while confronting the context in a provocative way.

The architects discussed in this chapter demonstrate in various ways a certain tendency to break with traditional norms and reinterpret architectural conventions, pushing the Modernist project even further in that quest towards radical forms that take their cue from Constructivist, Suprematist, or other avant-garde movements from the turn of the 20th century. And while they might share with High-Tech architects a similar appreciation of technology and a faith in a 'progressive architecture', they differ in their interpretation and their emphasis on the formal aspect of the architectural project, privileging in a sense the aesthetic over the economical, and aiming as well for a new synthesis between art and architecture.

10 Neo-Expressionism in Architecture

Expressionism in architecture developed at the end of the First World War, and lasted until the mid-1920s. It was very much influenced by the movement which originated in the arts, triggered by the same rebellion against mechanisation and the great human suffering it provoked in that war. Inspired by Nietzsche, artists had already adopted a rebellious approach against social conventions from the early 1900s, with members of the seminal group *Die Brücke* playing an important role in this regard. Despite the peripheral role that it took in architecture at that time, Expressionism gave another impetus to modern architecture, which Sigfried Giedion intentionally ignored in his survey, in which he advocated a more objective approach in architecture. Some of the utopian drawings of Expressionist architects metamorphosed in the early 1920s into actual buildings, under architects like Erich Mendelsohn, Bruno Taut, and Hans Scharoun, as well as the architects of the 'Amsterdam School' which included Michel de Klerk, Johan van der Mey, and Piet Kramer. Expressionism was perceived as the dialectical opposite, the latent Dionysian 'other', to the dominant paradigm of the times, that is, the 'New Objectivity' first promoted by Hermann Muthesius and later by Walter Gropius. The main principles of Expressionism may be summarised as the upholding of individual artistic expression, freedom of experimentation, and the quest for the realisation of the 'total work of art'.[1] Some of its ideological premises, as articulated by Bruno Taut in *Alpine Architektur*, also incorporated a utopian vision of a socially progressive world, designed on the principles of transparency and manifested in the crystalline beauty of glass architecture, envisioning life in a pacifist community spreading over wide territories.

A number of architects of the post-Second World War period were influenced by, if not directly involved in, the early Expressionist movement, while some of them also moved towards a synthesis between the two poles of artistic innovation and standardised production which were at the roots of the famous Werkbund polemic between Henry van de Velde and Hermann Muthesius in 1914. It is worth noting that Walter Gropius and Bruno Taut were among those who supported van de Velde's position at that time, against the approach towards 'standardisation' promoted by Muthesius. Among those who figured prominently in this group was Hans Scharoun, whose masterful Berlin Philharmonie (1957–63) was a late concretisation of these ideals, and became a reference for all subsequent concert halls that aimed to deviate from classical types. Some historians also attributed the late work of Le Corbusier, specifically his Chapel at Ronchamp, to Expressionism, in addition to Jørn Utzon's Sydney Opera House (1959–73), Eero Saarinen's David S. Ingalls Skating Rink at Yale (1958) and TWA terminal (1962), Giovanni Michelucci's Church of San Giovanni (1962), and Luigi Moretti's Villa La Saracena (1957).[2]

Expressionism did not die in the 1920s. The period of the 1960s and 1970s witnessed an Expressionist revival, starting with the epic work of Hans Scharoun, continuing with Eero Saarinen in America, and culminating with Frank Gehry and Zaha Hadid in our times. What unites all these architects is a common desire to explore new forms, to overcome the limitations of traditional typologies, and more often than not, to proceed in a rather intuitive way from a rough schematic that encapsulates a certain mood or vision, to a concrete realisation that breaks all norms, aiming towards a 'sublime' vision of space.

Despite being relegated to the bench of the accused during the heyday of Post-Modernism, Scharoun's legacy was later recognised, especially after consideration of his public projects, namely the Philharmonie and the State Library, both major landmarks in Berlin that were implanted within an empty field that had been completely stripped of its urban fabric after the Second World War. The Berlin Philharmonie (1956–63) (fig.10.1), with

NEO-EXPRESSIONISM IN ARCHITECTURE

10.1 Hans Scharoun, Berlin Philharmonie, Berlin, Germany, 1956–63

its two halls connected by a horizontal element, was the first to be realised, followed years later by the State Library, which was clad in the same material: gold-coloured aluminium panels with a distinctive pattern, years before the return *en force* of ornamentation to architecture. The State Library (1964–78) (fig.10.2) appears like a large ship, with multiple decks that, on the interior, provide a free space, almost devoid of structural columns. Unlike traditional libraries, the building was not conceived as an arrangement of rooms, but rather, like the Philharmonie, as a 'vineyard' with cantilevering terraces. As Peter Blundell Jones observed, several contemporary architects looked back at

above

10.2 Hans Scharoun, Staatsbibliothek, Berlin, Germany, 1964–78

left

10.3 Bolles + Wilson, Münster City Library, Münster, Germany, 1987–93

Scharoun's work with admiration, and assimilated many of his lessons, namely Günther Behnisch, Jacques Herzog, and Pierre de Meuron, as well as Julia Bolles and Peter Wilson. The latter's Münster Library (1987–93) (fig.10.3) reinterpreted Scharoun's language in its irregular plan and its overall organisation as a composition of distinct areas that communicate with each other, while differentiating between the different uses through spatial form and materiality.

FRANK GEHRY: FROM BRICOLAGE TO COMPLEX FORMS

Frank Gehry, who was among the star architects to be included under the 'Deconstructionist' label, was candid about his ambivalence towards this association. He expressed his bewilderment at the philosophical discourse of Eisenman, confessing his ignorance of its theoretical foundations.[3] In many of his works, Gehry betrayed more of a 'bricoleur' approach, as clearly seen in his early work: the renovation of his house in Venice, California (1978) (fig.10.4), where he introduced the use of unconventional materials such as chain-link fences and off-the-shelf components; or the University of Iowa Advanced Technology Laboratories (1992) (fig.10.5), a design consisting of a long rectangular block, fronted by a collection of cubical elements which appear to be arbitrarily thrown around, like dice on a table. In explaining this particular project, Gehry referred to the theme of 'crystals', articulating a very personal approach to form-making:

> I looked at a lot of crystalline shapes. The shape at the top that has become boatlike or fishlike (whichever you like) is the support lab [. . .]. So I took advantage of it and started to mold the shape. [. . .] We simplified some of the pieces. And because the pipe canyon had a solid wall, I was able to make this kind of sculptural form, which I wanted to put on the street to animate it. [. . .][4]

In his statements, Gehry reaffirmed that the design process should remain firmly in the hands of the architect, who follows the intuitive method of an artist, but where the tools vary from those

10.4 Frank Gehry, Gehry House, Venice, California, USA, 1978

10.5 Frank Gehry, Iowa Advanced Technology Laboratories, University of Iowa, Iowa City, Iowa, USA, 1992

of radical slicing through the site (as with Zaha Hadid), to those of a creative bricoleur who often resorts to fetishes like the fish-form in order to animate his work, giving it a zoomorphic or anthropomorphic dimension. In the Office Building

MODERN ARCHITECTURE IN A POST-MODERN ERA

in Prague (1995) (fig.10.6), Gehry resorted to a playful collage of two vertical elements engaged in a sort of dance, translated in a historical context that could well sustain a modern variation on the Baroque. Quite aptly, it was baptised the 'Fred and Ginger' building, reminiscent of a classic musical. Thus, Gehry took pleasure in breaking with traditional types, transcending Euclidean geometries to expand his formal language, even introducing sculptural elements into the design which would later morph into architectonic shapes. His obsession with the 'fish' motif was evident in many of his designs, and its development as a large metallic sculpture for the Olympic Village in Barcelona (1992) ushered the use of aeronautical software to develop these complex forms. Furthermore, his association with artists at an early stage indicates a particular tendency to blur the boundaries between architecture and art. In fact, in the introduction to his collection of schematic drawings, Gehry confessed:

> I came to architecture through fine arts, and painting is still a fascination to me. Paintings are a way of training the eye. You see how people compose a canvas. The way Bruegel composes a canvas, or Jasper Johns. I learned about composition from their canvases. I picked up all those visual connections and ideas. And I find myself using them sometimes.
>
> [. . .] I have always felt that artists and architects do similar things. That there is a moment of truth in which you decide what color, what size, what composition. How you get to that moment of truth is different and the end result is different.[5]

This statement clearly alludes to the intuitive, artistic approach that the architect followed in his design process, inspired by various figures from the pre-modern to the current period, and later associating contemporary artists in his projects.

Gehry's move towards an overt Expressionist style of irregular forms that would mark his later phase started well before the celebrated Guggenheim in Bilbao, with the Vitra Design Museum (1989) (fig.10.7), where the building emerges as a result of a sculptural play, twisting shapes that culminate in a composition that

10.6 Frank Gehry, Vlado Milunić, Office Building (Fred and Ginger/Dancing House), Prague, Czech Republic, 1995

10.7   Frank Gehry, Vitra Design Museum, Weil am Rhein, Germany, 1989

differs from his earlier work. The Guggenheim in Bilbao (1993–7) (fig.10.8) was the masterpiece that propelled Gehry on the global scene and defined his 'signature style'. Located in a city that was undergoing an economic recession, the building made an immediate impact, drawing thousands of visitors and giving a much-needed boost to the economy. The 'Bilbao Effect' was born.

Gehry won this project after an invited competition that pitted him against Coop Himmelb(l)au and Arata Isozaki. The final choice of the site gave the architect additional artistic licence to propose a building of great magnitude, a 'ship' that landed ashore, perhaps as masterfully contorted as Boccioni's sculptures. As one reviewer noted, the building 'scrolls and coils its way along the riverside, its boggling conflation of titanium-clad forms shimmering serenely like a pile of improbably huge fish or a fractured tinfoil flower'.[6] The metaphors for this complex construction abound, from a heap of fish to a ship, to floral forms and other figures that all seem to imply connotations that transcend architectural tropes. On the interior, the effects of this formal manipulation are equally felt, with an entrance that leads to an exploding atrium space, around which the gallery spaces are arranged over multiple floors. The largest gallery spreads horizontally and extends eastward along the promenade, dedicated to various installations and to a site-specific work by Richard Serra. This complex work, which

10.8   Frank Gehry, Guggenheim Museum, Bilbao, Spain, 1993–7

NEO-EXPRESSIONISM IN ARCHITECTURE

left, exterior and interior
10.9   Frank Gehry, Walt Disney Concert Hall, Los Angeles, California, USA, 1991–2003

below
10.10   Frank Gehry, MIT Stata Center, Cambridge, Massachusetts, USA, 2004

originated out of a series of handmade paper and cardboard models, could not have been realised without the new tools generated by the digital revolution, which the architect appropriated and developed to meet his objectives.

The Walt Disney Concert Hall in Los Angeles (1991–2003) (fig.10.9) represents an iteration of the Bilbao style adapted to a philharmonic hall. The building was designed as a single volume, with a simple rectangular plan for the main concert hall, surrounded by a free-flowing space that includes the lobby and other services. The irregular composition of the whole results from this space that wraps around the main body, giving the architect the opportunity to create a distinctive form, covered in reflective stainless-steel panels which give it the appearance of a large sculpture in an urban setting. In the main concert hall, curvilinear planes of Douglas fir wood unify the interior surfaces, and provide a contrast to the metallic exterior. The MIT Stata Center (2004) (fig.10.10) is yet another variation aiming to create a complex and multi-coloured collage of different forms and materials: cubes, prisms, cylinders, and amorphous shapes, all collide in different ways but coalesce in the end to integrate a complex building programme that includes classrooms, laboratories, cafeteria and lounge spaces, meeting rooms, and public spaces. While the building presents a non-conformist facade to the main street, it still respects the street alignment while breaking up around the internal courtyard, where the different towers create an irregular aggregation. Inside this labyrinthine complex, which is articulated around the different towers, spaces flow into each other, ramps move smoothly between one level and

201

another, with individual lounge areas overlooking the atrium space. Some of the building sections are covered in metallic cladding, matt grey or glossy metal, others in bright yellow panels, while some sections are clad in traditional brick.

EXPRESSIONIST VARIATIONS

Zaha Hadid's later work, after the Rosenthal Center, includes several spectacular examples which demonstrate a latent Expressionism. An example of this is the Guangzhou Opera House in China (2004–10) (fig.10.11), a project that is described by the architect as a composition of twin boulders, washed and perfectly smoothed by the elements. The break-up of the project into two separate elements, only touching at one point and separated by an outdoor plaza, is somewhat reminiscent of the similar strategy that Moneo employed at the Kursaal in San Sebastian. But whereas the latter used hard-edge geometrical forms poised slightly off-balance, Hadid's Opera House is composed of curvilinear shapes that take an organic form. The granite and glass-clad envelope reveals at some points the underlying steel structure, and gives the complex its pebble-like smoothness. One of the two 'boulders' contains the larger opera hall and its attendant functions, while the smaller one houses a multi-purpose hall. The smooth curves of the Opera House interior, with its stalactite lighting, evoke the earlier Expressionist works of Hans Poelzig, among others.

left

10.11   Zaha Hadid Architects, Guangzhou Opera House, Guangzhou, China, 2004–10

below

10.12   Ma Yansong – MAD Architects, Harbin Opera House, Harbin, China, 2010–15

In a similar vein to Hadid, Ma Yansong of MAD Architects designed the Opera House in the northern Chinese city of Harbin (2010–15) (fig.10.12), as part of a master plan for the city. The Opera House is the focal point of the Cultural Island, consisting of a grand theatre and a smaller one. The building was designed around two spherical volumes, each accommodating one of the theatres and embedded within a sculptural form that takes the shape of a large tent, perforated by a large oculus that admits light to the foyer. This external envelope, which is intended to mimic the undulating landscape surrounding it, is covered by white panels of aluminium, smoothly joined to render the whole envelope into one continuous, plastic surface. The foyer is flooded by the light coming through the large oculus and filtered through the thick grid of the skylight, while the peripheral walls are transformed into sinuous curtain walls of glass. Inside this large white space, an element of contrast is introduced by the natural wood cladding which covers the central stairways and circulation areas overlooking the atrium. The interior of the main theatre, with its proscenium and sidewalls, also presents a warm contrast to the

10.13 MAD Architects, Ordos Museum, Ordos, China, 2005–11

atrium, enveloped by Manchurian wood panelling, emulating a finely sculpted 'total work of art'.

MAD's early work, such as the Ordos Museum in China (2005–11) (fig.10.13), also played on the same tune of plasticity in architecture. As the architect states, the building appears to have landed on its site from another world; it gives the illusion of a 'timeless architecture in a modern city of ruins'. Situated in the Mongolian region, in a city that has been urbanised over the past decades, the museum forms the centrepiece of a new master plan. The mysterious egg-shell, covered in stripes of metallic panels that emulate traditional cladding, presents in its copper colour a contrast to the interior – all-white sinuous surfaces that offer themselves to the percolating light, coming in through various apertures. The metaphors inside are of canyons connected by bridges. While claiming to draw inspiration from local traditions and the primordial elements of the landscape, the architect nevertheless produces a futuristic building of high complexity, which acknowledges its debt to Buckminster Fuller's experiments in domical structures. In another proposal for a Culture Park for Shenzhen, the architect makes explicit his architectural intentions:

> I want to create a surreal atmosphere, so that the people who visit, relax or exercise here have the possibility of engaging in a dialogue with the past and the future. Time and space are dissolved and placed against each other, manifesting a sense of weightlessness, and unrestrained imagination.[7]

The intention to dissolve time and space brings us back to one of the fundamental paradigms of the Modern Movement, as expressed by Sigfried Giedion in his lectures. Yet in this case, the dissolution takes place through a 'plastic' rendering of architectural forms that transcend the geometric limitations of traditional architecture. The work of MAD, as well as of Zaha Hadid, seems bent on this 'transgression' that the Expressionists were the first to propose, but could not realise at the time.

The exuberant style of Santiago Calatrava may also be considered under this angle, although the architect-cum-engineer is sometimes associated with the High Tech movement, given his predilection to develop sophisticated structural systems which, in themselves, become the form givers for the architectural project. Calatrava's disposition for scientific analysis and the study of mechanics, combined with an innate interest in the human anatomy, earned him a comparison with Antonio Gaudí.[8] Commenting on the voluminous number of sketches and drawings in his archives, which represent human and animal anatomy, Alexander Tzonis compared them to Leonardo da Vinci's studies. And in a similar vein, these drawings served Calatrava as a supplement to his vigorous investigation of forms and of the mechanisms that allow movement in the human body. It is another form of thinking, through analogy, which complements the process of analytical thinking.[9]

In addition to the large number of innovative designs he developed for bridges and infrastructural works, such as airport terminals and train sheds – among them his signature design for the Alamillo Bridge in Spain (1987–92), culminating with a most spectacular design for the World Trade Center Terminal – Calatrava was also responsible for some major civic projects like the Zurich University Law Library (1989–2004), the Auditorio de Tenerife (1991–2003), the City of Arts and Sciences in Valencia (1991–6), the Opera House of Valencia (1996–2006), and the Bodegas Ysios Winery (1998–2001). In these works, an Expressionist tendency is manifest, which brings to mind the work of Erich Mendelsohn and Eero Saarinen, coupled with the ingenuity of Pier Luigi Nervi.

The City of Arts and Sciences in Valencia (1998–2009) (fig.10.14) is composed of two main elements: a planetarium, which takes the form of a large globe, and a science museum, configured as an exoskeletal longitudinal structure. The planetarium is covered by a concrete shell, tapering down to incorporate pivoting stems that activate a foldable system of steel and glass panels, which can be opened to reveal the building's interior. Standing apart from this large hyperboloid shell, with its eye in the middle, is the equally spectacular science museum, a 240-metre-long pavilion composed of repetitive profiles along its length that hold the segmental roof of the building, with lateral bracing provided by five tree-like concrete pillars. The northern facade is a continuous glass and steel curtain wall opening onto a cathedral space, while the southern facade presents a more complex array of concrete support systems, angled towards the main building. The Opera House of Valencia, built in proximity to the City of Arts and Sciences, presents another example of the great skills of the architect in producing a monumental sculpture, able to accommodate under its roof – which resembles a medieval warrior's helmet – three auditoria. The main auditorium is dedicated to the opera hall, located in the centre of the composition with its stage and accessory functions. A secondary auditorium for chamber music occupies the western end, and a larger, semi-covered auditorium occupies the eastern end. The main structure is made of concrete, left bare on the interior and exterior, and fitted in the interior spaces for optimal acoustical performance. The Bodegas Ysios Winery (fig.10.15) is another example of Calatrava's Expressionist tendency. The building is based on a simple linear organisation, formed by two walls, almost 200 metres in length, with a sinusoidal shape in plan as well as in elevation. The walls are clad in wood, while the roof is composed of thick laminated wood-beams, clad in aluminium. The structure presents a stretched profile of a wavy surface, accentuated by the shadows cast through the roof beams, somewhat echoing the lines of the mountains in the background.

The Paris Philharmonic Concert Hall (2007–15) (fig.10.16) by Jean Nouvel showed another direction by the French architect, radically different from his more restrained Institut du Monde Arabe, or the imposing Louvre Museum of Abu Dhabi. Nouvel went one step further in this case, creating a spectacular building which would complement the Parc de la Villette, and, in the words of the architect, would form 'a horizontal sheltered garden beneath the building, punctuated follies, reflections of shade in the shiny architectural surfaces, the creation of a "la Villette hill", a walkable mineral relief which, following the example of the Buttes-Chaumont, forms an observatory over the urban landscape'. Featuring a central orchestra pit surrounded by Scharoun-type vineyard seating, the floating balconies are unified by sweeping curves that give the interior its distinctive character. The exterior reveals a clash of planes and curved elements glowing under the light, clad in aluminium panels with silver, pearly textures.

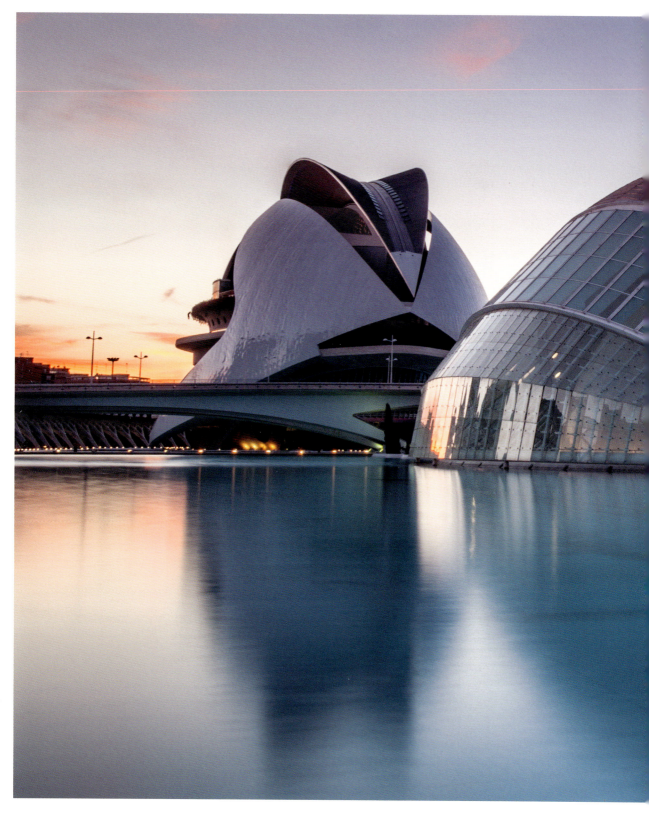

10.14 Santiago Calatrava and Felix Candela, The City of Arts and Sciences, Valencia, Spain, 1998–2009

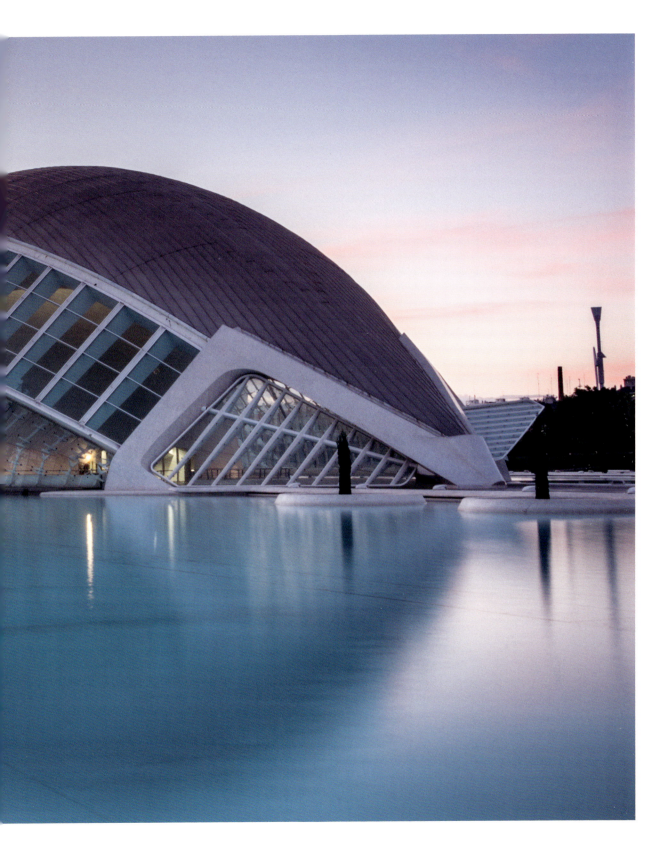

10.15   Santiago Calatrava, Bodegas Ysios Winery, Araba, Spain, 1998–2001

10.16   Jean Nouvel, Paris Philharmonic Concert Hall, Paris, France, 2007–15

The Elbphilharmonie Hamburg (2001–16) (fig.10.17) by Herzog & de Meuron raises the contemporary Expressionist tendency to an even higher pitch. This major restoration project accommodates a philharmonic hall, chamber music hall, restaurants, and bars, in addition to residential apartments, a hotel, and parking facilities, all into an existing base which has been overlaid by a complex volume. The architects restored the old buildings that constituted the Kaispeicher warehouses, turning them into a plinth for the upper addition, accommodating mainly the parking spaces as well as some accessory functions. The main addition, lifted on top of this base and extruded from it, provides a clear contrast to the brick compound, composed of glass facades with a swirling roofline that evokes the Berlin Philharmonie. Visitors are led through a long escalator to an upper-level lobby, sandwiched in-between the old and new sections. The Grand Hall constitutes the heart of the complex and follows the same vineyard layout as its Berlin predecessor. The meandering glass walls in the lobby lead the visitors up a series of steps to the main concert hall. The exterior of the new addition is clad in large glass panels, some of which are characteristically shaped like the gills of fish, intended, in the words of the architects, to transform the building into a 'gigantic, iridescent crystal' which changes in appearance according to the time of the day.

Herzog & de Meuron offered a different approach with the Caixaforum in Madrid, a building that was partially restored to house a private museum established by the Caixa Bank corporation. Expanding the existing industrial structure by building another structure on top of it that appears extruded from the building below, and clad in copper to emphasise the contrast, the architects created a stimulating synthesis between the old and the new, combining them to create a landmark building, which faces off the main avenue with a side wall covered by greenery. While the original facade of the power plant was preserved, the building was gutted on the interior to make room for the various functions, from exhibition galleries to auditoria and entertainment spaces, its base completely cut out to make room for an open foyer that extends to the plaza outside, and its ceiling formed by a composition of triangular metal sheets that evoke the crooked spaces of *The Cabinet of*

10.17 Herzog & de Meuron, Elbphilharmonie Hamburg, Hamburg, Germany, 2001–16

Dr Caligari. In contrast to this Expressionist ground level, the gallery interiors provide a neutral, white background space for the display of artwork, while the stairway creates another element of contrast reminiscent of the fluid curves of Erich Mendelsohn.

Another example of their Expressionist approach is the Vitrahaus (2006–9) (fig.10.18), designed for the Vitra company at Weil am Rhein, Germany, as an exhibition space for their furniture products. In a neighbourhood already occupied by Gehry's Vitra Museum, and the landmark Fire Station by Zaha Hadid, Herzog & de Meuron conceived a distinctive structure which results from the stacking of several horizontal slabs – each slab an abstraction of the 'typical house' with its pitched roof – and terminating at each end with a fully glazed profile. The irregular stacking of these units, piled one on top of the other over five storeys, yields unusual interior spaces, especially at the areas of their vertical intersection. In order to accentuate these intricate spaces, the whole building is rendered

209

MODERN ARCHITECTURE IN A POST-MODERN ERA

10.18   Herzog & de Meuron, Vitrahaus, Weil am Rhein, Germany, 2006–9

in white on the interior, with the exception of the wooden flooring, while the exterior is all clad/painted in black, with the exception of the ground level base, clad again in wood panels.

A more contextual approach was taken by Barozzi Veiga in their design for a Philharmonic Hall for the city of Szczecin in Poland (2007–14) (fig.10.19). In this case, the building was located at the heart of the old city, built on the site of the old Konzerthaus which was destroyed during the Second World War. As the architects acknowledge, the building emerges from its context, influenced by the pitched roofs and towers that dot the city skyline:

> The building is charged with expressive power, concentrated in the pattern that gives shape to the roof and its crowning perimeter. This power is the result of the influence of certain Central European expressionist architectures. From the outside, the building is perceived as a weightless volume in which the aluminium and glass facade – sometimes translucent, sometimes opaque – transmits expressive qualities depending on its use.[10]

The building thus reflects symbolically the old town in its rhythmical repetition of the rooftops, rendered in a glass-clad structure. The design brings to mind the Expressionist tendencies of the 1920s as well as the 'glass utopias' realised here in a new 'crystal palace'. The facade was designed to create the impression of an abstract, homogeneous surface that would glow at night. The vertical structure behind the glass panelling is a double-skin that provides acoustic insulation as well as natural ventilation. Inside, two auditoria are composed on a rectangular layout, opening onto a large foyer. In contrast to the white walls of the lobby and hallways, the concert halls are like finely crafted mineral pieces, with a gold-leaf cladding that transforms them into a sacral interior space.

Other projects – such as the Phoenix Central Park Gallery in Sydney, Australia (2014–19)[11] (fig.10.20), designed as a collaboration between Durbach Block Jaggers and John Wardle – also manifest a Neo-Expressionist tendency that results from the intentional twisting of the envelope to project a rich textural quality. The playful articulation of the brick surfaces – at times straight, at others curved and jagged – recalls the work of the German Expressionist architect Fritz Hoeger, who similarly manipulated this material to create expressive facades. The combination of two functions – a main gallery and a performance space – further provided an opportunity for a synthesis of contrasts, which was well brought under a unified scheme by the architects. While the main cultural

10.19   Barozzi Veiga, Szczecin Philharmonic Hall, Szczecin, Poland, 2007–14

210

NEO-EXPRESSIONISM IN ARCHITECTURE

venue, the gallery, was conceived as a series of neutral rooms with cast-in-place concrete for the floors and walls, mediated by plaster walls for the exhibition areas, the performance space is shaped as a bell, lined with wooden strips.

In contrast to the hard-edge, irregular compositions that some Neo-Expressionist architects adopted in their work, others opted for more organic, bulbous forms that were given the 'Blob' designation, whereby the complex functions that would make up the programme would be wrapped up, as it were, in one continuous envelope. Such is the case of Future Systems' Selfridges Department Store in Birmingham (1997–2003) (fig.10.21) where a large department store is enclosed within a continuous curvilinear surface, covered by 15,000 small, shiny aluminium discs that give the structure a futuristic outlook and an instant iconic status. The few curvilinear openings that cut through this largely opaque envelope offer glimpses of its interior. In plan, the amorphous shape of the building responds to the site limits, and creates a soft edge that wraps around the corner. While some have saluted its distinctive profile, others were critical of its lack of contextuality, imposing itself in close proximity to the old St Martin's Church. Similar in shape to the Selfridges in Birmingham, yet even more provocative to its context, is the 'friendly alien' Kunsthaus Graz (1999–2003) (fig.10.22) by ex-Archigram member Peter Cook, in collaboration with Colin Fournier. This project is another large 'blob' that sits tightly in the midst of the traditional red-roof houses of the historic city of Graz. Covered by a blue-coloured skin that operates as a multimedia device, projecting museum activities to the outside, the museum incorporates two large superposed exhibition spaces, inscribed within its amorphous structure. From the street side, the building appears unconventional, but does not reveal its full magnitude unless seen from above, with the enveloping surface punctured by a number of cylindrical skylights.

Another building type, the skyscraper, was also reimagined by some architects to express a new aesthetic in design. For Studio Gang, led by Jeanne Gang, the skyscraper was reconfigured as an expression of waves in their Aqua Tower in Chicago (2004–10) (fig.10.23), superposed as a series of layers over its 82 floors, creating an organic form

10.20 Durbach Block Jaggers Architects/John Wardle Architects, Phoenix Central Park Gallery, Sydney, Australia, 2014–19

10.21   Future Systems, Selfridges & Co. Department Store, Birmingham, UK, 1997–2003

10.22   Peter Cook and Colin Fournier, Kunsthaus Graz, Graz, Austria, 1999–2003

10.23   Studio Gang, Aqua Tower, Chicago, Illinois, USA, 2004–10

that is supposedly designed to improve interaction among its inhabitants. Another irregular tower was designed by the same firm for a high-rise in San Francisco. MIRA (2020) was conceived as a twisting tower with a revolving and repetitive sequence of bay-windows wrapping around the structure. The twisting manoeuvre was also designed with a view to improve both the building's response to environmental criteria and its energy performance.

Sou Fujimoto's L'Arbre Blanc in Montpellier (2014–19) (fig.10.24) is another irregular composition based on a circular plan, with multiple balconies cantilevering out like tree branches in every direction. The 17-storey tower, all finished in white, offers each unit a generous outdoor space, with some of the balconies cantilevering up to seven metres beyond their base. Similar to Hans Scharoun's high-rise residential project Romeo and Juliet in Stuttgart (1954–9), this residential tower based on an irregular plan layout aims to avoid the stereotypical, rectangular slab that became the template for such projects.

While the visionary drawings of the early Expressionist architects could not be realised at the time, due to the lack of both technical as well as financial means, the Neo-Expressionists in our own times had the benefit of both: new technical means for the generation and realisation of complex forms, within a global economy that espoused innovative and iconic architecture as a stimulant to economic growth, epitomised in what came to be known as the Bilbao Effect. This gave an additional impetus towards the rise of 'signature-style' projects, promoted through popular media, which even prompted some artists and fashion designers recently to enter the field of architectural design as 'stylists' of high-end domestic and commercial projects. This trend, epitomised in the work of some studios, revived the notion of *Gesamtkunstwerk* – that is, comprehensive design across the spectrum, from silverware and furniture to architecture, translates into an idiosyncratic approach that plays well on the keyboards of the sublime and the fantastic.

10.24   Sou Fujimoto, L'Arbre Blanc, Montpellier, France, 2014–19

11 The Minimalist Aesthetic

The Minimalist aesthetic appeared in art and architecture at different periods, advocating different agendas. Whereas Minimalism in architecture gained in momentum in the 1990s, building upon the legacy of Modernist masters from the 1920s, Minimalism in art emerged in the 1960s with artists Carl Andre, Donald Judd, Sol LeWitt, Robert Morris, and Dan Flavin, who advocated the rejection of traditional media such as painting and sculpture, and attempted to dissociate their work from the European art of the 20th century. Yet despite these attempts, one can still draw some parallels between their work and their predecessors, especially the ready-mades of Marcel Duchamp or the Black Square of Kazimir Malevich, which had already reduced the artwork to its degree-zero of expression. In one of the first anthologies on this subject, the critic Gregory Battcock asserted that Minimal Art is not necessarily a negation of the past, nor a nihilistic act:

> Minimal style is extremely complex. The artist has to create new notions of scale, space, containment, shape, and object. He must reconstruct the relationship between art as object and between object and man. Negative space, architectural enclosure, nature, and the mechanical are all concerns of the Minimal artist, and as such become some of the characteristics that unify the movement.[1]

The works that came to represent this new direction in art were in many cases installations that used what appears to be simple forms in repetitive patterns, laid out in a way as to provoke a different experience of space. Carl Andre's installation, *Lever* (1966), is a case in point. Composed of a linear arrangement of 137 unjointed firebricks, this horizontal 'sculpture' ran across the floor of the Jewish Museum in New York, touching one of the walls perpendicularly.

In another installation, Andre used simple metal sheets, laying them on the floor, without any further elaboration. The *Tenth Copper Cardinal* (1973) was composed of ten plates of copper laid out on the ground in two rows, with the shorter side aligned with the rough stone wall of the garden. Andre stressed that his work is decidedly 'atheistic, materialistic, and communal', and that it does not attempt to express any metaphysical meanings. This radical reinterpretation of the concept of sculpture was intended to dissociate the artistic object from any contextual or symbolic association, forcing the viewer to confront it in its pure, simple materiality.

Dan Flavin, on the other hand, focused on using the industrially produced neon lights as elements in various compositions. His works evolved as studies of light that are specific to the exhibition space. Spaces became modulated by the particular placement and colour of the neon lights. The *Nominal Three (to William of Ockham)* (1964), which was first installed at the Green Gallery in New York, was based on a simple arithmetic progression of one, two, then three white neon lights, standing upright at the middle and corners of the space. The neutrality of colour and the dedication to William of Ockham implied certain meanings beyond the projected neutrality they presumed to espouse. Donald Judd's constructions evolved into mass-produced identical units disposed in particular arrangements, such as the series of identical boxes mounted on the Leo Castelli Gallery wall in New York City (1968), or his *Untitled* (1969), which is composed of ten identical elements of stainless steel, mounted like a ladder onto the wall. Judd later moved to the remote town of Marfa in Texas, presenting larger pieces that were reproduced in series, such as the 15 untitled works in concrete (1980–84), all uniformly cast like large altar pieces sitting in the landscape.

In turn, Sol LeWitt's geometric forms, mostly monochromatic cubical elements, were arranged in series in different combinations and scales. As for Robert Morris, his elaboration of geometric forms translated them into larger units, configured to engage with the exhibition walls and corners, or suspended over the exhibition space such as the *Hanging Slab* (cloud) of 1964. Morris' *Box with the Sound of Its Own Making* (1961) can be seen as a forerunner to Peter Zumthor's Swiss Sound Pavilion, which was designed by the architect for the World Expo in Hannover (2000). Although very different in scale, Morris' small box was conceived to play out the sounds recorded in the process of its construction. In hindsight, Zumthor's Swiss Sound Pavilion may be seen as a large-scale piece of Minimal art that comes very close to the work of the Minimal artists of the 1960s.

There is definitely an ambivalent relation between what is labelled as 'Minimal Art' and what was later defined as 'Minimalist Architecture', which does not call for a simple extrapolation.[2] The former is decidedly anti-modern, or at least attempting to go beyond the limits of Modern Art, while the latter espouses the principles of modern architecture, taking them to a higher level of refinement. The association of Minimalist architecture with a reduction to essentials was also not on the agenda of Minimal artists. The two movements also appeared at different times, with Minimalist architecture entering the discourse in the 1990s, largely based on a renewed interest in the legacy of early Modernism and specifically the work of Mies van der Rohe; Minimal art, on the other hand, appeared on the scene in the 1960s, and was superseded by other artforms by the end of the 1970s. One of the early manifestations of this revived interest in Minimalist architecture was the dedication of a whole issue of *Architectural Design* to the new trend, followed by a series of conferences and publications on the topic,[3] and most significantly the rehabilitation of its father figure, Mies, through a major exhibition at the MoMA in New York.[4] Mies' Barcelona Pavilion was regarded in this respect as one of the first icons of Minimalist architecture, and this building – which was set up for the International Exhibition of 1929 and subsequently demolished – was resurrected and rebuilt on the same grounds in 1986. Yet, as some critics would argue, Minimalism in architecture transcended the earlier preoccupations with technique and materiality, as in the case of Mies, to take on other aspects and qualities, as for example in the aesthetic tendencies of Herzog & de Meuron, or the phenomenological attributes of Peter Zumthor's work.

These major differences between Minimalist art and Minimalist architecture led some critics to favour instead the use of the designation 'Essential Minimalism' for architectural projects that espouse a language of simple geometry, smooth surfaces, elimination of ornament, and a return to the authenticity of materials. This reductive approach was often associated with a 'cleansing' of architecture from the superfluous, in an ascetic move that in some cases carried within it a latent critique of consumerism, which paradoxically favoured this new style for several commercial projects.[5]

TADAO ANDO AND FRANCESCO VENEZIA: MINIMALISTS AVANT-LA-LETTRE?

Even before reaching the decade of the 1990s, several architects were already working in a Minimalist idiom, without expressly presenting their work under this label. The Japanese architect Tadao Ando's work is often cited in this regard, favouring an abstract reduction to the essential elements of architecture: floor, walls, and ceilings, rendered in finished concrete that bears the traces of its formwork. The Koshino House in Ashiya (1984) is one example of this approach where the project is reduced to two parallel elements joined by an underground passage: one wing contains a double-height living room, while the longest slab contains the bedrooms. The Chapel on the Water in Hokkaido (1988) (fig.11.1) renders the prayer hall into a simple monochromatic space, enclosed by bare walls on three sides, while the altar is located in front of a transparent wall, overlooking the water pond, in a perfect juxtaposition of nature and architecture.

Minimalism in architecture also appeared in projects that involved restoration of old structures. The Italian architect Francesco Venezia was the author of the restoration of the Museum in Gibellina Nuova (1980), where he operated like a

11.1 Tadao Ando, Chapel on the Water, Hokkaido, Japan, 1988

surgeon, restoring the facade of the old palace of Di Lorenzo as part of a new museum, composed with alternating strips of stone cladding, incorporating large panels of the old walls, like a mosaic. Venezia's other works, like the IUAV Materials Testing Laboratory (1995), exhibits his Minimalist approach, with an opaque structure of concrete, clad uniformly with large stone panels, and receiving light from a central skylight. The interiors feature evocative spaces and the building as a whole is far from what a technical facility would normally be reduced to. The project for an Open Air Theatre in Salemi, Italy (1986), in which Venezia collaborated with Roberto Collova and Marcella Aprile, shows another dimension where architecture merges with the landscape to express a timeless character. The town of Salemi had suffered an earthquake, but also from emigration that left much of the village desolate and in ruins. Such was the fate of the Church of Carmine, with only two arches of its cloister still standing. The architects proposed to turn this central area into an urban park, as a main locus to regenerate the area. The remaining ruins were transformed in the process into protective walls for the garden, which evolved into an amphitheatre surrounded by a series of enclosing walls and pathways, like the sacred precinct of a temple that has been levelled to the ground. The choice of materials, from travertine to sandstone, added another dimension that made this new construction blend into its surrounding topography. Venezia produced another work in the same spirit: the pavilion for the XXI Triennale of Milan (2016). This pavilion appears like an abstract walk-through sculpture, providing a bench against the main wall for a moment of respite. It featured no entryway, but simply a path through the space towards a small chapel separated from the main element, housing the work of the artist Ettore Spalletti. The pavilion was constructed almost completely of wood panels with some inserts of travertine, while the exterior of the chapel was clad in travertine.

THE MINIMALIST AESTHETIC

HERZOG & DE MEURON'S EARLY WORKS

Some of the early works of Herzog & de Meuron would also fall under the same lens, especially projects such as the Stone House in Tavole, the Goetz Foundation, the Ricola Warehouse, and the Studio Remy Zaugg. The architecture of Herzog & de Meuron, like that of many great architects, evolved across time, but there is one constant theme that seems to pervade all their work: an attempt to negotiate the boundaries between art and architecture. This persistent thread led them to collaborate with certain artists, as well as to conceive the architectural project as a mediator between different realms. Critics have made the associations between their work and that of Minimalist or conceptual artists, thus elevating the architectural project, despite its sometimes mundane appearance, to attain the level of artifice. This is especially evident in the Ricola Warehouse and the Eberswalde Technical School Library, where the appropriation of photographic images, imprinted onto the concrete or etched over glass panes, reintroduces ornamentation into the architectural work, but as a contemporary, two-dimensional graphic representation.

The Stone House in Tavole (1985–8) is an exercise in austerity, where the house was conceived as a simple rectangular plan subdivided by two axes into four quadrants. The exterior is clad in rough limestone, packed in horizontal layers and inscribed by a concrete frame. This 'packing' of the rough stone in an elementary way within a precisely defined framework creates a contrast between industrial and primitive construction techniques, harking back to some Minimalist artworks like Robert Smithson's metal boxes. As Kurt Foster aptly observed, Smithson's 'Non-Site' installation (1968) intentionally removed the stones from their 'natural' site, placing them within bins like geological specimens. Similarly, Herzog & de Meuron's stacking of rough stones is not intended to allude to a vernacular association, but rather aims to present the material in its roughness, as it has been extracted from nature, and placed in contrast to the concrete frame.[6] This presentation of materials in their rough condition found another translation in the Dominus Winery in Napa Valley

11.2 Herzog & de Meuron, Dominus Winery, Napa Valley, California, USA, 1995–8

(1995–8) (fig.11.2). The winery was conceived as a simple rectangular volume as well, with various functions arranged in a linear order, behind a porous envelope of steel gabions filled with rocks. The resultant effect is of a building that blends into the landscape, appearing like a long and imposing retaining wall – a line in the ground. This radical statement would contrast dramatically with the conceptions of other wineries, such as Graves' famous Clos Pegase in the same region; and like its predecessor, the Stone House in Tavole, it refers to some of the conceptual themes of Minimal art.

The concept of setting a block of glass, stone, or concrete in the midst of a landscape, like a piece of art, manifested itself with the Goetz Foundation in Munich (1989–92) and the Studio Remy Zaugg in Mulhouse (1995–6). The Goetz Foundation (fig.11.3) was designed as a free-standing volume to house a private art gallery, surrounded by a park. The gallery appears as a simple box, the lower level clad in translucent glass, overlaid by a second storey clad in birch wood and crowned by a clerestory. The Studio Remy Zaugg was designed as a plain concrete box with two roof overhangs, similar in spirit to the Ricola Warehouse, but on a smaller scale. The fair-faced concrete box sits in the middle of the landscape with skylights flush into the roof, in addition to wide bays that open towards the landscape. The weathering effects on the plain

11.3 Herzog & de Meuron, Goetz Foundation, Munich, Germany, 1989–92

concrete surface add another layer to the structure, which presents itself like a large sculpture set in the middle of a garden.

Other projects by Herzog & de Meuron further explored the idea of placing an object in the middle of landscape, or an urban context, with a view to adding another layer to the form, represented in these cases by a contemporary ornamental representation, as in a graphically printed surface. This experiment first appeared with the Ricola Warehouse in Mulhouse (1993), a production and storage facility designed on a flexible open plan: a box with its two flaps open. The rough concrete texture of this large object – which recalls the sculptures of Donald Judd – is contrasted with a screen-printed polycarbonate surface, featuring a plant motif, allowing light into the interior and creating a visual effect reminiscent of the lithographs of Andy Warhol. Although ornament returns here in a new form, it does not overshadow the abstraction of the form. Critics noted that this 'strange facade' shares more affinities with the work of artists like Gerhard Richter than with the work of Le Corbusier, Venturi, or Koolhaas.[7] The overlaying of an ornamental pattern as a defining element of the facade, which some critics also related to Gottfried Semper's theory, reappears in another format with the Eberswalde Technical School Library in Germany (1994–9) (fig.11.4), where a series of images selected by the photographer Thomas Ruff were imprinted in horizontal bands over the surface of the building, turning it into a mediatised box that displays these images during the day and projects them on glazed horizontal strips at night. One may also draw a certain affinity between this structure and Robert Venturi's pop-inspired Market Street building at Drexel University in Philadelphia.

The work of Herzog & de Meuron, although difficult to categorise, nevertheless betrays a continuous attempt to achieve a conceptual architecture, with different aesthetic expressions. As one critic noted, their work definitely takes some of its cues from American Minimalism, and their aesthetic direction confronts the traditional in an incisive manner, while utilising some of its elements.[8]

11.4   Herzog & de Meuron, Eberswalde Technical School Library, Eberswalde, Germany, 1994–9

PETER ZUMTHOR: TOWARDS A PHENOMENOLOGICAL MINIMALISM

Another master of Minimalism, Peter Zumthor, came to architecture through an initial training in carpentry, hence his intimate connection with craftsmanship. His approach is marked by attention to architecture as an art of construction – which brings him closer to the 'Neo-Rationalist' architects – but imbued with a phenomenological sensitivity that one can detect in his architectural writings.[9] Zumthor, in fact, speaks of a search for the essence of things, for primordial qualities found 'in the things themselves', of a return to the basic elements that architecture is made of, namely structure, materials, spatial relationships, emptiness, and light. As he states: 'To me, buildings can have a beautiful silence that I associate with attributes such as composure, self-evidence, durability, presence, and integrity, and with warmth and sensuousness as well; a building that is being itself, being a building, not representing anything, just being.'[10]

Zumthor searches for the artistic spark, as he says, between the reality of things and the imagination. Reality remains a fundamental platform on which the artistic work, and architecture as art, plays itself. His sources of reference are varied, and range from the novels of Peter Handke, which inspired some of Wim Wenders' movies, to the paintings of the great realist Edward Hopper, to the writings of the philosopher Martin Heidegger. His seminal work is without question the Thermal Baths in Vals (1990–96) (fig.11.5), a project that propelled him on to the international scene. Built on a site in the mountainous village of Vals in Switzerland, the baths were designed to complement an existing hotel built in the 1960s. The commune, which was the proprietor of the project, insisted on a building that would fit within its context, to which Zumthor responded with a project that buries itself in the ground, appearing simply as a series of planted terraces that extend the hotel's outdoor area. Zumthor's defining conceptual sketch is emblematic of his Minimalist approach: stripes of charcoal-marks define a set of square spaces, all arranged within a rectangular block, articulating a balance between solids and voids. The complex thus emerges naturally from the terrain as a set of spaces that lead the visitor from one thermal bath to another, organised around a central area and opening up to the landscape through selective apertures, and then again through a large outdoor pool area. The entry to the baths emphasises its cavernous character, starting from the lobby of the hotel and then proceeding through a subterranean passageway to the main foyer. Slits in the wall at

11.5   Peter Zumthor, Thermal Baths, Vals, Switzerland, 1990–96

11.6　Peter Zumthor, Kunsthaus Bregenz, Bregenz, Austria, 1989–97

the roof level introduce light to the interior spaces. The load-bearing structure consists of solid walls of concrete, layered with thin strips of Gneiss stone extracted from the region, which renders the whole building in a dark grey tone. The composition of rooms within larger rooms recalls the design strategy of Louis Kahn, where the spaces also become a manifesto on light and sensorial qualities.

Similar to the Thermal Baths in Vals, the Kunsthaus in Bregenz (1989–97) (fig.11.6) originated from a simple schematic that defines a light-flooded interior space framed by three black marks: three free-standing walls erected in a Miesian manner to define the interior space. Light once again played a role here in the generation of the museum, drawing it in a diffused manner into the interior spaces. The facade of the main building consists of a double layer of etched glass shingles which give the building its appearance as a light box. Designed as a self-supporting steel framework, this glass curtain wall is double-layered, with a void separating the internal and external elements, allowing daylight to penetrate to the first underground level, while accommodating the lighting system that illuminates the building at night. The gallery spaces are framed by a composition of concrete walls which carry the floor slabs and stand as silent witnesses within an abstract interior space. All supporting functions are housed separately in a smaller building, which includes a library, museum shop, cafe, and administrative offices.

The Bruder Klaus Field Chapel in Mechernich, Germany (2007) is not a complex structure by any means, yet it confirms even more the architect's search for essentials, which leads in the end to a phenomenologically inspired Minimalism. The

221

chapel was designed for a private farmer who wished to honour the local patron, Saint Klaus. The commission appealed to Zumthor, who undertook it to create a chapel that embodies a new interpretation of religious space. From the outside, the chapel stands as a rectangular pillar of sand-tinted concrete, chamfered at one of its edges, like a vertical sculpture amidst the agricultural field. The concrete was poured in layers, giving it a distinctive texture. On the interior, the chapel walls were lined in a curvilinear fashion with strips of local pine trees, which were then set on fire to burn slowly. Once removed, the burnt timber left its marks on the concrete surfaces. A single oculus at the top allows light to penetrate into this dark interior, evoking a sense of mystery.

MINIMALISM IN SWITZERLAND AND GERMANY

Working in a similar vein to Zumthor, the Swiss architect Peter Märkli has also contributed works of similar austerity, such as his small museum of La Congiunta in Ticino (1992) (fig.11.7), dedicated to the work of the sculptor Hans Josephsohn. The small museum, consisting of a set of concrete boxes of equal width but differing heights, laid out in sequence in the rural field, provides a bare background for the sculptures, some of which are hung as reliefs on the walls, while others are free-standing on pedestals set off-centre in the main hall. The texture of the concrete work – poured in layers that leave traces of the construction process – contrasts with the steel joists that carry the metallic roof and express the rough character of the building, in tune with the artwork. Light enters through a skylight cut along the length of the building. From the outside, the building exudes a primitive simplicity, like a piece of art by Donald Judd, sitting in the middle of nature. As stated by Marcel Meili:

> The building's monolithic character informs its position in the landscape. [. . .] The building engages the ground and the prolific vegetation without a base, in the same way that prepared stone steles are rammed into the earth as fence posts in this area. The form asserts its position in the massive topography but does not lay a greater claim to its function's uniqueness than the small factories and the churches in the valley or the magnificent bridges across the Ticino [. . .][11]

11.7 Peter Märkli, La Congiunta, Giornico, Ticino, Switzerland, 1992

11.8 Christian Kerez, Chapel in Oberrealta, Grisons, Switzerland, 1992–3

Originally from Venezuela, Christian Kerez completed his studies at the ETH in Zurich before opening his practice, which has been marked by a distinctly 'objectivist' spirit that in some cases veers towards the Minimalist. The small project for a chapel in Oberrealta in Switzerland (1992–3) (fig.11.8) is one of his early works, standing on a plateau above the Rhine Valley, like a silent witness to the passage of time. The chapel takes the form of an 'original hut', a pitched roof structure that does not, however, emulate timber construction but rather moulds the whole form in concrete without any articulations between ground, walls, and roof. This 'typical' construction evokes, by its sheer simplicity, the work of Minimalist artists and acts like a sentinel over the landscape. Inside the chapel, the bare interior corresponds to the exterior, while a single vertical slit into the concrete wall, facing the open entrance, brings rays of light dramatically into the interior. This slit in the wall takes on a discreet symbolic significance in the small religious edifice.

An earlier project in which Kerez collaborated with Meinrad Morger and Heinrich Degelo was the Kunstmuseum Liechtenstein (2000), a building that sits as a 'black box' upon the site. Built of concrete and clad in black basalt stone, the structure features horizontal windows which open up to the outside at selective points. The interior contrasts with the exterior. Plain white surfaces provide neutral backgrounds for the display of the art collection, divided among six exhibition rooms, arranged around two opposed staircases. Kerez's design for a House with One Wall in Zurich (2007) constitutes another example of his Minimalist tendency in design, where the building is rendered as a glass box, supported on an internal structure of concrete walls. This house is actually a building divided into two separate apartments, with the stairways placed alongside the load-bearing party wall in a somewhat irregular composition. The conditions of the site resulted in a trapezoidal-shaped building, sliced along the middle, to allow for the two apartments which share a similar configuration, based on a composition of the domestic functions over three levels. The interiors feature a bare concrete structure, with the glass curtain wall framing all sides, and the stairway introducing an element of dynamism into a rather restrained space.

In another context, the Ohel Jakob Synagogue in Munich (2004–6) (fig.11.9) by Wandel Hoefer Lorch Architekten provides another variation on this theme, where a simplicity of architectural form – the paradigmatic square or cube – is translated into a composition of two elements: the base clad in rough travertine stone, overlaid by a smaller cubical element of steel and glass. This marriage of materials simultaneously provides a sense of gravitas, carrying historic associations, while also projecting a progressive outlook. The

11.9 Wandel Hoefer Lorch Architekten, Ohel Jakob Synagogue, Munich, Germany, 2004–6

left

11.10 Sergei Tchoban and Sergey Kuznetsov, Museum for Architectural Drawing, Berlin, Germany, 2013

right

11.11 Alberto Campo Baeza, Gaspar House, Cádiz, Spain, 1990–92

main synagogue building stands in the middle of the plaza as a modern monument, connected to a community centre which forms part of the complex.

In another context, the Museum for Architectural Drawing in Berlin (2013) (fig.11.10) by Sergei Tchoban and Sergey Kuznetsov provides an interesting conclusion to a stretch of row-houses, with a composition of blocks piled one on top of the other forming the spaces of this four-storey structure on a narrow site. The blocks of coloured concrete, with their slight declinations and the etched drawings on their almost opaque facades, appear like a Minimalist statement.

ALBERTO CAMPO BAEZA AND THE PURITY OF A WHITE ARCHITECTURE

Many architects reject categorising their work under a specific designation, and some, of course, are hard to classify into a single category. Alberto Campo Baeza is one case among many and, despite the fact that the majority of his work really exudes a Minimalist character, he expressly rejected this denomination, preferring instead to talk about an 'essential' architecture that draws its main raison d'être from the interrelated concepts of ideas, light, and space.[12] Yet this search for essentiality resonates as well with a constant reference to the Miesian idiom of 'Less is More', supplemented by his preference for simple forms which evoke a silence that counters the noisiness of contemporary life and which represent 'a sincere architecture that seeks to achieve everything with almost nothing'.[13] As Manuel Blanco observed, Campo Baeza's work is an attempt to 'construct an architecture of absence with light', to create spaces for reflection, meditation and withdrawal from the world. But it is also an architecture that complements its landscape, often resulting in iconic buildings.[14] And in a sense, these iconic elements, whether boxes standing in the landscape, or platforms covering the architectural space, appear like Minimalist artworks.

Starting with his early works, the Turegano House in Madrid (1988) – which he designed as a cubical volume – is separated internally by a stairway between a public area containing on different levels the living, dining, and study areas – interrelated in a Loosian fashion – and the private areas of bedrooms. The spatial character of this house testifies to a preoccupation with the playful articulation of spaces, while the abstract aspects are accentuated by the almost windowless street facade, revealing the mass of the cubical form. The Gaspar House in Cádiz (1990–92) (fig.11.11) further indicates this preoccupation with abstract forms, rendered in a neutral 'white' colour. In this case, the house was configured on a square-grid plan with the inner sanctum surrounded by an enclosing wall. The central space features a higher roof than the enclosing volumes, creating a sense of hierarchy. On either side of the central hall, two rectangular courtyards are punctuated by a symmetrical composition of lemon trees, creating a contrast between the natural and the artificial. From the outside, the house appears like a neutral box, without any external openings, set in the middle of the landscape.

above, left

11.12 Alberto Campo Baeza, Asencio House, Cádiz, Spain, 1999–2001

above, right

11.13 Alberto Campo Baeza, House of the Infinite, Cádiz, Spain, 2012–14

The Asencio House, also in Cádiz (1999–2001) (fig.11.12), reiterates the thematic of the white box in the middle of a sacred precinct, with an enclosing wall providing privacy and breached only at the pool side, allowing a natural extension to the landscape. Inside, the square plan of the house is divided into four quadrants, with the typical separation between served and serving spaces, and the playful articulation of spaces on the upper level overlooking the ground level, the whole thing rendered in a pristine white that accentuates further the role of light in shaping and revealing the interiors. The series of houses that Campo Baeza designed throughout the years, in the same idiom, reached perhaps their epitome in the House of the Infinite in Cádiz (2012–14) (fig.11.13), a masterpiece that faces the ocean, embedded in its sloping site, with its rooftop perforated at select areas for light, providing access through a stairway cut into the horizontal plane, drawing people down to the lower levels. The house thus appears as a mere platform, like an installation by Carl Andre, or as described by the architect: 'an infinite plane facing the infinite sea, an acropolis of stone, in Roman travertine'.

Campo Baeza's output was not restricted to designing houses, but extended to various institutional and commercial projects. Yet even in such cases, the architect persisted in his search for the 'essentials', subjecting architecture not to the prescriptions of functionality, but to higher aesthetic ideals. With the exception of some projects where

THE MINIMALIST AESTHETIC

the client or programme requirements demanded otherwise – such as his Public School for San Sebastian de los Reyes in Madrid (1983), where the overall form, brick construction, and organisation betrays a Rossian approach – the majority of his other public works remain committed to this search for essentials. This is evident, for instance, in his Zamora Office Complex in Zamora, Spain (2004–12) (fig.11.14), where an office building was projected for a site near the historic cathedral, sharing the same public square. Facing the cathedral and respecting the outline of the former convent's garden, the architect designed a walled enclosure of local stone, inserting the office functions within a glass box set inside the enclosing walls, only abutting them on one side of the precinct. The office complex reveals again a Miesian influence, perfecting the idea of a glass curtain wall with its double layer of large glass panes, while on the exterior deferring to the historic context with its solid stone walls.

11.14   Alberto Campo Baeza, Zamora Office Complex, Zamora, Spain, 2004–12

227

VARIATIONS ON MINIMALISM

The two Spanish architects Fuensanta Nieto and Enrique Sobejano have also produced a number of masterpieces, chief among which figures the Madinat-al-Zahra Museum. Their approach to design draws on multiple sources, principally the memory of recollections and impressions gathered through different times, and subjected to a random process of selection. They explained it in these terms:

> Shedding everything that is not strictly necessary and knowing when to stop in time, before the meaning of a work begins to blur, is for us one of the most suggestive metaphors for the patient process manifested in our work as architects.[15]

And later:

> Immersed in a meta-architecture, which always unconsciously ends up referring to itself, in which projects and works form a feedback loop and thus become the features of those following them, we find ourselves enmeshed in our own personal process. We delete letters from the text at random, we take one step back, we try to halt at just the right point. In this way we arrive at a concrete architecture, one reduced to its specific means, to built aphorisms designed for a certain place and its memory.[16]

While the process they describe indicates a conscious effort to reduce architecture to its essential elements, these elements are by no means devoid of meaning. On the contrary, some of these elements evoke certain associations with the present or the past, and give architecture its greater value. Such is the case of the Madinat-al-Zahra Museum in Córdoba (1999–2009) (fig.11.15), where the architects acted like archaeologists, keen to unravel the multiple layers of the site, to preserve what was there, and compose a new structure that would not in any way compete with the existing ruins. The museum was conceived as a place to display the archaeological findings from one of the most important archaeological sites of Arab-Hispanic culture. It blended seamlessly into

right, top

11.15   Nieto Sobejano Arquitectos, Madinat-al-Zahra Museum, Córdoba, Spain, 1999–2009

right, bottom

11.16   Nieto Sobejano Arquitectos, San Telmo Museum Extension, San Sebastian, Spain, 2005–11

the landscape by embedding itself into the ground, demarcated by a wall that wraps around the rectangular plan, almost mimicking the organisation of the old city. The excavated ground served as a base for the new design, composed on a grid with all the main functions (auditorium, exhibition spaces, archives) organised around an open courtyard slightly off-centre, and accessed through a long ramp that brings visitors down one level below the ground. Concrete walls, Corten steel roof panels, and limestone paving evoke the colours and textures of the old city.

In another context, the architects applied their sensitive approach to produce a building that engages in a dialectical relation with its context. The San Telmo Museum Extension (2005–11) (fig.11.16) – located on the seashore of Mount Urgull in San Sebastian, not far from Moneo's Kursaal – is an extension designed to add spaces to the historic Dominican monastery which had been converted into a museum. Conceiving of the project as a 'boundary', or an inhabited wall that runs along one of the sides of the monastery, the new addition acts as a mediator between nature and artifice, as it plays the role of a buttress against the cliff, providing access through a stairway to the hilltop. After a careful restoration of the existing cloister, church, and chapels, the architects proceeded to insert their extension, an irregular longitudinal form which sets itself back from the monastery, only to re-connect at the very end. The new extension thus provides additional room for public spaces, an assembly hall, a library, and service areas. The visual impact of the new construction was mediated by a 'vegetal' wall, a facade of perforated aluminium sheets supporting greenery, designed in collaboration with artists Leopoldo Ferrán and Agustina Otero. This 'artificial-natural' facade concretises the idea of dialogue between nature and art, as it is further transformed at night,

11.17   Fran Silvestre Arquitectos, House on the Castle Mountainside, Ayora, Spain, 2010

through the illuminated irregular patterns of the perforated panels, into an artistic installation that complements the historic building.

Fran Silvestre's work owes a lot to one of his mentors, Álvaro Siza, at whose office he worked after graduating from the University of Valencia. Yet the purity of his forms also owes some debt to the Minimalist style of Alberto Campo Baeza. His House on the Castle Mountainside in Ayora, Spain (2010) (fig.11.17) is an example of this precise manipulation of elements to create a consistent piece of art. Like an abstract sculpture with slightly Cubist undertones, the building is conceived as three layers that slightly shift as they adapt to the site, articulating the piano nobile in the composition, while in the end condensing all floors into a single white volume that fits into the rocky mountainside. In clear contrast to the vernacular architecture around it, which consists of traditional two-storey houses covered in stucco, the white prism distinguishes itself by its formal composition and distinct colour. This approach towards a purist architecture that adapts to its different site constraints was followed by Silvestre in a number of other projects, among them the Pati Blau House in Valencia (2020). This rather small house occupies a limited area of the site, enclosed by a protective wall to allow for a generous patio space, as in traditional houses of North Africa and Islamic Spain. The two-storey house has a smaller footprint on the ground level, while cantilevering a section of the patio on the second floor. The purity of the white volumes, inside and out, is only contrasted by the blue of the outdoor pool, and the greenery of the garden.

The work of the Portuguese brothers Francisco and Manuel Aires Mateus also betrays this search for essentials. Introducing their work, Alberto Campo Baeza spoke of a 'Handful of Air', borrowing this Nazarene proverb to describe one of their early works, the House in Alenquer (1999–2001), where the walls appear like simple devices constructed to 'contain the air in between'.[17] The house, indeed, is an unusual composition of an object placed within the enclosure of the old ruins, which have been reinforced and whitewashed, to become the defining boundary of the space. Inside this precinct, a rectangular slab has been positioned, housing the public areas on the ground floor and the private areas on the first floor, with projecting 'boxes' that add to the area of the bedrooms. A semi-public space is thus created between the old walls and the new object, which serve for recreational activities, also enclosing a swimming pool. The whole building is whitewashed, with pristine interiors that offer their surfaces to the play of light.

The House in Brejos de Azeitao in Setubal (2000–2003) followed a similar aesthetic, although the configurations would differ based on the programme, site, and other constraints. The House in Brejos is another example of restoration, where the architects transformed a former warehouse into a contemporary habitation, keeping the structure of the old building and inserting within its walls a cluster of cubicles containing the bedrooms. These white cubicles – which project over the main floor – cantilever off a set of walls at the ground level that delimit the public space, and are accessible through two sets of stairs parallel to the longitudinal walls of the warehouse. They appear suspended and opposed to each other in a state of tension, like abstract elements of an artistic installation. Their finish and colour, in clear contrast to the wooden roof, and their autonomous presence vis-à-vis the walls of the old structure further accentuate this strong statement. The house is thus transformed into a well-scripted and well-delimited set of relations between autonomous units, that nevertheless contrive together to form a well-balanced whole. Even their project for an elderly housing community at Alcacer do Sal in Portugal (2010) was conceived as a series of white boxes, arranged over three-tiers in a linear fashion, like a necklace, around the site, alternating between solids and voids in a checkerboard fashion. The voids translate into openings of different sizes based on the geometry of the site, and turn into outdoor patios.

The project for a Faculty of Architecture in Tournai, Belgium (2017) (fig.11.18) gives another perspective on the work of these architects at an institutional level. Yet again, the building was conceived as a simple white volume based on a cross plan, with one of the transepts missing, inserted within its context. The main access is through an off-centre porch, cut out from the cubical element that sits between two adjoining brick buildings. The whole ensemble is thought of as a playful articulation of subtracted elements within plain, cubical volumes, transforming the openings into distinctive elements that emphasise the forms while bringing light in measured ways into the interiors. The Centro de Artes de Sines in Portugal (2005) provides a slight variation on the Mateus brothers' language, this time cladding the exteriors with a local sandstone, somewhat similar to Siza's approach in the Santiago de Compostela museum. In contrast to the white interiors of this elaborate project, the stone cladding brings the project into a more intimate relationship with its context in this small coastal town. The building is split into two halves that are inserted within the urban fabric, separated by an alley, yet joined below ground. In one of the sections is located the main auditorium, while the other section comprises the exhibition galleries, library, and offices. The opaque walls of the enclosure only allow light through slits in the wall, or through the ground-level openings along the internal alleyway. This gives the building its monumental character, while the layering of stones brings it down to the scale of the street.

Fabrizio Barozzi and Alberto Veiga – who designed the Philharmonic Hall in Szczecin, Poland – recently completed the Musée Cantonal des Beaux-Arts in Lausanne (2011–19) (fig.11.19) that features a radically different direction. Compared with the 'Expressionistic' articulation of the Philharmonic Hall, the Lausanne Museum has a more restrained appearance, like a monolithic block of concrete, articulated by vertical fins on its main facade, and running parallel to the railroad tracks. The other facades of the building present a plain structure without openings. Built on the location of industrial buildings, the new museum also occupied part of the railway station. The scheme thus incorporated some of the elements of the old structure, principally the large arched window facing the entrance hallway and rendered in white stucco, which gives the foyer the appearance of a church nave. The large

11.18 Francisco and Manuel Aires Mateus, Faculty of Architecture in Tournai, Tournai, Belgium, 2017

above and left

11.19   Barozzi Veiga, Musée Cantonal des Beaux-Arts, Lausanne, Switzerland, 2011–19

arch provides a passageway, leading the visitors through its grand stairway to the upper levels. The galleries are all organised in a linear fashion, connected on the upper floors by the void of the foyer that structures the circulation. The whole interior is rendered in a Minimalist way, with white walls and floors, except for the galleries where the floors are of natural wood. Skylights illuminate the upper-level galleries, giving the spaces a distinct character.

The British designer John Pawson left his aesthetic touch on several works, ranging from the design of everyday objects, to renovations of historical buildings, to new houses. After spending an initiation period in Japan, working under Shiro Kuramata, Pawson attended architecture school at the AA in London, but left before completing his studies to take on several interior design projects, eventually completing a number of houses. Pawson's Abbey of Nový Dvůr in the Czech Republic (1999–2004) figures as one of his masterpieces. Occupying a large area of farmland in a remote part of Bohemia, the monastery was composed within an existing complex of ruins and dilapidated buildings. The existing courtyard configuration was revived as the footprint of the main cloister complex, with the existing manor house restored to form the west wing and to house the offices and the novitiate, while the remaining derelict structures were replaced by new buildings, dominant among which is the main church. The overall design draws on the principles of Cistercian architecture, with its emphasis on light, simple forms, and balanced proportions. A barrel-vaulted passageway with a glazed facade surrounds the cloister, and provides a covered circulation route that links all the different functions. The main church crystallises these principles, with the light filtering through the walls, illuminating the bare white interiors. The south wing, which has also been restored, houses the refectory on the ground level, and the dormitories on the upper level. Shower cubicles and lavatories stand in rhythmic order below the original timber roof of the building. The contrast between the new installations, in their pure white rendering, and the natural wood evokes the dialectic between modernity and tradition, brought together in a convincing synthesis.

Pawson's Okinawa House in Japan (2016) is another example of an architecture that draws on the essentials. The site for this single-family home is a small lot on a cliff-top on the island of Okinawa, where the owners spend their summer and winter holidays. The programme called for a place with a sense of expansiveness. The design traces the diagonal footprint of the plot, combining single- and double-height spaces within a form that is closed and tapered to the rear, but opens up at the front, with its ground-floor level raised to optimise the sightlines to the ocean.

Dominique Perrault's monument to the labour of the intellect, the Bibliothèque nationale de France (1989–95) (fig.11.20) is another grand statement of Minimalist architecture. The library project was conceived, in this case, as four prisms, each an L-shape building standing at a corner of a large, rectangular open court, like open books, with gleaming facades of glass curtain walls. Beyond the simple metaphor of the open book, the towers appear in a sort of silent conversation with each other, like an arrangement of pieces placed on a plateau by a Minimalist artist.

While the tendency towards Minimalism seems largely to be a European affair – especially pronounced in the works of Swiss, Spanish, and Portuguese architects – this tendency was not in any way confined to these countries. It spread throughout the world, and can be detected in the work of various architects, among whom we may note Steven Holl, Tod Williams and Billie Tsien, Kazuyo Sejima and Ryue Nishizawa.

Unlike his other projects, Steven Holl's Nelson-Atkins Museum of Art in Kansas City (1999–2007)

11.20   Dominique Perrault, Bibliothèque nationale de France, Paris, France, 1989–95

THE MINIMALIST AESTHETIC

left, exterior and interior
11.21 Steven Holl, Nelson-Atkins Museum of Art, Kansas City, Missouri, USA, 1999–2007

below
11.22 Tod Williams and Billie Tsien, Barnes Foundation, Philadelphia, Pennsylvania, USA, 2012

(fig.11.21) takes a decidedly Minimalist turn. Set in the midst of a large park, Holl's design was conceived to add exhibition spaces to the existing Neo-Classical building. Yet instead of projecting a typical extension that would abut the existing building, Holl set out to install a sequence of elements running along one side of the existing museum while keeping their distance, and acting as skylights that bring light into the underground spaces which are all connected in a linear fashion, and again to the main building. These independent and irregular 'lenses' are in fact simple lightwells that are double-glazed and illuminated at night, like light-sculptures set in the landscape. The interiors reflect this luminous character on white walls and circulation paths, the latter composed within a maze of spaces that are open on different levels, to allow for this visual transparency to percolate through the various levels.

Tod Williams and Billie Tsien, who came to prominence with their American Folk Art Museum in New York (2001–demolished 2014), produced another masterpiece, the Barnes Foundation in Philadelphia (2012) (fig.11.22). This large museum takes the form of a stone-clad podium on which rests a glazed volume, a 'light box' that glows at night, and cantilevers at one end of the building. Located on the Franklin Parkway, the building turns a slight angle to the street. A tripartite composition defines the new museum, with a gallery housing the art collection, an L-shaped element containing the support functions, and a courtyard in between. The Barnes collection is housed in the new gallery space, which replicates the scale of the original museum in Merion, in accordance with the founder's testament. Besides the impressive 'light box' visible from a distance, it is the rectangular slabs that anchor the building to the site which give it its distinctive character, clad by large panels of grey limestone and hung on a steel armature, with the panels being spaced in rhythmical bands, leaving vertical gaps to accentuate the rhythm.

above

11.23   SANAA, Museum of Contemporary Art, Kanazawa, Japan, 1999–2004

right, exterior and interior

11.24   SANAA, Rolex Learning Center, Lausanne, Switzerland, 2010

SANAA, founded by the Japanese architects Kazuyo Sejima and Ryue Nishizawa, has consistently employed a Minimalist approach to design which seeks to generate architectural conceptions from basic schemata, or 'diagrams'. Anthony Vidler saw in these operations a reduction that transforms architecture itself to the status of a diagram, or rather succeeds in transforming the diagram into a built work of Minimalist aesthetics, without much in terms of additions.[18] The Museum of Contemporary Art in Kanazawa (1999–2004) (fig.11.23) is emblematic of this direction. It is essentially a pure diagram rendered into a building that contains a variety of spaces. Inscribed within a large circular shape around 110 metres in diameter, the museum is a composition of diagrams within diagrams, with all the internal functions configured as square, rectangular, or circular spaces within the larger template. The template preserves its slim peripheral outline, which translates into a glass curtain wall. The spaces within, of different heights in some instances, perforate the roof and establish a hierarchy that attenuates the overall abstract character of the complex. At night, the interiors project a ring of light that wraps the building continuously.

The Rolex Learning Center in Lausanne (2010) (fig.11.24), built on the campus of the Polytechnic University to provide spaces for a learning laboratory, follows a slightly different strategy. Spread over one single space of 20,000 square metres, it provides a network of functions, social spaces, study areas, and outdoor spaces, spread over an undulating surface of gentle slopes and terraces, composed around a series of internal patios, with almost invisible supports for its complex curving roof.

This diagrammatic Minimalism appears again in their New Museum of Contemporary Art in New York (2002–7) (fig.11.25) which was built in the Bowery district, an old neighbourhood on the Lower East Side with industrial buildings from the turn of the century. Without prescribing to the context in terms of its typology, the new building was conceived like an artistic sculpture: a stack of seven white boxes of different proportions, set back slightly one from the other to allow for skylights and outdoor spaces. A rectangular unit, housing a tight stairway, elevator, and service core, runs perpendicular to the main street, and slightly off the edge of the sidewall. This core element organises circulation through the ten storeys of the building, which vary in footprint according to their position. The building is based on a steel structure, which allows for column-free spaces, while the interior walls of polished concrete offer a contrast to the lightness of the aluminium cladding on the exterior. This aluminium mesh gives the building its contemporary industrial character, while on the ground level, the cladding gives way to a transparent glazed facade that invites visitors in and provides an open connection to the streetscape.

Ryue Nishizawa's independent design for a museum on Teshima Island in Japan (2010) (fig.11.26), in collaboration with Japanese artist Rei Naito, takes this Minimalist aesthetic to another level, dissolving the project in its landscape. The small museum was conceived as a drop of water in a green landscape, taking the form of a large saucer perforated by two large oculi at either end, bringing light and air freely into the interior. The large shell is made of a thin layer of whitewashed concrete, also reflected in the colour of the floor, giving this space a luminous, ephemeral presence.

Finally, it would be a major omission not to mention a project that translated a competition brief for a monument into a project that combined architecture and landscape design, with a powerful, Minimalist message. Maya Lin's Vietnam Veterans Memorial (1982) (fig.11.27) – a commission won through a competition while still a student at Yale – occupies an important place in the history of monuments. Her approach was to cut through the site with two walls of black granite acting like retaining walls and allowing visitors to walk though this installation that would carry the names of all the fallen soldiers. Despite initial public opposition to this Minimalist statement which eschewed any overt symbolic references to patriotism or heroism, the memorial turned out to be one of the greatest popular successes of the 20th century. Worthy of note is Lin's reference to Edwin Lutyens' Memorial to the Missing of the Somme, to which she was coincidentally exposed at a lecture by Vincent Scully a few weeks before the competition submission, and which she cited as a source of inspiration. Scully's description of that monument presented it as a journey towards the awareness of loss, which the young architect tried to translate into a new experience of space, and a Minimalist one at that.

11.25 SANAA, New Museum of Contemporary Art, New York, USA, 2002–7

11.26 Ryue Nishizawa, Teshima Art Museum, Teshima Island, Japan, 2010

11.27 Maya Lin, Vietnam Veterans Memorial, Washington, DC, USA, 1982

12 New Directions in Contemporary Architecture

Over the past few decades, a large number of architectural practices emerged around the world, committed to experimentation with new methods, techniques, and materials, leading to innovative projects and buildings. This experimental approach originated with the pioneering works of architects like Frank Gehry, Rem Koolhaas, and Zaha Hadid, and evolved with other practices like Coop Himmelb(l)au, Morphosis, Future Systems, Foreign Office Architects, and many others, reflecting a regained optimism in the profession, similar to the period that accompanied the advent of modern architecture in the 1920s. This 'new spirit' in architecture was coupled with a belief in the capacity of innovative buildings to resolve environmental and even social problems. In their attempts to transcend previous architectural conventions, these practices managed in many cases to reach a synthesis between the opposite poles of Modernist functionalism and Post-Modernist historicism, aiming towards radical forms that are original while also engaging the public semantically in various ways.

The works considered in this chapter may be divided into three main tracks: one, those projects that blur the boundaries between art and architecture, intent on re-engaging architecture within its larger 'aesthetic' dimension; two, those that rely on new tools and technologies for the development of complex forms, which I have dubbed as 'Hyper-Modern'; and three, projects that address the great ecological challenge of the century.

TOWARDS A NEW AESTHETICS

Recent works by some of the most innovative architectural practices have indicated a revival of ornament as a way to respond to the absence of meaning, that is 'semantics', in modern architecture. This return of ornament triggered a number of essays and publications on the topic, and seems to recapitulate one of the major objectives of Post-Modernism, yet relying on the new digital means of production instead of reviving age-old craftsmanship or resorting to historicist motifs.[1] In reaction to abstract, unadorned surfaces, this return to ornamentation gave back to the architectural surface its lost aura, and seemed to coincide with the evolution of design trends around the world, from product to fashion design, which overruled the Bauhaus search for 'Gute Form' in favour of a celebration of aesthetic diversity, pluralism, and personal expression.[2]

The role of new technologies, principally the imaging techniques that accompanied the development of new design software, cannot be overlooked in this ornamental revival. As outlined by Antoine Picon, experimentation with these new techniques generated a variety of ornamental types from pixelation to tessellation, with the resultant ornamentation being embedded into the surface of the building and forming an integral part of it. In some cases, this even led to the radical result of turning the structure itself into an ornamental sculpture, as in the famous Olympic Stadium in Beijing by Herzog & de Meuron, dubbed the 'Bird's Nest' (2008).[3] Despite the complex variety of different techniques used in the ornamental revival, we may categorise them in two major trends: graphical imprints applied to the surface, or formal ornaments that are integral to the construction of the surface. The former can be seen as a contemporary reinterpretation of the Venturian paradigm – explored in various projects from the ISI Corporation in Philadelphia (1978) to the Ponte dell'Accademia in Venice (1985) – whereas ornament as integral to the surface owes more to the new techniques of production in what some observers have termed as the 'reconciliation' of technique and ornament.[4]

12.1   Herzog & de Meuron, Brandenburg University of Technology Media Centre and Library, Cottbus, Germany, 1998–2004

Applied ornament appears in different forms in the work of Herzog & de Meuron, from their original application of ornamental motifs on the Ricola Production and Storage Building in Mulhouse, France (1992–3), to the Eberswalde Technical School Library in Germany (1994–9), and the Brandenburg University of Technology Media Centre and Library in Cottbus (1998–2004) (fig.12.1). While some of these works have already been discussed under the lens of 'Minimalism', they also highlight another dimension that indicates an interest in ornamentation through imprinted graphical patterns on glass panes or concrete panels, as in the case of Eberswalde. In some cases, the architects collaborate with visual artists like Thomas Ruff, who selected images from his collection to be uniformly repeated on the four facades of the Eberswalde Library. While remaining true to their Modernist approach to form-making, the architects attempted in these projects to dematerialise the building through manipulation of its

left, top

12.2   Wiel Arets, Utrecht University Library, Utrecht, the Netherlands, 1997–2004

left, bottom

12.3   Herzog & de Meuron, De Young Museum, San Francisco, California, USA, 1999–2005

below

12.4   David Adjaye, Smithsonian National Museum of African American History and Culture, Washington, DC, 2016

surface. In the case of the Brandenburg Library, the building form was organically shaped to respond to the surrounding landscape, while standing as a landmark in its context. While the amoeba-shaped plan of the library appears to be fortuitous and purely expressionistic, the architects insisted that the plan developed in response to a study of the movement flows through the library, providing for reading rooms of different sizes, heights, and orientations, with a large spiral staircase connecting the different levels. A printed 'white veil' featuring texts in different languages provides a screen that wraps around the building.

On a similar note, Wiel Arets' design for the Utrecht University Library (1997–2004) (fig.12.2) featured a rectangular block covered by panes of glass, printed with a stylised pattern based on the papyrus plant, which reflects on the origins of writing. Besides their representational function, the imprinted surfaces reduce the light entering the library and give the building its distinctive quality. The John Lewis Department Store in Leicester by Foreign Office Architects (2008) incorporated a double-glazed surface that wraps around the building, with both surfaces imprinted with the lace motif inspired by the traditions of this once major textile-production city. The facade effectively becomes a 'skin' with textile connotations that recall Semper's theory of architecture.

An example of ornamentation that is integral to the building surface can be seen in Herzog & de Meuron's De Young Museum in San Francisco (1999–2005) (fig.12.3). The different elements of this three-block museum are united by the external surface, with its copper sheets that are perforated in a smooth gradation of circular openings, almost like pixels.

David Adjaye's Smithsonian National Museum of African American History and Culture (2016) (fig.12.4) followed a similar design approach, as far as its envelope, to the one developed earlier for the Aïshti Department Store in Beirut, Lebanon (2015). The museum was built on one of the last sites of the National Mall in Washington, DC, and was to include a theatre, exhibition galleries, and administrative functions. The architect envisaged turning the building into a medium for the dissemination of cultural narratives on a problematic history, which translates into a museum-cum-

left, exterior and interior

12.5 Neutelings Riedijk, Institute for Sound and Vision, Hilversum, the Netherlands, 2006

right

12.6   Neutelings Riedijk, Veenman Printing Works, Ede, the Netherlands, 1997

below

12.7   Neutelings Riedijk, MAS Museum, Antwerp, Belgium, 2010

memorial and community centre. The building was wrapped with an ornamental bronze-coated lattice which filters the light entering the building, as a reference to the textile heritage of the African-American community. A spiralling ramp leads visitors to the below-ground level where the theatre is located, in addition to a 'contemplative court' which is lit from above by a large oculus, featuring a waterfall that flows into a reflection pond.

In affirmation of the 'ornamental principle', the Dutch practice of Neutelings Riedijk published a collection of their works under the evocative title of *Ornament and Identity*.[5] In this the architects presented their work as pluralistic, heterogeneous, and diverse, not subscribing to a single approach or method. In some cases, these are platonic solids that have been ornamented by graphic signs; in others, they are buildings that display spectacular heads and tails, all with a propensity to 'speak, sigh, whisper, and declaim'. Recalling Charles Jencks' original call for a pluralistic architecture that responds to the local culture and identity by creating meaningful buildings, the architects espoused a synthetic direction that would be abstract yet figurative, tectonic and ornamental, and that would lead to a new version of Post-Modernism that was not tied to past stylistic trends, but reflected its own time. It is in this sense that they define the facade of their buildings as an artistic 'canvas' on which images can be etched or applied, as in the Institute for Sound and Vision in Hilversum (2006) (fig.12.5), where the facade of this complex cubical volume housing the visual archives of the Netherlands becomes a glowing display of images collected from the archives, selected by the graphic designer Jaap Drupsteen – a 'wunderkammer' of images on display.

An earlier project by Neutelings Riedijk, the Veenman Printing Works in Ede (1997) (fig.12.6), features an open space configuration housing the printing factory and the corresponding offices in a large warehouse structure with a sloping roof. In order to give the building an appropriate expression that reflects its function, the architects resorted to applying a series of letters over the facade, which form part of a poem by K. Shippers, wrapping around the building. With the assistance of a graphic designer, Karel Martens, the envelope was configured as a series of individual panels of glass, each imprinted with one letter, and clamped on a framework of glazing bars. Other projects by Neutelings Riedijk are less graphic, but nevertheless attempt to express through specific symbolisms, a certain story. This is the case of the MAS Museum in Antwerp (2010) (fig.12.7), located on the harbour. Its distinctive silhouette, a stack

MODERN ARCHITECTURE IN A POST-MODERN ERA

above

12.8   Kumiko Inui, Dior Ginza Shop, Tokyo, Japan, 2003–4

below

12.9   Valerio Olgiati, Atelier Bardill, Scharans, Switzerland, 2005–7

of alternating red Indian sandstone blocks and glass panels, features upon closer look a set of ornamental motifs: a human 'hand' derived from the city coat of arms, reproduced and affixed to each stone panel. The architects appealed to history through the idea of a vertical funerary monument that expressed the city's past, while also projecting a transparent image through the undulating curtain of glass.

Kumiko Inui's design for the Dior Ginza shop in Tokyo (2003–4) (fig.12.8) appears like a synthesis of the two approaches. Composed of a double skin – the outer skin of perforated aluminium sheets and an inner skin of imprinted glass panels – it projects the image of the famous Dior handbags, with their chequered patterns. A more abstract rendering of the integrated ornamental facade can be seen in Valerio Olgiati's Atelier Bardill in Scharans, a small town in Switzerland (2005–7) (fig.12.9), which was situated on a plot that was occupied by a barn. Respecting the context guidelines, the architect proposed a monolithic volume with a pitched roof that accommodates both the living quarters and the atelier of the artist, its brown-coloured concrete facades etched with an ornamental motif cast into the surface.

HYPER-MODERNISM

Much of the work discussed above was experimental in nature, although the emphasis was placed on its symbolic dimension. In this section, projects that were more distinctly experimental in nature are presented, moving towards what we may call a 'Hyper-Modernism', hereby defined as the breaking of traditional norms and subverting of normative types, driven by a futuristic approach that draws on various sources.[6] In a sense, the projects that fall within this ambit all seek to supersede, or go beyond Modernism, by exacerbating some of its fundamental principles like functionality, technological aptitude, and environmental responsivity.

The Constructivist/Surrealist influences that informed the early work of Rem Koolhaas somehow receded into the background of later projects, which became more focused on instrumental articulations of complex programmes. The

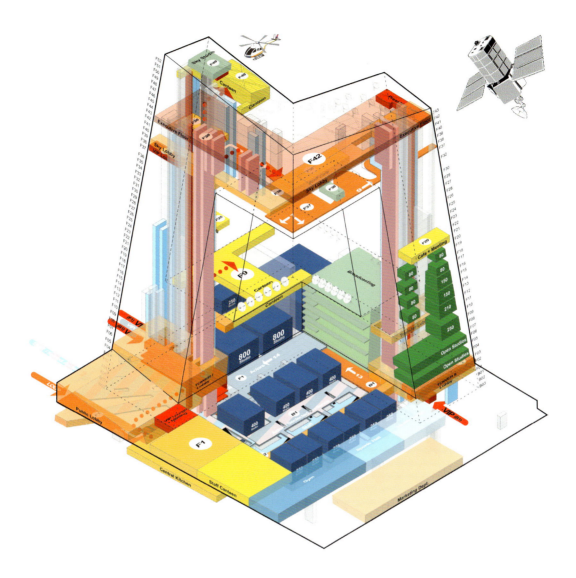

12.10   OMA, CCTV – Headquarters, Beijing, China, 2002–12

CCTV tower in China (2002–12) (fig.12.10) is a case in point, where the architect explored new arrangements that avoid the traditional typology of the skyscraper, creating a building that presents a novel interpretation of a mega-office complex. Instead of a vertical structure, the complex is conceived as a continuous loop, with two main towers slightly tilted at each end and connected at the base by an L-shaped platform, and again at the top. This innovative structure posed a major structural challenge, with the slab at the top cantilevering over a 75-metre span. The first tower serves mainly as an office space, while the second contains the media production facilities, connected at the top by the administration and entertainment functions. The structural forces at play are expressed on the facades, where the web of steel elements results from the stress analysis. In one of

12.11   OMA, Seattle Central Library, Seattle, Washington, USA, 1999–2004

the informative drawings that show the functional distribution across this complex, the different colour-coded blocks lend additional importance to the role that the 'diagram' reclaims in the generation of the architectural project, a method that was rendered obsolete during the period of Post-Modernism.

The same method dictated the development of the Seattle Central Library (1999–2004) (fig.12.11) where the analysis of the programme – in this case the main activities of a library, the systems of archiving, as well as a study of new patterns of public usage – dictated the form of the building. The form emerges out of its site as an extruded volume, integrating the different functions which have been segregated according to the different uses. The central space is the large lobby at main entrance level, which acts as a public forum, reminiscent of the great public spaces of central train stations from where one could access the auditorium at the lower level or the ramps that lead to the upper spaces. The building is conceived in section as a composition of layers: five layers of stability, as the architect defines them, and four layers of instability, superposed in an irregular fashion, with the diagonals connecting their edges to close the polyhedron. The five regular compartments include the administration at the top, the spiral block that encompasses the bookstacks arranged along a continuous spiral, meeting spaces, staff, and parking. In-between are sandwiched the irregular spaces that house the reading rooms, 'mixing chamber', the large foyer, and the children area. The building is thus conceived as a series of platforms, each dedicated to a cluster of functions. The articulated surface of this large monolithic polyhedron is uniformly covered by a mesh of steel and glass, revealing through its transparency the internal functions.[7] As noted by Gargiani, the library is conceived as an 'abstract machine', a 'formal diagram, on a par with those of Van Berkel and Bos, and MVRDV'. The arbitrary shifting of floors is geared towards creating an 'ideal diagram' to represent the public library in its contemporary form, in the mediatic era.[8]

Massimiliano and Doriana Fuksas who designed the Maison des Arts in Bordeaux (1994–9), which exhibited more of a Minimalist aesthetic, followed another path in their sophisticated Ferrari Operational Headquarters and Research Centre in Modena, Italy (2004). This elegant complex, with its Miesian slabs floating above each other, covered by ponds, conjures an image of technical precision and complex spatial interrelations, a far cry from what a 'sensational' proposal could have been made for the manufacturer of luxury racing cars. A more experimental approach appears in their later projects such as the Lycée Georges Frêche in Montpellier (2007–12) (fig.12.12), which marks a clear demarcation from their earlier language, towards an architecture of curvilinear, fluid forms accentuated by metallic panels. This comes as a clear reaction against the geometry of platonic shapes and is more in tune with what became known as an architecture of 'blobs'. The building, which appears as one continuous structure enveloped by panels of anodised aluminium, is in reality composed of two elements: one L-shaped and another Y-shaped volume, interconnected at various levels. For the Tbilisi Public Service Hall – a complex that houses a number of governmental functions, including the National Bank of Georgia, the Ministry of Energy, and the Civil and National Registry Agency – Fuksas resorted to a composition of seven glass-clad blocks, covered by a series of tree-like canopies supported on steel posts, creating a dialogue between rectilinear and curvilinear forms. In a more recent work, the Music Theatre and Exhibition Hall at Rhike Park, also in Tbilisi, Georgia (2010–17) (fig.12.13), the architects deployed an assortment of unconventional forms, consisting of two funnel-shaped volumes, each containing one part of the programme and connected at the rear end of the site. The two 'periscopes' are clad in steel and glass panes on a tessellated pattern, with a large glass oculus at their front end that offers a view of the landscape.

Influenced at its beginnings by High-Tech architecture, Odile Decq's work is characterised by its unconventionality and its attempt to explore new spatial relations. Her GL Events Headquarters in Lyon, France (2014) is an example of structural complexity that translates into a transparent building containing offices and meeting spaces, cantilevering over the boardwalk. The complex is composed of two parallelepiped volumes, almost at 90 degrees to one another, forming a large atrium space and anchored by three pylons that carry the exposed crossbeams which support the different floors. Decq's earlier project, a competition she won to expand the MACRO Museum in Rome (2001–10) (fig.12.14), built within an existing Art Deco brewery, exhibited similar features of exposed steel elements that carry the floors and suspended walkways, in a colourful collage of elements that negotiate their place within a dynamic interior. The entrance to the building is at the corner of two main avenues, through a garden lined with trees, and contrasting with the mysterious interior, which receives indirect lighting from the roof skylight. At the heart of the composition lies a small auditorium, clad in red-lacquered wood, like a jewel in the middle of the lobby space, surrounded by the suspended circulation bridges. While the lobby and the adjoining spaces are given a characteristic 'modern' rendition in black, red, or grey, the galleries are mostly contained in the existing old building with a neutral white for the display of artworks. On the exterior, the building presents a restrained glass-curtain wall, which rises behind the existing, old facade of the brewery.

12.12 Massimiliano and Doriana Fuksas, Lycée hôtelier Georges Frêche, Montpellier, France, 2007–12

above

12.13 Massimiliano and Doriana Fuksas, Music Theatre and Exhibition Hall, Rhike Park, Tbilisi, Georgia, 2010–17

left

12.14 Odile Decq, MACRO Museum, Rome, Italy, 2001–10

One of the most prominent disciples of Koolhaas to emerge on the international scene is the Danish architect Bjarke Ingels. Ingels followed Koolhaas in 'advertising' his design approach through an unusual publication blending fact with fiction, data with analysis, and in his particular case, turning the publication into a comic strip book. The publication *Yes is More: An Archicomic on Architectural Evolution*[9] is emblematic of BIG's approach to architectural design as an experimental, playful process where anything can be attempted, and where, in his own words, architecture can find the middle ground between a naïve utopian thinking on the one hand, exemplified by the avant-garde, and a sterile pragmatism, advocated by traditional corporate architecture. The first pages of this autobiographical monograph show the architect as a fearless innovator moving around in a large loft space where teammates are spread out in an unconventional way around large tables overlaid with computers, drawings, and models. In this playful and jovial atmosphere, Ingels opens up with a statement calling for an inclusive architecture, unburdened by the 'conceptual monogamy of commitment to a single interest or idea':

> An architecture where you don't have to choose between public or private, dense or open, urban or suburban, atheist or Muslim, affordable flats or football fields.

> [. . .] A pragmatic utopian architecture that takes on the creation of socially, economically and environmentally perfect places as a practical objective.

> Yes is More, Viva la Evolucion[10]

The reliance on accidental happenings, on the element of chance, and on the notion that architecture does not need to be a 'serious business', is nowhere better exemplified than in the first project featured in this catalogue and ironically titled: 'Found in Translation', in indirect reference to a popular film. Here, Ingels relates how a proposal that originated as a fortuitous idea for the Danish Pavilion at the Shanghai Exhibition was rejected, only to be taken up by a Chinese developer who was seduced by its associations. The proposal, which was based on the exhibition mascot, as two legs in marching condition, was read by the businessman as a Chinese character signifying 'people'. The pavilion was thus transformed into a split tower containing a hotel, apartments, a congress centre, and other functions. The 'Tower of the People' would thus be developed in Shanghai, emanating from an accident of translation.

Also characteristic of Ingels' playful approach is the Lego House in Denmark (2017) (fig.12.15), conceived as a museum, exhibition centre, and space for Lego activities. The building is a composition of blocks superposed on top of each other like a Lego construction, resulting

12.15   Bjarke Ingels Group, Lego House, Billund, Denmark, 2017

left, top

12.16   Bjarke Ingels Group, The Mountain Housing, Copenhagen, Denmark, 2008

left, bottom

12.17   Bjarke Ingels Group, CopenHill, Copenhagen, Denmark, 2011–19

right

12.18   Bjarke Ingels Group, Business Innovation Hub at the University of Massachusetts, Amherst, Massachusetts, USA, 2019

in a pyramidal form around eight storeys high, and centred around an internal plaza illuminated through the voids between blocks. Ingels' catalogue of work is a collection of spectacular projects of different scales and in different contexts, without any consistent thread between them, other than the celebration of playful experimentation aimed towards formal innovation, always stressing creative solutions to exceptional problems. In some cases, a tendency towards a playful arrangement of modules prevails, as in the Lego House; in other cases, a topological translation of data into organic or crystalline compositions takes place, as in the 'Battery', a project of redevelopment of a district of Copenhagen intended to merge three neighbourhoods, including entertainment functions, offices, and a religious centre (unrealised project). In other instances, the outcome is a result of urban vectoral forces that manipulate the form into a twisted parallelepiped, as in the National Bank of Iceland (unrealised).

Among the noteworthy, realised projects by Ingels figures the large housing project in Copenhagen, baptised 'The Mountain' (2008) (fig.12.16), somewhat reminiscent of Safdie's Habitat '67, yet articulated in a completely new way. Instead of the rough concrete of the latter, this one is an ecologically inspired complex of 80 modular units, designed on an inclined grid that rises up like an artificial mountain, clad in wood and featuring a green outdoor space for each unit. The space underneath the housing units is dedicated to parking and the facades facing the roads are clad in perforated aluminium plates, designed to form a reproduction of Mount Everest. Another example is the incinerator plant in Copenhagen, baptised as CopenHill (2011–19) (fig.12.17), which turned a conventional waste plant into a multi-functional building, including administrative offices, entertainment functions, and an educational centre, as well as a rooftop bar and gardens for visitors. The huge artificial mountain was covered by a slanted roof that doubles as a ski slope and hiking trail.[11]

Ingels' dexterity in formal manipulation also shows itself in the Business Innovation Hub at the University of Massachusetts at Amherst (2019) (fig.12.18). Designed as an appendix to the Isenberg School of Management, the area of the new volume doubles that of the school, adding new spaces for education, informal gatherings, and workshops. The new building was conceived as a cylindrical drum, a doughnut with an outdoor courtyard space at the centre that connects to the original rectangular slab. The regular, copper-clad vertical pilasters that rhythmically surround the facade gradually fall down as they approach the old building, transforming into a triangular elevation on that side, where one of two entrances is located. Daylight filters through the pilasters to illuminate the multi-storey atrium, which forms the heart of the new building, also doubling as a venue for ceremonies, banquets, and career fairs. From a different perspective, the Musée Atelier Audemars Piguet (2020) was designed as a spiral-

shaped building rising up out of the site in Vallée de Joux in Switzerland, to contain the watchmaker's museum and ateliers, next to the historic original building. The spiral-shaped building is formed of two concentric spirals, with load-bearing glass walls that offer a panoramic view of the landscape. The rooftop is covered by a grass canopy, turning the building into a large sculpture. Inside, the curved glass walls channel the visitors through the building, where the slanted floors create a gradient effect, leading towards the centre. Two ateliers are incorporated within the museum, offering visitors a direct view onto the watchmakers' craft.

The work of Marion Weiss and Michael Manfredi spans a whole spectrum of projects from landscape to specific interventions, and also varies in terms of its stylistic approach, from a conventional Modernism to more futuristic projects, as in their Krishna Singh Center for Nanotechnology at the University of Pennsylvania (2013) (fig.12.19). This is an impressive architectural intervention on the edge of the campus, housing labs and classrooms in a U-shaped plan, with the two wings cantilevering over the courtyard space. An internal gallery, which houses the stairways and lobbies, rings the building providing visual access to the interior, framed by a metal-panelled facade of glass that reflects the surrounding buildings and glows at night.

Foreign Office Architects, led by Farshid Moussavi and Alejandro Zaera-Polo, appeared on the international scene with a winning proposal for the Yokohama International Port Terminal (1995–2002) (fig.12.20). This 'topological' structure adapted itself to the harbour and to the movement of passengers by adopting a curvilinear profile that turns the building into an artificial landscape. The building is organised over three levels connected by ramps: starting with the car parking, followed by a middle floor of administrative functions (including shopping areas, restaurants, and so on), finally leading to the observation deck. The complex

12.19   Marion Weiss and Michael Manfredi, Krishna Singh Center for Nanotechnology, University of Pennsylvania, Philadelphia, Pennsylvania, USA, 2013

12.20   Foreign Office Architects, Yokohama International Port Terminal, Yokohama, Japan, 1995–2002

structure of concrete girders and steel plates provides for large free spans that allow for smooth movement through the complex. The building's main attraction remains perhaps its dissolution into the harbour landscape, offering an alternative vision for large infrastructural projects of this type.

The Yas Hotel in Abu Dhabi (2007–10) (fig.12.21) by Asymptote (Hani Rashid and Lise Anne Couture) provides an example of an innovative approach to the design of a large hotel complex, which in this case was broken down into different units, straddling a Formula One track. Rather than thinking of it as a functionalist tower, the hotel takes on a horizontal profile, with a large curvilinear canopy of glass – almost like a necklace of luminous beads – covering the whole ensemble. The interior also features the same streamlining, drawing the dynamism of the exterior into the internal spaces.

The monumental Tianjin Binhai Library in China (2017) (fig.12.22) by MVRDV takes the concept of monumentality to another scale, after Mecanoo's Delft Library of 1995 and OMA's Seattle Public Library of 2004. Here, the architects proposed a large space that merges between public zones, reading areas, and auditoria in a spectacular composition that simulates the pattern of waves on its interior. These waves, formed by the cascades of bookshelves that surround the main atrium, ascend from the ground level all the way to the top, displaying the millions of books that are normally arranged in repetitive stacks, to become the main feature – the ornamental supplement that gives this space its character. The building was conceived on a basic rectangular template that was then carved out internally to create the large atrium, surrounded by multi-levels of shelving. Within the atrium stands a spherical volume containing the

12.21 Asymptote – Hani Rashid and Lise Anne Couture, Yas Hotel, Abu Dhabi, UAE, 2007–10

12.22 MVRDV, Tianjin Binhai Library, Tianjin, China, 2017

auditorium, crowned by a large circular skylight. The bookshelves are accessed through continuous stairways that wrap around the space, following the same contour lines, doubling as seating areas and extending all the way to the ceiling. Light penetrates into this illuminated cavern through the skylight, as well as the two main facades that have been shaped by the carved-out atrium. The uniform texture and pristine-white colour of the interior space evokes a surreal space, accentuated by the spherical form that landed on the ground level. Supporting educational facilities were arranged along the edges, with additional facilities, such as archives, placed in the basement. The Tianjin Binhai Library succeeded in overturning the classical typologies of public libraries, by conceiving the design into a plastic, sculptural modelling of space that blurs the boundaries between served and serving areas, expanding the public realm to cover the larger part of this monumental building.

UN Studio created an iconic landmark in Stuttgart for the Mercedes-Benz Museum (2001–6) (fig.12.23). The aerodynamic form of this museum reflects the technological image of the automotive manufacturer, and it would not be too far-fetched to draw connections between the design of cars and the design of the building, which appears like a giant mechanical apparatus. Visitors are drawn into the ground level of the building, to be lifted up to the last level through elevators within the central atrium, from which they commence a gradual descent through the three loops that compose the interior space, arranged around the central atrium. The cars are exhibited on these elliptical platforms, around the central core. The external envelope expresses the cyclical movement on the interior, with the structure clad in aluminium panels, interspersed by wide bays of glass that reveal the structural system.

One of the major catalysts of this new tendency for innovation in architecture is the movement known as Parametricism. Parametricism was promoted by Patrik Schumacher as the style that would supposedly supersede all styles, in a Hegelian fashion, and signal the advent of a new age in architecture. While many of the architectural works covered above, such as the Mercedes-Benz Museum by UN Studio, relied on parametric modelling to resolve complex structural requirements, the definition of Parametricism was left to Schumacher who articulated his theoretical framework in two large volumes, advocating the elevation of this new paradigm into what he termed an 'epochal style' that would resolve the 'crisis' of Modernism, which in his opinion sprouted temporary episodes such as Post-Modernism, Neo-Historicism, and Deconstructivism.[12] Schumacher presented the work of Zaha Hadid Architects

12.23 UN Studio, Mercedes-Benz Museum, Stuttgart, Germany, 2001–6

as exemplary of this new style in architecture, which, in a manner that also recalls Le Corbusier's ambitious proposals, would extend into urbanism. Schumacher presented his firm's urban proposals for a business park for 150,000 persons in Singapore (2001–3), the master plan for Bilbao (2004), and the master plan for the Kartal-Pendik district in Istanbul (2006) as examples of this radical futuristic approach to urban planning.

THE ECOLOGICAL CHALLENGE AND THE PATH TO SUSTAINABLE DESIGN

Many of the 'High-Tech' architects of the 1960s to the 1990s already harboured an 'ecological' agenda which aimed at using technology in the service of sustainability, devising strategies for 'recycling' buildings, adopting flexible spatial organisations that reduce excessive use of resources, and ultimately developing new techniques to reduce energy use in buildings. These ideas were in some ways the legacy of the great experimental engineer Buckminster Fuller, who influenced many of these architects, as well as Reyner Banham's ideas about the ecological challenges of our epoch. Such concerns became even more pressing with the environmental problems that emerged in the 1990s. With the Commerzbank Headquarters in Frankfurt (1991–7) (fig.12.24), Norman Foster ushered in the ecological agenda in the field of office towers. The building is presented as the 'first ecological office tower', with a design strategy that emphasises natural lighting and ventilation, reducing the reliance on active energy systems. A variety of winter gardens were incorporated in the design, which revolves around a central atrium space, spanning every four storeys. Foster also moved towards an ecological architecture with a regionalist twist, in his plan for Masdar, a city in the middle of the desert in the United Arab Emirates, which was projected to become the first carbon-neutral city. So far, only the Masdar Institute (2007–15) (fig.12.25) has been realised, which incorporates laboratories, offices, and residential units, with additional functions covering entertainment, sports, and leisure facilities. The design incorporates a number of passive and active environmental strategies, such as 'brise-soleil' shading devices, a farm of photovoltaic panels that

12.24   Foster + Partners, Commerzbank Headquarters, Frankfurt, Germany, 1991–7

produces the energy needed for the complex, water collection and recycling, in addition to responsive landscaping. The residential structures feature a contemporary version of the traditional 'mashrabiya' screen-windows, built of glass-reinforced concrete, allowing light and air to filter through without excessive heat intake. The curvilinear sand-coloured facades of the residential buildings form a counterpart to the more functional blocks of the laboratories, and present an architecture with a regionalist touch.

In his illustrated manifesto, *Cities for a Small Planet*,[13] Richard Rogers laid out the groundwork for what constituted his philosophy of architecture, which provides a good perspective on the concerns and motivations behind his work. Grounded on a social awareness of the role played by cities in the

12.25 Foster + Partners, Masdar Institute, Masdar, Abu Dhabi, UAE, 2007–15

formation of civic culture, and taking stock of the multiple problems facing them in light of projected growth as well as the intensive consumption of resources and energy, Rogers called for architects to take an active role in addressing these pressing issues. Architecture, in his account, needs to adopt sustainability as a core value, incorporating new technologies geared towards the reduction of energy consumption and pollution. As illustrations of this approach, Rogers gave the example of the design for the Law Courts in Bordeaux, as well as the Lloyd's of London building, discussed earlier.

A seminal project that illustrates the new awareness of environmental issues is the Federal Environment Agency in Dessau by Sauerbruch Hutton (1998–2005) (fig.12.26). This project was destined to house the main agency in charge of devising strategies for environmental protection and sustainability, and thus would act as a manifesto for sustainable architecture. Active and passive systems were incorporated to ensure the reduction of energy consumption as well as the overall carbon footprint of the building complex. Located in a former industrial zone, the building access is through an open forum, a crescent-shaped transparent space, covered by skylights. Offices are arranged along a curvilinear path that draws a loop around the extended atrium space – the inner courtyard – with bridges crossing the two sides for ease of communication between different offices. Inside this organic composition, a landscape of natural elements with a variety of natural materials is transformed into an ecological garden. The building combines a compact volume with a high degree of thermal insulation, coupled with the use of renewable energy sources. In particular, it benefits from the use of a large geothermal heat exchange system that runs below ground, moving hot air back into the building in wintertime, and cool air in summertime. In addition, solar panels on the roof collect energy. Building materials were chosen according to their ecological value, with panel facades entirely of timber, a renewable resource.

A similar approach was taken by Behnisch Architekten for the Unilever Headquarters in Hamburg (2009), a large complex of office spaces for an agri-food company, and part of the redevelopment of the HafenCity area industrial zone. Instead of a typical office block, the architects opted for a longitudinal slab supported on a steel structure and clad in a double layer of glass. Like the Federal Environment Agency in Dessau, the design relies on the bioclimatic thermal exchange that circulates the air into the building from the exterior to the underground, reducing the dependence on mechanical heating and air-conditioning. The interior is designed around a large central atrium that serves as a meeting and recreational space for the employees, with open views towards the office areas which receive additional light from the skylights.

12.26   Sauerbruch Hutton, Federal Environment Agency, Dessau, Germany, 1998–2005

In addition to the projects by Renzo Piano mentioned in previous chapters, one recent project featured a more direct translation of the ecological imperative: the California Academy of Sciences (2000–2008) (fig.12.27). Located in a natural park in San Francisco on the site of the former academy, the new structure takes the form of a large rectangular slab with an undulating roof covered by vegetation, mostly native plants and wildflowers. Water is collected on the roof and reused, while sunlight is modulated through a system of louvres to ensure optimal heat transfer to the interior. Apart from its sinuous roof incorporating skylights and

left

12.27   Renzo Piano, California Academy of Sciences, San Francisco, California, USA, 2000–2008

below

12.28   Dominique Perrault, EWHA Womans University, Seoul, South Korea, 2004–8

domical inflections, which covers the planetarium, rainforest, and aquarium functions, the building has no expressive architectural features: it appears like a large, well-structured box, containing the variety of functions from exhibition spaces to educational facilities, all under one roof. The roof is framed by a glass canopy covered by thousands of photovoltaic cells that generate part of the energy used for the building.

Dominique Perrault's EWHA Womans University in Seoul, South Korea (2004–8) (fig.12.28) represents another example of earth-covered architecture. The architect devised this building as two strips of green zones covering the functions below, with an artificial ravine slicing through the blocks, providing a public space and a pedestrian path, as well as the main sources of light for the embedded functions. The longitudinal facades are glass-curtain walls, with passageways and stairways running alongside them, to allow daylight into the interiors. The architect intended to create an environmentally responsive complex, which relies on geothermal energy for most of its operation.

The preoccupation with energy consumption and economical structures has become a regular staple for many practices, even those with a more avant-garde agenda, such as MVRDV. Their public library for the town of Spijkenisse in the Netherlands (2011) is a case in point. Built to house the town library, this pyramidal structure of timber beams and glass was fitted with a sophisticated system of passive energy control, in addition to a

12.29 Alonso Balaguer Arquitectos Asociados, Richard Rogers, Nuevas Bodegas Protos Winery, Peñafiel, Spain, 2004–8

modulated facade system to control heat transfer. A number of other projects showed a similar emphasis on natural, replenishable materials like wood, and on passive energy systems, to reduce the carbon footprint. The Rossignol Headquarters in La Buisse, France (2009) by Hérault Arnod Architectes features an undulating roof of wooden strips, covering a large space that is partitioned into production facilities, offices, and recreation areas. Clerestories in the roof structure bring light to the interior, while rainwater is collected, treated and reused in the service areas. Similarly, the Nuevas Bodegas Protos winery in Peñafiel, Spain (2004–8) (fig.12.29) by Alonso Balaguer Arquitectos Asociados, in collaboration with Richard Rogers, was designed as a series of parabolic, wood-laminated vaults covering a triangular plan of three main floors, with the wine production and storage located below ground level. The building reduces the impact of temperature changes through its reinforced concrete structure and absorbs heat through the tile-covered roof.

The Kroon Hall at Yale University (2009) (fig.12.30) is another major example of ecologically responsive architecture, introducing a richer palette of materials, including local stone, wood, and concrete. The building was designed by Michael Hopkins with intelligent systems to regulate light, heat, and air intake and to reduce energy consumption, with an interior covered in durable red oak wood panels giving it a warmer character. It was oriented southward to collect

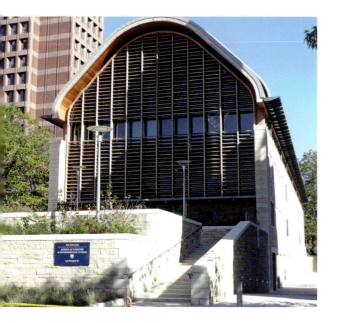

left

12.30   Michael Hopkins, Kroon Hall, Yale University – School of Forestry and Environmental Studies, New Haven, Connecticut, USA, 2009

right, top

12.31   Stefano Boeri, Bosco Verticale, Milan, Italy, 2007–14

right, bottom

12.32   Stefano Boeri, Shenzhen Rehabilitation Center, Shenzhen, China, 2020–

heat, with louvres on the interior to reduce direct sun exposure. The roof also allows natural daylight in, stocking energy through photovoltaic cells that cover it. Rainwater is collected and drained to a purification system and reused.

A different approach towards mitigating the effects of climate change and reducing the consequences of carbon emissions was taken by the Italian architect Stefano Boeri, with a series of proposals for a Green Architecture. The first example of his 'vertical forest' is the two towers designed for Milan, the Bosco Verticale (2007–14) (fig.12.31), part of a larger urban renewal. These vertical forests feature more than 500 trees and 15,000 plants and shrubs that grow on the surfaces or the slabs of the towers, replacing the traditional cladding with a veneer of vegetation designed to promote biodiversity. The diversity of plants and shrubs creates a microclimate that absorbs carbon dioxide, produces oxygen, and protects against pollution. While traditional suburban development also favours the distribution of buildings within a natural environment, the vertical forest concept implements an anti-sprawl strategy that reduces expansion and favours densification and a better use of resources. Boeri's approach won him several projects, from Italy to Albania to China, the latest being a project for a Rehabilitation Center in Shenzhen (2020–) (fig.12.32). The 'ziggurat' type of development features green areas on the different roof levels, which transform these spaces into therapeutic gardens for the patients.

On the margins of these architectural practices, new tendencies emerged that have called for a revival of the social dimension of architecture. The Chilean architect Alejandro Aravena, who won the Pritzker Prize in 2016, was rewarded largely for his socially-minded projects such as the master plan for Constitución, a district that was devastated by an earthquake in 2010. In that context, Aravena initiated a participatory process in which the population would be solicited about major planning measures, such as the development of a forestation plan to counter future tsunami threats. Villa Verde, a large housing settlement, also in Constitución, was part of the master plan to reconstruct the city and comprised a series of identical half-storey houses with the typical pitched roof profile. The houses were designed with a low-budget, appearing incomplete, with the prospect of allowing the owners, mostly middle to lower-middle classes, to complete the other half of the house at a later time. The half-house is equipped with basic utilities, electro-mechanical equipment, and plumbing, allowing the families to move in at a minimal cost. This approach provided a feasible way for the population to be housed within a short timeframe, as well as the opportunity to leave their personal imprint on the remaining section of the house.

The same format was applied to another project in Mexico, Elemental Monterrey (2008–10) (fig.12.33), which consisted of 70 houses, built

12.33 Alejandro Aravena – ELEMENTAL, Elemental Monterrey, Nuevo Leon, Mexico, 2008–10

within an open frame that would allow for future expansion. The housing project was arranged on a rectangular plot, around an internal courtyard. Yet unlike Villa Verde, the houses here were covered by a flat horizontal roof, connecting the whole ensemble. Somewhat reminiscent of Siza's Bouça Housing Complex of the 1970s, each house is accessed through an external stairway that leads to the first level open loggia. These open loggias would be closed, eventually, by extensions built by the individual owners, each given its distinctive colour and material that would contrast with the overall white scheme of the complex. Aravena also designed projects that built on the legacy of Modernism in Latin America, taking it to another dimension. One example is his Centro Tecnologico at the Catholic University in Santiago, Chile (2003–6), where the architect turned a regular commission for a computer centre into a remarkable structure that responds to climatic conditions by twisting the regular curtain wall into a slightly angled facade, as well as creating a double layer to reduce the greenhouse effect, all within a very tight budget. A single glass skin covers the whole facade, separated from a fibre-cement internal wall by a ventilation space. In addition to this geometric play on the facade, which breaks it into a cubical formation at the top, the interior features a variety of spaces with different treatments and colours, expressing a certain dynamism resulting from 'chance encounters' that counters the image associated with such spaces.

In a similar vein to Aravena, a number of architects – working mostly as members of collectives – attempted to address the social conditions in other parts of the world, as in Niger, where the Article 25 practice has been working to design small schools for children of all ages. Their project for Niamey Urban Community (2022) is exemplary in its prioritisation of local crafts and materials, reviving the vernacular traditions of building while supplementing them with innovative systems to create a passive design system that attenuates the high temperatures. The structures are composed of repetitive modular units of walls and barrel vaults, built of local Laterite stone, and covered by a secondary metal roof, inspired by the work of Francis Kéré, which allows for air circulation and for a double layer of insulation.

CONCLUSION

It is evident from this survey that modern architecture did not die in 1973, as Charles Jencks proclaimed. The impetus that was given to it by the contestations from within and without the discipline led to a variety of transformations, ushering in new paradigms in its continuing evolution. And while the efforts of some architects to single out one major paradigm as the way of the future remains a highly contested proposition, the possibility for a hybrid architecture that synthesises between technological innovation, environmental sustainability, and cultural/contextual appropriateness may be the most likely projection for an architecture of the future.

It transpires from what has preceded that there were several directions or themes under which each project could be analysed or categorised, and that these specific tendencies were not necessarily exclusive, with many architects operating across different paradigms, depending on the context and the specific requirements of the project in question. With the exception of some architects who were committed to a particular direction, many have moved across the lines from Post-Modernism, to Minimalism, or to Hyper-Modernism. This has led some critics to contest the notion of categorisation as a legitimate means to analyse contemporary architecture.

It is also clear from this survey that the majority of built works that continue to receive greater attention are still those that are built in the main centres of what were geographical locations of industrial development, that is, Europe and the United States, in addition to Japan. Yet new areas of architectural activity have also surfaced in China and South Korea, as well as in Africa and the Arabian Gulf, and the emerging republics of the former Soviet Union, all of which have benefitted from globalisation and have attempted to employ architecture – perhaps much like the countries of the developing world in the 1950s – as an emblem of their newly gained economic and political clout. In the process, the 'star architect' phenomenon was born to accompany this surge in interest in signature styles that bestow instant iconic status and world-recognition to various cities around the globe.

On another note, the recent momentum to address the question of diversity in architecture has prompted architectural reviews, conferences, and professional prizes to pay long overdue attention to the architectural production of figures that were historically considered on the margins of the profession, namely women architects and minorities. This increasing exposure is certain to bear fruit, potentially prompting a different approach to architectural practice that will engage political, social, and environmental challenges in an equitable and sustainable way, in which architects would be called upon to play once again a critical role.

Notes

PREFACE

1   Manfredo Tafuri, 'Introduction: The Historical Project', in *The Sphere and the Labyrinth*, MIT Press, Cambridge, MA, 1990.
2   In this volume, I use the term 'Modernism' to denote, specifically, modern architecture, not Modernism in general.

1   MODERNISM AND ITS DISCONTENTS

1   Bruno Zevi, *Towards an Organic Architecture*, Faber & Faber, London, 1949.
2   Zevi, *Organic Architecture*, pp 66–76.
3   Frank Lloyd Wright, 'Lecture to British Architects' [1939], in Zevi, p.66.
4   Zevi, *Organic Architecture*, p.72.
5   According to Zevi, even a master such as Wright could sometimes fall prey to this tendency, as in the case of the S.C. Johnson Building where columns appear like trees; see Zevi, p.73.
6   Zevi, *Organic Architecture*, p.75.
7   Zevi, *Organic Architecture*, pp 75–6.
8   Bruno Zevi, *The Modern Language of Architecture*, University of Washington Press, Washington DC, 1978. The original Italian version appeared in 1973 as *Il linguaggio moderno dell'architettura*.
9   Zevi, *Modern Language*, pp 71–3.
10   Zevi, *Modern Language*, pp 55–63.
11   Zevi, *Modern Language*, p.67.
12   For more on van Eyck's role, see Francis Strauven, *Aldo van Eyck: The Shape of Relativity*, Architectura & Natura, Amsterdam, 1998, Chapters 6 and 8.
13   Van Eyck completed a lengthy manuscript, c.300 pages, which elaborates on some of his ideas on architecture: *The Child, the City and the Artist – An Essay on Architecture – The Inbetween Realm*. Yet this work, completed around 1962, was not published in his lifetime.
14   Van Eyck and his Team X colleagues were involved in this periodical from 1959 until 1963.
15   The article appeared in Dutch as 'het verhaal van een andere gedachte', *Forum*, no.7, Special Issue (1959). For a discussion of this article, see Strauven, *Aldo van Eyck*, pp 339–406.
16   Strauven, p.345.
17   Aldo van Eyck, 'Kaleidoscope of the Mind', *VIA*, University of Pennsylvania (1968), p.94.
18   'Kaleidoscope of the Mind', p.95.
19   Amos Rapoport, *House, Form and Culture*, Foundations of Cultural Geography, Prentice Hall, Englewood Cliffs, NJ, 1969.
20   Bernard Rudofsky, *Architecture without Architects*, MoMA, New York, 1965. Aldo van Eyck published his first article on the 'Architecture of the Dogon', in *Architectural Forum* (September 1961), pp 116–21 and p.186. This was followed by an article on 'The Pueblos', in *Forum*, no.3 (August 1962), pp 95–114, and again in *Ekistics*, vol.15, no.89 (April 1963), pp 240–41. 'A Miracle of Moderation' was later published in conjunction with two articles by Paul Parin and Fritz Morgenthaler on the Dogon culture in *VIA*, University of Pennsylvania (1968), pp 96–132; and re-published in Charles Jencks and George Baird (eds), *Meaning in Architecture*, George Braziller, New York, 1970, pp 170–213.
21   Paul Parin and Fritz Morgenthaler published their study in a joint work, with Goldy Patin-Mattey: *Die Weissen denken zuviel: psychoanalytische untersuchungen bei den Dogon in Westafrika*, Atlantis, Zurich, 1963. Another work by the same authors was published in English as *Fear thy Neighbor as Thyself: Psychoanalysis and Society among the Anyi of West Africa*, University of Chicago Press, Chicago, 1980.
22   Joseph Rykwert, 'The Idea of a Town', *Forum*, no.3 (1963), pp 99–148. The same essay was published again by Drukkerij & Uitgeverij, Hilversum, c.1965; and in its final edition by Faber & Faber, London, 1976.
23   For a detailed discussion of this work, see Chapter 9 in Strauven, pp 407–23.
24   Aldo van Eyck, 'The Image of Ourselves', *VIA* (1968), pp 125–31.

25 Van Eyck actually borrowed this notion from the Swiss architects Rolf Gutmann and Theo Manz, who expressed it in the CIAM 9 papers, 1952. The Swiss architects based it on Martin Buber's notion of 'Gestalt gewordene Zwischen' in *Urdistanz und Beziehung*.

26 '[. . .] night and day – the short cycle – points to another cycle – the long one – for every 24 hours the sun dies and is born again. I mean childhood and old age. Socially, emotionally, and economically – hence also in architecture and planning – this cycle is as pitifully misrepresented as the other natural cycles are. It embraces the meaning of many twin phenomena – beginning and end; movement and rest; change and constancy; transience and immutability; life and death.' 'The Image of Ourselves', p.127.

27 'The Image of Ourselves', p.127.

28 It is interesting to note here the distinction between van Eyck's and Alexander's observations on the city. Alexander, who attended as a guest the Team X meeting at Royaumont in 1964, later published his article 'A City Is Not a Tree' partly in response to van Eyck's discussion of the analogies between leaf-tree and house-city. For more on this, see van Eyck in 'The Image of Ourselves', *VIA* (1968), fn 8, p.130.

29 See Liane Lefaivre and Alexander Tzonis, *Aldo van Eyck: Humanist Rebel*, NAI, Rotterdam, 1999; and Strauven, *Aldo van Eyck: The Shape of Relativity*.

30 For a detailed discussion of this project, see Strauven, pp 284–325. At the CIAM congress in Otterlo, in 1959, van Eyck discussed the three traditions, giving as an example of the first, the Temple of Nike on the Acropolis; of the second, Van Doesburg's contra-constructions of 1923; and of the third, photos of the village of Aoulef in the Algerian Sahara; see Strauven, p.350. In another article, van Eyck gave a variation on this, with the Greek Temple as illustrating the first, a drawing by van Doesburg for the second, and an Indian Pueblo for the third; see *VIA*, no.1 (1968), p.95.

31 Jencks and Baird, *Meaning in Architecture*. The first section of this book contained five seminal essays by Charles Jencks, Françoise Choay, Gillo Dorfles, and Geoffrey Broadbent, while the second and third parts contained a number of essays by George Baird, Aldo van Eyck, Kenneth Frampton, Joseph Rykwert, and others. This collection stands as an interesting work of reference on this topic, which included indirectly related essays, such as the analysis of the Dogon villages in Africa.

32 Charles Jencks, 'The Architectural Sign', in Geoffrey Broadbent, Richard Bunt and Charles Jencks (eds), *Signs, Symbols and Architecture*, Wiley, New York, 1980, pp 71–118.

33 Jencks, 'The Architectural Sign', pp 83–4.

34 Geoffrey Broadbent, 'Meaning into Architecture', in Jencks and Baird, p.55.

35 Broadbent, 'Meaning into Architecture', p.56.

36 Broadbent, p.72.

37 Broadbent, p.73.

38 Christian Norberg-Schulz, *Genius Loci: Towards a Phenomenology of Architecture*. The book was first published in Italian as *Genius Loci – paesaggio, ambiente, architettura* by Electa in 1979. It is interesting to note here that the Italian subtitle differs from the one chosen for the English edition and does not include the reference to Phenomenology.

39 Martin Heidegger, *Poetry, Language, Thought*, Harper & Row, New York, 1971.

40 Heidegger, *Poetry, Language, Thought*, p.110. Two drawings were used to illustrate the 'figural quality': the first, a drawing by Louis Kahn, the second, by Michael Graves, titled 'On the way to figurative architecture', pp 132, 134.

41 Heidegger, p.135.

42 Alexander's *The Timeless Way of Building* (1979), *A Pattern Language* (1977), and *The Oregon Experiment* (1975) were all published by Oxford University Press.

43 Stephen Grabow, *Christopher Alexander: The Search for a New Paradigm in Architecture*, Oriel Press, Stocksfield, 1983.

44 Grabow, *Search for a New Paradigm*, p.45.

45 D'Arcy Wentworth Thompson, *On Growth and Form*, Cambridge University Press, Cambridge, 1917.

46 See Grabow, Chapter XVI, 'Construction', pp 161–73.

47 This debate took place at Harvard University on 17 November 1982. First published in *Lotus International*, no.40 (1983), pp 60–68. Reposted at http://www.katarxis3.com/Alexander_Eisenman_Debate.htm.

2 THE ARCHITECTURE OF *BÉTON BRUT*

1 Reyner Banham, 'The New Brutalism', *The Architectural Review* (December 1955), pp 354–61.

2 'An Interview with Marcel Breuer', *Connection – Visual Arts at Harvard* (Fall 1966). Quoted in Isabelle Hyman, *Marcel Breuer Architect: The Career and the Buildings*, Harry Abrams, New York, 2001, p.150.
3 Hyman, *Marcel Breuer Architect*, p.227.
4 Robert McCarter, *Louis I. Kahn*, Phaidon, London, 2005, p.172.
5 McCarter, *Kahn*, p.276.
6 Tom Wilkinson, 'Diego Portales University in Chile by Rafael Hevia, Rodrigo Duque Motta and Gabriela Manzi', *The Architectural Review* (6 October 2015).
7 Grafton Architects, 'Space for Time', *Irish Review*, no.51 (Winter 2015), pp 23–7.

3 NEO-RATIONALISM

1 See Cristiana Mazzoni, *La Tendenza: Une avant-garde architecturale italienne, 1950–1980*, Editions Parenthèses, Marseille, 2013, pp 53–9.
2 Aldo Rossi, *The Architecture of the City*, MIT Books, Cambridge, MA, 1982, p.23.
3 Rossi wrote the preface to Benedetto Gravagnuolo's *Adolf Loos: Theory and Works*, Idea Books, New York, 1982.
4 Daniel Libeskind, '"Deus ex Machina"/"Machina ex Deo": Aldo Rossi's Theater of the World', *Oppositions*, no.21 (Summer 1980), pp 3–23.
5 Alberto Ferlenga (ed.), *Aldo Rossi: The Life and Works of an Architect*, Könemann, Cologne, 2001, pp 270–71.
6 Ignasi de Solà-Morales, 'Critical Discipline' (review of Giorgio Grassi's *La arquitectura como oficio*, 1980), reprinted in *Oppositions Reader: Selected Readings from a Journal for Ideas and Criticism, 1973–1984*, Princeton Architectural Press, Princeton, NJ, 1998.
7 Solà-Morales, 'Critical Discipline', p.665.
8 Solà-Morales, p.669.
9 See Luciano Semerani, 'Introduction', *The School of Venice*, Architectural Design, vol.55, no.5/6, London (1985).
10 Gregotti's *Il Territorio dell'architettura*, 1962, was never translated into English. A short essay by Gregotti on the Territory was included in the *Architectural Design* volume, *The School of Venice*.
11 See Lejla Vujicic's analysis of Gregotti in 'Architecture of the Longue Durée: Vittorio Gregotti's Reading of the Territory of Architecture', *Architectural Research Quarterly*, vol.19, no.2 (2015), pp 161–74.
12 Vittorio Gregotti, 'Territory and Architecture', *The School of Venice*, Architectural Design, vol.55, no.5/6, London (1985), pp 28–34.
13 Gregotti, 'Territory and Architecture', pp 28–34.
14 Gregotti, pp 28–34.
15 Rob Krier, *Urban Space*, Rizzoli, New York, 1979.
16 David Chipperfield, 'Composition', in Rik Nys (ed.), *Form Matters*, exh.cat., Walther König Verlag, Cologne, 2009, pp 73 and 102.
17 Adrian von Buttlar, 'Greek Analogies: On the Historical Semantics of the James-Simon-Galerie', in *James-Simon-Galerie Berlin*, Walther König Verlag, Cologne, 2019, pp 43–59.

4 POST-MODERN ARCHITECTURE

1 The term 'Post-Modernism' was first coined by Charles Jencks in an article for the AA Files in 1975. See Murray Fraser and Joe Kerr, *Architecture and the 'Special Relationship': The American Influence on Post-War British Architecture*, Routledge, London, 2007, p.388. The term actually originated in literary studies in the United States during the 1950s and 1960s: see Jürgen Habermas, 'Post-Modern Architecture', *9H*, no.4 (1982). For a comprehensive analysis of Jencks' writings on this topic, see my article, 'Charles Jencks and the Historiography of Post-Modernism', *The Journal of Architecture*, vol.14, no.4 (2009), pp 493–510.
2 Jean-François Lyotard, *La Condition postmoderne: Rapport sur le savoir* [The Postmodern Condition: A Report on Knowledge], Minuit, Paris, 1979. Lyotard chose the term 'Post-Modern' as he found it in currency in North America as, for instance, in the writings of Daniel Bell, *The Coming of Post-Industrial Society*, 1973; Ihab Hassan's *The Dismemberment of Orpheus: Towards a Postmodern Literature*, 1971; and Michel Benamou and Charles Caramello's *Performance in Postmodern Culture*, 1977, among others.
3 Lyotard, *La Condition postmoderne*, Chapters 6 and 7.
4 Lyotard, Chapter 14.
5 In architecture, the term 'Post-Modernism' was first used by Charles Jencks in the title of his

book, *The Language of Post-Modern Architecture*, Academy Editions, London, 1977. Jencks was rather 'pluralistic' in his interpretation of Post-Modernism, and his definition of the nascent movement took on several variations. Yet the label of Post-Modernism in architecture stuck mainly to a particular 'style', the Neo-Classical. This is due in great part to Jencks himself, as well as to others who promoted the Neo-Classical style as being the Post-Modern style par excellence, among them Paolo Portoghesi (b.1931) and Andreas Papadakis (1938–2008). The latter played an important role as the editor of the influential periodical *Architectural Design*, which devoted no less than 24 issues to Neo-Classical architecture and related themes during the 1980s alone.

6   Charles Jencks, *The Language of Post-Modern Architecture*, 6th edn, 1991, p.108. For a description of Piazza d'Italia, see also pp 116–18.

7   Jencks, *The Language of Post-Modern Architecture*, 1991, p.142.

8   Paolo Portoghesi, *Postmodern: The Architecture of the Postindustrial Society*, Rizzoli, New York, 1983.

9   Francesco dal Co, 'The Architecture of Carlo Scarpa', in *Carlo Scarpa: The Complete Works*, Electa/Rizzoli, New York, 1985, p.34.

10   Manfredo Tafuri, 'Carlo Scarpa and Italian Architecture', in *Carlo Scarpa: The Complete Works*, pp 72–95.

11   See Stanislaus Von Moos, 'Introduction', in *Venturi, Rauch & Scott Braun: Buildings and Projects*, Rizzoli, New York, 1987, pp 24–7.

12   James Stirling, 'Ronchamp: Le Corbusier's Chapel and the Crisis of Rationalism', *The Architectural Review*, vol.191 (1992), pp 62–7.

13   See, for instance, Anthony Vidler's 'Introduction', in *James Frazer Stirling: Notes from the Archives*, Yale Center for British Art and the Canadian Centre for Architecture in association with Yale University Press, New Haven, CT, 2010, pp 23–7.

14   Anthony Vidler, 'Losing Face: Notes on the Modern Museum', *Assemblage*, no.9 (June 1989), pp 40–57.

15   A version of this chapter had appeared in *Postmodernism on Trial*, Academy Editions, London, 1990, a special issue of *Architectural Design*. This issue also signalled the end of the movement, with another essay by David Harvey titled 'Looking Backwards on Postmodernism', pp 10–12.

5   REGIONAL MODERNISMS

1   There was much debate regarding the proper terminology to use in characterising this trend in modern architecture. For more on this, see Macarena de la Vega's 'Revisiting Quotations: Regionalism in Historiography', Paper presented at SAHANZ Conference, Australia, November 2017.

2   Alexander Tzonis and Liane Lefaivre, *Critical Regionalism: Architecture and Identity in a Globalized World*, Prestel, Munich, 2003.

3   Kenneth Frampton, 'Towards a Critical Regionalism', in Hal Foster (ed.), *The Anti-Aesthetic: Essays on Postmodern Culture*, Bay Press, Seattle, WA, 1983, pp 16–30.

4   Alan Colquhoun was one of the first to critically adress 'critical regionalism', retracing its historical roots to the 18th century and the development of Romanticism. One of the byproducts of this was the various oppositions articulated as society/community and civilisation/culture, which reappear in the current discourse as an opposition of the universal/local, or industrial/local. See Alan Colquhoun, 'The Concept of Regionalism', in Gülsum Baydar Nalbantoglu and Wong Chong Thai (eds), *Postcolonial Spaces*, Princeton Architectural Press, Princeton, NJ, 1997, p.17.

5   Another critical account of the concept of 'critical regionalism' and its specific application to the work of Luis Barragán was given by Keith Eggener; see his 'Placing Resistance: A Critique of Critical Regionalism', *Journal of Architectural Education*, vol.55, no.4 (May 2002), pp 228–37.

6   Rafael Moneo, 'Museum for Roman Artifacts, Merida, Spain', *Assemblage*, no.1 (1986), pp 72–83.

7   Juan Navarro Baldeweg, 'A Resonance Chamber', in *Juan Navarro Baldeweg*, Gingko Press, Corte Madera, CA, 2001, p.12.

8   See Geoffrey Baker, 'Antoine Predock and the Search for an Authentic Architecture', in *Architectural Monographs*, no.49, Wiley-Academy, Chichester, 1997, pp 8–15.

9   Antonio Toca Fernández, 'The Work of Luis Barragán: Looking and Seeing', in *Barragan: The Complete Works*, Princeton Architectural Press, Princeton, NJ, 1996, pp 13–19.

10   Francis Kéré, in discussion with James Morris, 'Building on Architectural Traditions of the Sahel', 15 July 2020, https://www.metmuseum.org/blogs/now-at-the-met/2020/francis-kere-james-morris-sahel-architecture.

6 THE TECHNOLOGICAL PARADIGM

1   On Banham's theory, see Nigel Whiteley, *Reyner Banham: Historian of the Immediate Future*, MIT Press, Cambridge, MA, 2002.

2   Reyner Banham, *Theory and Design in the First Machine Age*, The Architectural Press, London, 1960 (repr. MIT Press, 1992), p.328.

3   Whiteley, *Reyner Banham*, Chapter 3.

4   The fascinating story of the development of the Centre Pompidou can be traced in two publications: Nathan Silver, *The Making of Beaubourg: A Building Biography of the Centre Pompidou*, MIT Press, Cambridge, MA, 1994, and the more recent *Centre Pompidou: Renzo Piano, Richard Rogers and the Making of a Modern Monument* by Francesco dal Co, Yale University Press, New Haven, CT, 2016.

5   Renzo Piano, *Logbook*, The Monacelli Press, New York, 1997, p.40.

6   https://www.jeannouvel.com/en/projects/fondation-cartier-2/.

7   For a detailed review of the Sainsbury Centre, see Angus Macdonald, *High Tech Architecture: A Style Reconsidered*, The Crowood Press, Marlborough, 2019, pp 91–105.

8   Macdonald, *High Tech Architecture*, p.154.

7 THE CONTINUING LEGACY OF MODERNISM

1   From John Summerson in 1943, who described Niemeyer's work as a new 'kind of Baroque', to Nikolaus Pevsner in 1961, who saw in his work a 'revolt against rationalism', associating him with Jørn Utzon and Hans Scharoun as part of a 'new post-modern anti-rationalism'. For a comprehensive study of Niemeyer, see Styliane Philippou, *Oscar Niemeyer: Curves of Irreverence*, Yale University Press, New Haven, CT, 2008. Specifically, her introduction: 'Much more than parrots and banana trees', pp 8–17.

2   See Vittorio Magnago Lampugnani, 'Richard Meier, European Architect', in Alessandro Gubitosi and Ferruccio Izzo (eds), *Richard Meier: Architecture/Projects 1986–1990*, Centro Di, Florence, 1991.

3   Quoted in Philip Jodidio, *Richard Meier*, Taschen, Cologne, 1995, pp 156–8.

4   For a critique of the Getty project, see Murray Fraser and Joe Kerr, 'Beyond the Empire of Signs', in Iain Borden and Jane Rendell (eds), *InterSections: Architectural Histories and Critical Theories*, Routledge, London, 2000, pp 125–49.

5   Colin Rowe, 'Mannerism and Modern Architecture', reprinted in *The Mathematics of the Ideal Villa and Other Essays*, MIT Press, Cambridge, MA, 1976, pp 29–58.

6   See Peter Testa, 'The Architecture of Alvaro Siza', unpublished dissertation, Massachusetts Institute of Technology, 1984, pp 29–30. Testa observes: 'This complex construction goes beyond the perspectival distortions of the Roman Baroque examples and the circumscribed experiments in simultaneous vision of Picasso's pre-1940 works. While the means employed are different, the relational structures developed in the Siza house would appear to lie closer to Picassos's [sic] later works which, as Leo Steinberg has convincingly argued, include a systematic exploration of the spatial environment. The "contractile, expansive, collapsible space" of these works is not unlike the spatial matrix of Siza's construction in which multiple viewpoints and perspectives are combined with a multiplicity of forms.'

7   Rafael Moneo, *Theoretical Anxiety and Design Strategies in the Work of Eight Contemporary Architects*, MIT Press, Cambridge, MA, 2004, pp 200–251.

8   For a detailed discussion of this competition, see Pierluigi Nicolin, 'Minimal Architecture and Aesthetic Shock', *Lotus International*, no.70, Electa, Milan (October 1991), pp 52–69.

9   Hans Ibelings, *20th Century Architecture in the Netherlands*, NAI, Rotterdam, 1995.

8 THE PROJECT OF DECONSTRUCTION

1   Christopher Norris and Andrew Benjamin (eds), *What is Deconstruction?* Academy Editions, London, 1988.

2   Norris and Benjamin, *What is Deconstruction?*, p.40.

3   Mark Wigley was also the author of *Derrida's Haunt: The Architecture of Deconstruction*, MIT Press, Cambridge, MA, 1993, a work that addressed the Derridean discourse without explicitly attempting to connect it to any architectural 'projects'.

4   Jonathan Culler, 'Jacques Derrida', in John Sturrock (ed.), *Structuralism and Since: From Lévi-Strauss to Derrida*, Oxford University Press, Oxford, 1979, p.172.

NOTES

5   Jacques Derrida, *Of Grammatology*, trans. Gayatri C. Spivak, Johns Hopkins University Press, Baltimore, MD, 1976.

6   In this respect, Derrida defined the notion of an 'architecture of architecture': 'Let us not forget that there is an architecture of architecture. [. . .] This naturalized architecture is bequeathed to us: we inhabit it, it inhabits us, we think it is destined for habitation, and it is no longer an object for us at all. But we must recognize in it an *artefact,* a *construction*, a monument. It did not fall from the sky; it is not natural, even if it informs a specific scheme of relations to *physis*, the sky, the earth, the human, and the divine. This architecture of architecture has a history; it is historical through and through. Its heritage inaugurates the intimacy of our economy, the law of our hearth (oikos), our familial, religious and political "oikonomy", all the places of birth and death, temple, school, stadium, agora, square, sepulchre.' In Jacques Derrida, 'Point de Folie – Maintenant L'Architecture. Bernard Tschumi: La Case Vide – La Villette, 1985', *AA Files*, vol.12 (Summer 1986), p.65.

7   Derrida, 'Point de Folie – Maintenant L'Architecture', p.69.

8   Peter Eisenman, 'Cardboard Architecture: House I and House II', in Arthur Drexler (ed.), *Five Architects*, Oxford University Press, Oxford, 1972, pp 15–24.

9   Peter Eisenman, 'Aspects of Modernism: Maison Dom-ino and the Self-Referential Sign', *Oppositions*, vol.15/16 (1980), pp 119–28.

10   Peter Eisenman, 'The Futility of Objects: Decomposition and the Processes of Differentiation', *Harvard Architectural Review*, vol.3 (Winter 1984), pp 65–82.

11   Peter Eisenman, 'The Representations of Doubt: At the Sign of the Sign', *Rassegna*, vol.9 (March 1982); reprinted in *Eisenman Inside Out: Selected Writings 1963–1988*, Yale University Press, New Haven, CT, 2004, pp 143–51.

12   Peter Eisenman, 'The End of the Classical, the End of the Beginning, the End of the End', *Perspecta*, vol.21 (1984), pp 154–72; reprinted in *Eisenman Inside Out*, pp 152–68.

13   Peter Eisenman, *Fin d'Ou T Hou S*, Architectural Association, London, 1985.

14   Jeffrey Kipnis discussed the play on words in this title, which could alternately signify 'find out house', 'fine doubt house', or even the French 'fin d'Aout', among other things. See Kipnis, 'Architecture Unbound', in *Fin d'Ou T Hou S*, pp 12–23.

15   Peter Eisenman, *Moving Arrows, Eros and Other Errors: An Architecture of Absence*, Architectural Association, London, 1986.

16   Derrida titled his chapter 'The End of the Book and the Beginning of Writing'.

17   See Franco Rella, 'Tempo della fine e tempo dell' inizio' [The Age of the End and the Age of the Beginning], *Casabella*, no.498/9 (January/February 1984), pp 106–8; and Jeffrey Kipnis, 'Eisenman/Robertson: Trasposizione di maglie urbane: un progetto per la Ohio State University', *Casabella*, no.498/9 (January/February 1984), pp 96–9.

18   Peter Eisenman, 'Misreading', in *Houses of Cards*, Oxford University Press, Oxford, 1987, p.167.

19   The term used by Eisenman at that time was 'decomposition'. Later, 'deconstruction' would supplement 'decomposition' in some of the discussions of his work.

20   Jeffrey Kipnis commented that this particular project came at a time when Eisenman's pursuit of the 'elusive' goal of structuralism was faced with doubts, and as he started his readings of Derrida. See Kipnis in *Fin d'Ou T Hou S*, pp 15–21.

21   Jean-François Bedard (ed.), *Cities of Artificial Excavation: The Work of Peter Eisenman, 1978–88*, Canadian Centre for Architecture, Montreal, 1994 and covered projects that date from 1978 to 1988. Incidentally, the Wexner Center for the Arts, which is a major work in this group (completed in 1989), was not included in this collection.

22   Jean-François Bedard, 'Introduction', in Bedard, *Cities of Artificial Excavation*.

23   See, for instance, Dianne Ghirardo's critique of Eisenman's project in 'Two Institutions for the Arts', in Ghirardo, *Out of Site: A Social Criticism of Architecture*, Bay Press, Seattle, WA, 1991. Ghirardo commented: 'Here, the site's *real* political history is repressed in favor of a decorative shell, perhaps the most compelling and powerful feature of the whole project. With its delicate craftsmanship and playful slices of tower, arch, and wall, in its Disneylandish caricature of the earlier structure, it effectively realizes the gloomy prognosis of Walter Benjamin about the aestheticization of politics. The fetishized structures are wittingly emptied of their history and rendered nothing more than cheerfully manipulable images that direct attention only to formal games.'

24 The previous works of Eisenman had exhibited equally word-playful titles. See above.

25 Jeffrey Kipnis and Thomas Leeser (eds), *Chora L Works: Jacques Derrida and Peter Eisenman*, The Monacelli Press, New York, 1997.

26 Derrida, in Kipnis and Leeser, *Chora L Works*, p.8.

27 From 17 September 1985 to 27 October 1987.

28 Jacques Derrida, 'Letter to Peter Eisenman [October 1989]', in Kipnis and Leeser, pp 161–5.

29 For more on these projects, see Andrew Benjamin (ed.), *Blurred Zones: Investigations of the Interstitial: Eisenman Architects, 1988–1998*, The Monacelli Press, New York, 2002.

30 For an analysis of Bernard Tschumi's theoretical project, see Louis Martin, 'Transpositions: On the Intellectual Origins of Tschumi's Architectural Theory', *Assemblage*, vol.11 (April 1990), pp 22–35.

31 Jacques Derrida, 'Point de Folie – Maintenant L'Architecture', pp 65–75.

32 Bernard Tschumi, 'Parc de la Villette, Paris', in *Deconstruction in Architecture: Architectural Design*, Academy Editions, London, 1988, pp 32–9.

33 Tschumi, 'Parc de la Villette, Paris', p.39.

34 Jacques Derrida, 'Letter to Peter Eisenman', in *Assemblage*, vol.12 (August 1990), pp 6–13.

35 In 'Between the Lines: Extension to the Berlin Museum', *Assemblage*, vol.12 (August 1990), pp 52–7.

36 The V&A competition was won by Libeskind, but in the face of mounting opposition and lack of funding support, the project was aborted. For more on this, see Charlotte Benton, '"An Insult to Everything the Museum Stands For" or "Ariadne's Thread" to "Knowledge" and "Inspiration"? Daniel Libeskind's Extension for the V&A and Its Context', *Journal of Design History*, vol.10, no.1 (1997), pp 71–91.

37 Mark Wigley, 'Deconstructivist Architecture', in Philip Johnson and Mark Wigley (eds), *Deconstructivist Architecture*, MoMA, New York, 1988, pp 16–17.

38 Mark Wigley, 'Deconstructivist Architecture', in Andreas Papadakis, Catherine Cooke, and Andrew Benjamin (eds), *Deconstruction*, Rizzoli, New York, 1989, p.133.

39 Mark Wigley, 'The Translation of Architecture: The Tower of Babel', in Andreas Papadakis (ed.), *Deconstruction III*, Academy Editions, London, 1990, p.12.

9 NEO-CONSTRUCTIVISM, NEO-SUPREMATISM AND THE RETURN OF THE AVANT-GARDE

1 Catherine Cooke, 'The Lessons of the Russian Avant-Garde', in Andreas Papadakis (ed.), *Deconstruction in Architecture*, *Architectural Design*, Academy Editions, London, 1988, pp 13–15.

2 See Roberto Gargiani, *Rem Koolhaas: OMA, The Construction of Merveilles*, Essays in Architecture, EPFL Press/Routledge, London, 2008, p.4.

3 Gargiani, *Rem Koolhaas*, p.7.

4 Gargiani, pp 166–7.

5 Gargiani gives another perceptive description of this work: 'The Grand Palais, like the Amsterdam Bourse, is an intentionally unalluring work in which the choice of materials and their arrangement continues to be driven, as in the works of Berlage, by a symbolic thrust, though no longer based on the principles of Viollet-le-Duc and Semper, but on the surrealist paranoid-critical method. In the amorphous urban landscape of rail lines, roads and highways, the Grand Palais seems to have landed by chance on the ground; it resembles no architecture or sculpture, precisely like a *merveille*; if anything, it gives the impression of being able to slowly move, from one moment to the next, like a tortoise or a giant mechanical contraption of Archigram.' Gargiani, p.182.

6 See Harry Francis Mallgrave and David Goodman, 'Pragmatism and Post-Criticality', in *An Introduction to Architectural Theory: 1968 to the Present*, Wiley-Blackwell, Chichester, 2011, pp 177–93.

7 Bart Lootsma, *SuperDutch: Architecture in the Netherlands*, Thames & Hudson, London, 2000, p.17.

8 Zaha Hadid, 'Recent Work', in Peter Noever and Regina Haslinger (eds), *Architecture in Transition: Between Deconstruction and New Modernism*, Prestel, Munich, 1991, pp 47–61.

9 Cooke, 'The Lessons of the Russian Avant-Garde', p.14.

10 Hadid, 'Recent Work', pp 48–9.

11 See the Landesgartenschau in Weil am Rhein, or the BMW Plant in Leipzig, completed in 2005.

12 See Catherine Cooke, 'The Development of the Constructivist Architect's Design Method', in Papadakis (ed.), *Deconstruction in Architecture*, *Architectural Design*, pp 21–37. Geoffrey Broadbent, in a sceptical essay on this topic, extended the sources of this new trend to include Dada and Cubism, in addition to the more recent work of the Situationists of the

1960s. See Geoffrey Broadbent, 'The Architecture of Deconstruction', in *Deconstruction: A Student Guide*, Academy Editions, London, 1991, pp 10–30.

13   Quoted in Cooke, 'The Development of the Constructivist Architect's Design Method' p.22.

14   Wolf Prix, 'On the Edge', in Andreas Papadakis (ed.), *Deconstruction III: Architectural Design*, Academy Editions, London, 1990, pp 65–70.

15   Quoted in: https://www.frac-centre.fr/_en/art-and-architecture-collection/coop-himmelb-au/open-house-317.html?authID=46&ensembleID=121.

16   See https://designmanifestos.org/coop-himmelblau-architecture-must-blaze/.

17   Anthony Vidler, 'Working the Language', in *Morphosis 1998–2004*, Rizzoli, New York, 2006, pp 32–3.

18   Anthony Vidler, 'The Baroque Effect', in *Eric Owen Moss: Buildings and Projects 2*, Rizzoli, New York, 1996, pp 6–11.

19   Eric Owen Moss, 'Gravity is only Temporary', in *Eric Owen Moss: Buildings and Projects 2*, pp 12–15.

10   NEO-EXPRESSIONISM IN ARCHITECTURE

1   For more on Expressionism in architecture, see Dennis Sharp, *Modern Architecture and Expressionism*, George Braziller, New York, 1966.

2   For a thorough discussion of Expressionism and its legacy, see Rosemarie Haag Bletter, 'Expressionism and the New Objectivity', *Art Journal*, vol.43 (Summer 1983), pp 108–20.

3   Frank Gehry, 'Keynote Address' to the Symposium on 'Postmodernism and Beyond: Architecture as the Critical Art of Contemporary Culture', held at the Beckham Center, California, October 1989. Reprinted in William J. Lillyman, Marilyn F. Moriarty, and David J. Neuman (eds), *Critical Architecture and Contemporary Culture*, Oxford University Press, Oxford, 1994, pp 165–86.

4   Gehry, 'Keynote Address', p.171.

5   Mark Rappolt and Robert Violette, 'Editors' Note', in *Gehry Draws*, MIT Press in association with Violette Editions, Cambridge, MA, 2004, p.7.

6   Catherine Slessor, 'Guggenheim Museum in Bilbao, Spain by Frank O. Gehry and Associates', *The Architectural Review* (12 December 1997).

7   See https://www.archdaily.com/942442/mad-reveals-the-shenzhen-bay-culture-park-masterplan?ad_source=search&ad_medium=search_result_all.

8   See Alexander Tzonis, *Santiago Calatrava: The Complete Works*, Rizzoli, New York, 2007, Chapter 1.

9   See Tzonis, *Santiago Calatrava*, Chapter 3.

10   See https://barozziveiga.com/projects/philharmonic-hall/b:v.

11   See https://www.dezeen.com/2020/09/04/phoenix-central-park-sydney-john-wardle-architects-durback-block-jaggers/?.

11   THE MINIMALIST AESTHETIC

1   Gregory Battcock, 'Preface', *Minimal Art: A Critical Anthology*, E.P. Dutton, New York, 1968.

2   Philip Ursprung, 'Minimalism & Minimal Art', in Ilka and Andreas Ruby, Angeli Sachs, and Philip Ursprung, *Minimal Architecture*, Prestel, Munich, 2003.

3   Maggie Toy, 'Aspects of Minimal Architecture', *Architectural Design*, Chichester, Wiley-Academy, 1994; and Josep Maria Montaner and Vittorio Savi, *Less is More: Minimalism in Architecture and the Other Arts*, Actar, Barcelona, 1996.

4   This was accompanied by the publication of two large monographs: *Mies in Berlin*, and *Mies in America*.

5   See Ilka and Andreas Ruby, 'Essential, Meta-, Trans-. The Chimeras of Minimalist Architecture', in Ruby, Ruby, Sachs, and Ursprung, *Minimal Architecture*.

6   See Kurt Foster, 'Pieces for Four and More Hands', in Philip Ursprung (ed.), *Herzog & de Meuron: Natural History*, Lars Muller Publishers, Zurich, 2002, pp 41–62.

7   See Harry Francis Mallgrave and David Goodman, *An Introduction to Architectural Theory*, Chichester, Wiley/Blackwell, 2011, Chapter 11.

8   See Robert Kudielka, 'Speculative Architecture: On the Aesthetics of Herzog & de Meuron', in Ursprung, *Herzog & de Meuron*, pp 279–88.

9   See, for example, Peter Zumthor, *Thinking Architecture*, Lars Muller Publishers, Zurich, 1998.

10   See 'The Hardcore of Beauty', in Zumthor, *Thinking Architecture*.

11   Mohsen Mostafavi (ed.), *Approximations: The Architecture of Peter Märkli*, MIT Press, Cambridge, MA, 2002, p.113.

12   See Alberto Campo Baeza, 'ESSENTIALITY: More with Less', in *Alberto Campo Baeza: The Built Idea*, Oscar Rieda Ojeda Publishers, Shenzen, 2015.

13   Campo Baeza, 'The Right White', in *The Built Idea*, p.33.

14 Manuel Blanco, 'Constructing the Architecture of Absence with Light', in *Alberto Campo Baeza: Idea, Light and Gravity*, Toto Publishing, Tokyo, 2009.

15 Nieto Sobejano, 'Meta-Architecture', in *Nieto Sobejano: Memory and Invention*, Hatje Cantz, Berlin, 2013, p.23.

16 Nieto Sobejano, *Memory and Invention*, p.26.

17 Alberto Campo Baeza, *Aires Mateus*, *2G* (International Architecture Series), no.28 (January 2004).

18 See Anthony Vidler, 'Diagrams of Diagrams: Architectural Abstraction and Modern Representation', *Representations*, no.72 (Autumn 2000), pp 1–20.

12 NEW DIRECTIONS IN CONTEMPORARY ARCHITECTURE

1 See, for instance, Greg Lynn, 'The Structure of Ornament', *Digital Tectonics* (2004), pp 63–68; Robert Levit, 'Contemporary Ornament: The Return of the Symbolic Repressed', *Harvard Design Magazine*, vol.28 (2008); and Farshid Moussavi and Michael Kubo (eds), *The Function of Ornament*, Actar, Barcelona, 2008.

2 Antoine Picon, in his analysis of this phenomenon in *Ornament: The Politics of Architecture and Subjectivity*, John Wiley, London, 2013, reflects on the age-old debate on the role of ornamentation in architecture, noting that the return of ornament in contemporary architecture is inseparable from the massive diffusion of the computer in the architectural profession, which opened up new perspectives for the development of ornamental forms out of complex textures and patterns. This was accompanied, according to Picon, by a weakening of the 'tectonic' approach in favour of an emphasis on the 'surface' structure, with the building envelope taking on a more important role. See Picon, *Ornament*, Chapter 1.

3 Picon, Chapter 1.

4 See Ben Pell, 'Introduction', in *The Articulate Surface: Ornament and Technology in Contemporary Architecture*, Birkhäuser, Basel, 2010.

5 Neutelings Riedijk Architects, *Ornament and Identity*, Hatje Cantz, Berlin, 2018.

6 The term 'Hyper-Modern' is defined, according to *Webster*, as 'Extremely Modern' and its first use goes back to 1904. According to Wikipedia: 'Hypermodernism is a cultural, artistic, literary and architectural successor to modernism and postmodernism in which the form (attribute) of an object has no context distinct from its function. Attributes can include shapes, colors, ratios, and even time. Unlike postmodernism and modernism, hypermodernism exists in an era of fault-tolerant technological change and treats extraneous attributes (most conspicuously physical form) as discordant with function.' While Hans Ibelings came closest to this concept in his *Supermodernism: Architecture in the Age of Globalization* (NAI, Rotterdam, 1998), the term 'Hyper-Modern' has been rarely used in architectural discourse. In an interview with Paul Virilio, the theorist answers a question posed on this subject by stating: 'As far as "hyper" or "super" modernism is concerned, I think we are not out of modernity yet, by far. I think that modernity will only come to a halt within the ambit of what I call the "integral accident". I believe that technical modernity, modernity taken as the outcome of technical inventions over the past two centuries, can only be stopped by an integral ecological accident, which, in a certain way, I am forecasting. Each and every invention of a technical object has also been the innovation of a particular accident. From the sum total of the technosciences does arise, and will arise a "generalized accident". And this will be modernism's end.' See John Armitage (ed.), *Paul Virilio: From Modernism to Hypermodernism and Beyond*, Sage Publications, London, 2000, p.25.

7 For more on this, see Ingrid Böck, *Six Canonical Projects by Rem Koolhaas*, Jovis, Berlin, 2015, pp 263–76.

8 See Roberto Gargiani, *Rem Koolhaas: OMA, The Construction of Merveilles*. Essays in Architecture, EPFL Press/Routledge, London, 2008, p.286.

9 Bjarke Ingels, *Yes is More: An Archicomic on Architectural Evolution*, Taschen, Cologne, 2009.

10 Ingels, *Yes is More*, pp 14–15.

11 As advertised by its architect, CopenHill is a 'blatant architectural expression of something that would otherwise have remained invisible: that it is the cleanest waste-to-energy power plant in the world. [. . .] As a power plant, CopenHill is so clean that we have been able to turn its building mass into the bedrock of the social life of the city – its facade is climbable, its roof is hikeable and its slopes are skiable. A crystal clear example of hedonistic sustainability – that a sustainable city is not only better for the environment – it is also more enjoyable for the lives of its citizens'; see https://www.dezeen.com/2019/10/08/big-copenhill-power-plant-ski-slope-copenhagen/.

12 See Patrik Schumacher, *The Autopoiesis of Architecture: A New Agenda for Architecture, Vol. II*, Wiley, Hoboken, NJ, 2012, Chapter 11.

13 Richard Rogers, *Cities for a Small Planet*, Faber & Faber, London, 1997.

Index

All numbers in *italics* indicate the presence of illustrations

Aalto, Alvar 10, 65, 87, 88, 93, 141, 145, 152
  Town Hall, Saynatsalo 87, *145*
Adjaye, David 245, 247
  Aïshti Department Store, Beirut 245
  Smithsonian National Museum of African American History and Culture, Washington, DC 245, 247, *245*
Ahrends, Burton and Koralek 67
Aires Mateus, Francisco and Manuel 230–33
  Centro de Artes de Sines, Sines 231
  elderly housing community, Alcacer do Sal 231
  Faculty of Architecture, Tournai 231, *232–3*
  House in Alenquer 230–31
  House in Brejos de Azeitao, Setubal 231
Alexander, Christopher 9, 12, 14–15
  Mexicali Housing project, Mexico 15
  Oregon Experiment, The 14
  pattern language 14–15
  Pattern Language, A 14
  Timeless Way of Building, The 14
Alonso Balaguer Arquitectos Asociados (ABAA) 267
  Nuevas Bodegas Protos winery, Peñafiel (with Rogers, R.) 267, *267*
Amateur Architecture Studio (Shu, W. and Wenyu, L.) see Shu, Wang
Ando, Tadao 32–3, 215–16
  Chapel on the Water, Hokkaido 215, *216*
  Chikatsu-Asuka Historical Museum, Osaka 33
  church on Mount Rokko, Kobe 33
  Izutsu House, Osaka 33
  Koshino House, Ashiya *32*, 33, 215
  Tomishima House, Osaka 33
Andre, Carl 214, 226
Antonakakis, Dimitris and Suzana 87, 89
  Archaeological Museum of Chios 87
  house and atelier, Oxylithos 87
Aravena, Alejandro 268, 270
  Centro Tecnologico, Catholic University, Santiago 270
  Constitución, master plan 268
  Elemental Monterrey, Monterrey 268, 270, *270*
  Villa Verde, Constitución 268
Archigram 114
Archizoom 170
Arets, Wiel 244, 245
  Utrecht University Library *244*, 245
Arolat, Emre 138–9, 141
  Museum Hotel Antakya, Antioch 138, *139*, 141
Article 25 271
  Niamey Urban Community, Niamey 271

Artigas, João Batista Vilanova 30
  School of Architecture and Planning, University of São Paulo 30
Arts and Crafts movement 10, 63
Arup, Ove 115
Asymptote (Rashid, H. and Couture, L-A.) 259, 260–61
  Yas Hotel, Abu Dhabi 259, *260–61*
Atelier Z+ (Wei + Bin) 158
  Sino French Centre, Tonji University, Shanghai 158
Aymonino, Carlo 39, 41
  Gallaratese, Milan *40*, 41, 43

Bader, Bernardo 33, 38
  Klostergasse Studio, Bregenz 38, *38*
Baker, Geoffrey 93
Baldeweg, Juan Navarro 91–3, 146
  Altamira National Museum and Research Centre, Santander 92
  Castilla y Leon Convention Centre and Exhibition Hall, Salamanca 92–3
Banham, Reyner 16, 23, 114, 263
  Theory and Design in the First Machine Age (1960) 114
Barclay and Crousse 99
  Archaeological Museum of Paracas 99, *99*
Bardi, Lina Bo 29, 131
  Social Service of Commerce, São Paulo 29, *29*
Barozzi Veiga 210, 231, 234, 235
  Musée Cantonal des Beaux-Arts, Lausanne 231, *234*, 235
  Szczecin Philharmonic 210, *210*
Barragán, Luis 95–8
  Efrain González Luna House, Guadalajara 95
  Egerstrom House and Stables (Cuadra San Cristóbal), Atizapán de Zaragoza 96, *96–7*
  own house, Mexico City 96
Barthes, Roland 166, 167
Bataille, Georges 166
Battcock, Gregory 214
Baudrillard, Jean 161
Bedard, Jean-François 161
Behnisch Architekten 265
  Unilever Headquarters, Hamburg 265
Behnisch, Günther 77, 195
Benjamin, Andrew 159
béton brut, the architecture of see Brutalism 16–38
Bin, Zhang see Atelier Z+
Bjarke Ingels Group (BIG) 255–8
  Battery, Copenhagen (project) 257
  Business Innovation Hub, University of Massachusetts, Amherst 257, *257*
  CopenHill, Copenhagen *256*, 257
  Lego House, Billund 255, *255*, 257

Mountain Housing, The, Copenhagen *256*, 257
  Musée Atelier Audemars Piguet, Vallée de Joux 257–8
  National Bank of Iceland (project) 257
  Tower of the People, Shanghai 255
  Yes is More: An Archicomic on Architectural Evolution (2010) 255
Blanco, Manuel 225
blob architecture 211, 251
Boeri, Stefano 268, 269
  Bosco Verticale, Milan 268, *269*
  Rehabilitation Center, Shenzhen 268, *269*
Bofill, Ricardo 79–85, 110, 112
  Arcades du Lac, Paris 79, *80–81*
  Echelles du Baroque, Paris 79
  Espaces d'Abraxas, Marne-la-Vallée 79, *82–3*
  Mohammed VI Polytechnic University, Ben Guerir 110, *112*
  Muralla Roja, Calpe 79, *79*
  Shepherd School of Music, Rice University, Houston 79, *84*, 85
Böhm, Gottfried 17–18, 19–20
  Bensberg Town Hall, Bergisch Gladbach-Bensberg 18, *20*
  Pilgrimage Church, Neviges 17–18, *19*
Bolles + Wilson 194–5
  Münster City Library *194*, 195
Borchers, Juan 30
  Electrical Cooperative, Chillán 30
Botta, Mario 49, 52, 54–5
  BSI Bank (formerly Gottardo Bank), Lugano 54, 55
  Evry, cathedral of 55
  Ligornetto, house at, Ticino 54–5
  Museum of Modern Art, San Francisco 55, *55*
  Single-Family House, Riva San Vitale 54, *54*
Breuer, Marcel 21–3, 28, 135
  Begrisch Hall, New York University, University Heights, Ohio 22, *22*
  Church of St. Francis, Michigan 23, *23*
  Grosse Pointe Public Library, Michigan 22
  Monastery of St. John, Minnesota 22–3
  Whitney Museum, New York 22
Broadbent, Goffrey 13
Brutalism 16–38, 107, 131
  in America 18, 21–9
  in Europe 16, 17
  in Germany 17–20
  in Latin America 29–31
  in the United Kingdon 16, 17
Buttlar, Adrian Von 61

Calatrava, Santiago 204–5, 206–8
  Bodegas Ysios Winery, Araba 205, *208*
  City of Arts and Sciences, Valencia 205, *206–7*
  Opera House of Valencia 205

281

Campo Baeza, Alberto 225–7, 230
   Asencio House, Cádiz 226, *226*
   Gaspar House, Cádiz 225, *225*
   House of the Infinite, Cádiz 226, *226–7*
   Public School for San Sebastian de los Reyes, Madrid 227
   Turegano House, Madrid 225
   Zamora Office Complex, Zamora 227, *227*
Canales, Fernanda 99–101
   Terreno House, Valle de Bravo 99, 101, *100*, *101*
Canella, Guido 39, 49
   Pieve Emanuele Civic Centre, Lombardy 49
Caruso St John 154–5
   Bremer Landesbank, Bremen 154–5, *155*
   Nottingham Contemporary, Nottingham 154, *154*
Chaderji, Rifaat 109
   Administration Offices for the Federation of Industries, Baghdad 109
Chipperfield, David 56–9, 61
   Am Kupfergraben, Museum Island Berlin *56*, 57
   James-Simon-Galerie, Museum Island Berlin 58–9, *59*, 61
   Museum of Modern Literature, Marbach am Neckar 56, *57*
   Museum in Naga 57–8
   Neues Museum, restoration of, Museum Island Berlin 58, *58*
   summer house, Galicia 57
Chomsky, Noam 160
CIAM (Congrès International d'Architecture Moderne) 11, 12, 62, 85, 86
Coderch, Josep Antonio 89
   La Barceloneta 89
   Rozes House, Girona 89
   School of Architecture in Barcelona, expansion of 89
Coenen, Jo 147
Collins, Peter 9
   Changing Ideals in Modern Architecture: 1750–1950 9
Colquhoun, Alan 9, 129
Constructivism, Russian 159, 167, 169–71, 173, 176, 178, 179, 187, 191, 248
   see also Neo-Constructivism
Cook, Peter 211, 212
   Kunsthaus Graz (with Fournier, C.) 211, *212*
Cooke, Catherine 170, 176–7
Coop Himmelb(l)au 169, 179–85, 198, 242
   Akron Art Museum, Ohio 180, *182–3*
   Blazing Wing 180
   BMW Welt, Munich 180, *182*, *184*
   Musée des Confluences, Lyon 182–3, *185*
   office penthouse, Vienna 169, 179–80
   Open House project for Malibu, California (Open Structures) 180, *181*
   UFA Cinema Multiplex, Dresden 180, *181*
Corbu, Père 72
Correa, Charles 106
   Gandhi Memorial, Ahmedabad 106
critical regionalism 87–8, 131, 142
   see also Regional Modernisms

Deconstruction 159–69, 170, 178, 195, 262
   philosophical foundation of 159
Decq, Odile 251, 254
   GL Events Headquarters, Lyon 251
   MACRO Museum, Rome 251, *254*
Deleuze, Gilles 165–6
Denys Lasdun 17, 18
Derrida, Jacques 159–61, 164–7, 169
   De la grammatologie (1967) 159, 160, 161
   L'Écriture et la différence (1967) 159
   La voix et le phénomène (1967) 159
   Margins of Philosophy (1972) 160
Doshi, Balkrishna 106, 107
   Sangath Office, Ahmedabad 107
Dudler, Max 51, 60, 61
   Jacob and Wilhelm Grimm Centre, Berlin *60*, 61
Duhart, Emilio 30
   CEPAL Building, Santiago 30
Durbach Block Jaggers and John Wardle 210–11
   Phoenix Central Park Gallery, Sydney 210–11, *211*

Eames, Charles and Ray 114, 129
   Case Study House 114, 129
Eisenman, Peter 15, 86, 131, 133, 159–66, 167, 169, 178, 195
   Aronoff Center for Design and Art, University of Cincinnati *164*, 165
   Canareggio, Venice 161
   Checkpoint Charlie (IBA Housing), Berlin 161, *162–3*
   Chora L Works (1997) 164
   Church of the Year 2000, Rome 165
   City of Culture of Galicia, Santiago de Compostela 164–5, *165–6*
   Deconstruction 160–66
   Fin d'Ou T Hou S (drawings) 161, 164
   Greater Columbus Convention Center, Ohio 165
   House El-Even Odd 160
   House series 160, 161
   Koizumi Sangyo office building, Tokyo 165
   Moving Arrows, Eros, and Other Errors (1986) 161
   'The End of the Classical, the End of the Beginning, the End of the End' (1982) 160, 161
   'The Representations of Doubt: At the Sign of the Sign' (1982) 160
   Wexner Center for the Visual Arts, Ohio 161, 163–4, *163*
Expressionism 17–18, 23, 55, 155, 156, 192, 196, 203–5, 209–10, 213, 231, 245
   see also Neo-Expressionism

Eyck, Aldo van 9, 11–12, 87, 147
   Amsterdam Orphanage 12
   Forum – The story of another idea 11
   Forum (journal) 11, 12
   Miracle of Moderation, A (publication) 12
   playgrounds for children 12
   The Child, the City and the Artist – An Essay on Architecture – The Inbetween Realm 12

Fehn, Sverre 89
   Nordic Pavilion, Venice Biennale 89
   Villa Busk, Bamble 89
   Villa Schreiner, Oslo 89
Fernández, Antonio Toca 96
Flavin, Dan 214
Foreign Office Architects (Moussavi, F. and Zaera-Polo, A.) 242, 245, 258–9
   John Lewis Department Store, Leicester 245
   Yokohama International Port Terminal 258–9, *259*
Foster, Norman (Foster + Partners) 122, 125–6, 127, 128, 129, 146, 263–4
   Carré d'Art, Nîmes 126, *127*
   Commerzbank Headquarters, Frankfurt 263, *263*
   HSBC headquarters, Hong Kong 125, 126, *126*
   IBM plant, Cosham (with Hopkins, M.) 129
   Masdar Institute, UAE 263, *264*
   Reichstag building, Berlin, restoration of 126, *128*
   Sainsbury Centre for the Visual Arts, Norwich 125, *125*
   Willis Faber & Dumas headquarters, Ipswich (with Hopkins, M.) 125, 129
Foucault, Michel 161
Frampton, Kenneth 9, 87–8, 142
Fujimoto, Sou 213
   L'Arbre Blanc in Montpellier 213, *213*
FUKSAS (Massimiliano and Doriana) 251, 252–4
   Ferrari Operational Headquarters and Research Centre, Modena 251
   Lycée Georges Frêche, Montpellier 251, *252–3*
   Maison des Arts in Bordeaux 251
   Music Theatre and Exhibition Hall, Rhike Park, Tbilisi 251, *254*
   Tbilisi Public Service Hall 251
Fuller, Buckminster 114, 125, 174, 204, 263
   Dymaxion House 114
Future Systems 211, 212, 242
   Selfridges Department Store, Birmingham 211, *212*

Gargiani, Roberto 170–71, 174, 251
Gehry, Frank 55, 159, 178, 192, 195–201, 242
   Fred and Ginger building/Dancing House, Prague (with Milunić, V.) 195–6, *196–7*
   Gehry House, Venice, CA 195, *195*

INDEX

Guggenheim in Bilbao 196, 198, *198–9*, 201
MIT Stata Center, Cambridge, MA *201*, 201, 203
University of Iowa Advanced Technology Laboratories 195, *195*
Vitra Design Museum, Weil am Rhein 196, 198, *198*, 209
Walt Disney Concert Hall, Los Angeles *200*, 201
Winton House, Minnesota 159
Giedion, Sigfried 9, 10, 78, 192, 204
Ginzburg, Moisei 77, 174, 179
Narkomfin building, Moscow 174
Grabow, Stephen 14
Grafton Architects 31, 155–7
London School of Economics 155–6, *156*
Luigi Bocconi University, Milan *156*, 157
University of Engineering and Technology, Lima 31, *31*
Grassi, Giorgio 39, 45, 47, 51
Public Library, Groningen 45
Student Housing, Chieti 45, 61
Graves, Michael 63, 70, 72–6, 86, 131, 133, 163
Benacerraf House addition, Princeton, NJ 72
Clos Pegase Winery, Napa Valley 75–6, *76*, 217
Disney Corporation, Miami 86
Humana Headquarters, Kentucky 63, 73, *74*, 75
Portland City Hall, Portland 63, 73, *73*
San Juan Capistrano Library, California 75, *75*
Snyderman House, Indiana 72–3, *72*
Villa Plocek, Warren Township, NJ 72–3, *72*
Gregotti, Vittorio 39, 47–9, 86
Il Territorio dell'architettura (1962) 47
territory, concept of 47–8
University of Calabria, Cosenza 47–9, *48*
Grimshaw, Nicholas 126–7, 129
British Pavilion, Seville's Expo '92 126–7
Waterloo International Terminal, London (with Hunt, A.) 126, 127, 129, *129*
Gropius, Walter 9, 10, 131, 135, 192
Bauhaus, Dessau 63
Gruppo 7 39
Gwathmey, Charles 131, 133

Hadid, Zaha 55, 170–71, 176–9, 192, 195, 203, 204, 242, 262–3
Guangzhou Opera House *202*, 203
Hong Kong Peak (project) 176–7, *177*
hotel on Hungerford Bridge (Malevich's Tektonik) 176
Prime Minister Residence, Dublin 176
Rosenthal Center for Contemporary Art, Cincinnati 176, 178, *179*
Vitra Fire Station, Weil am Rhein 177, *178*
Heidegger, Martin 12, 14, 159, 169, 220
Being and Time (1927) 159
Poetry, Language, Thought (1971) 14

Hejduk, John 131, 133
Henning Larsen 141
Royal Danish Opera, Copenhagen 141, *141*
Hérault Arnod Architectes 267
Rossignol Headquarters, La Buisse 267
Herzog & de Meuron 195, 209–10, 215, 217–19, 242–5
Brandenburg University of Technology Media Centre and Library, Cottbus 243, *243*, 245
Caixaforum, Madrid 209
De Young Museum, San Francisco *244*, 245
Dominus Winery, Napa Valley 217, *217*
Eberswalde Technical School Library (with Thomas Ruff) 217, 219, *219*, 243
Elbphilharmonie Hamburg 209, *209*
Goetz Foundation, Munich 217, *218*
Olympic Stadium in Beijing (Bird's Nest) 242
Remy Zaugg Studio, Mulhouse 217, 219
Ricola Warehouse, Mulhouse 217, 219, 243
Stone House, Tavole 217
Vitrahaus, Weil am Rhein 209–10, *210*
Hevia, Duque Motta, and Manzi 30–31, 33
The School of Economics and Business, Diego Portales University 30–31
High-Tech 114–30, 131, 170, 179, 180, 191, 263
Holl, Steven 152–4, 235–7
Art Building West, University of Iowa 152, *153*
Chapel in Seattle 152
Kiasma Museum of Contemporary Art, Helsinki 152
Knut Hamsun Centre, Hamarøy 152
Nelson-Atkins Museum of Art, Kansas City 235, *236*, 237
Visual Arts Building, University of Iowa 152, *153*, 154
Hollein, Hans 63, 86
Hopkins, Michael and Patty 129–30, 267–8
Hopkins house, London 129, *129*
IBM plant, Cosham (with Foster, N.) 129
Kroon Hall, Yale, Connecticut 267–8, *268*
Patera building system 129–30
Schlumberger Research Centre, Cambridge 130, *130*
Willis Faber & Dumas headquarters, Ipswich (with Foster, N.) 125, 129
Houben, Francine *see* Mecanoo
Hunt, Anthony 115, 127
Hybrid Brutalism 21, 24
Hybrid Modernisms 147–52
Hyper-Modernism 242, 248–63

IBA (International Building Exhibition) 86
Ibelings, Hans 147
Interbau 86
International Style 9, 114, 131

Internationale Bauaustellung *see* IBA
Inui, Kumiko 248
Dior Ginza shop, Tokyo 248, *248*
Isozaki, Arata 31–2, 63, 84, 85, 86, 146, 198
Kitakyushu Central Library, Fukuoka *84*, 85
Museum of Contemporary Art, Los Angeles 85, *85*
Oita Medical Center, Oita 31
Oita Prefectural Library, Oita 31, *32*
Ito, Toyo 158
Tod's Building, Tokyo 158, *158*

Jain, Bijoy (Studio Mumbai) 107–9
Ahmedabad Residence, Gujarat 107, 109
Carrimjee House, Satirje 107, *108*
Copper House II, Chondi 107
Palmyra House, Alibag 107, *108*
Jencks, Charles 13, 62, 63, 73, 86, 131, 247, 271
'Death for Rebirth' 86
Language of Post-Modern Architecture, The 86
Meaning in Architecture (Jencks, Baird) 13
Johnson, Philip 76, 159
AT&T headquarters, New York 76
Jourdan/Muller/Albrecht 86
Judd, Donald 214, 219, 222

KAAN Architecten 36, 37
Crematorium Siesegem in Belgium, The, Aalst 36, *37*
Kabbaj S., Kettani D., and Siana M. 109–10, 111
Taroudant University 109–10, *110*
Technology School of Guelmim 109, 110, *111*
Kahn, Louis 16, 23–6, 54, 55, 65, 106, 221
First Unitarian Church and School, Rochester, New York 23–4
parliament complex, Dhaka, Bangladesh 23, 26, *26*
Salk Institute, La Jolla, California 23, 24, *24–5*, 26
Yale Art Gallery, Connecticut 16
Kalach, Alberto (Taller de Arquitectura X) 36, 101
Jojutla School, Oaxaca 36, *36*, 101, *101*
Kallmann, McKinnell, and Knowles 26–7
Boston City Hall, Boston 26–7, *27*, 28
Kéré, Francis 110–13, 271
Benin National Assembly, Ouagadougou 111–12
National Park of Mali, Bamako 112–13
primary school in Gando 110–11, *112*
Kerez, Christian 223
chapel in Oberrealta, Grisons 223, *223*
House with One Wall, Zurich 223
Kunstmuseum Liechtenstein (with Morger and Degelo) 223
Khoury, Bernard 190–91
B-018 Nightclub, Beirut 190
Centrale, Beirut 190, *191*
Plot 450, Beirut 190–91, *191*

283

Kleihues, Josef Paul 51, 52–3, 85–6
  Archaeological Museum, Frankfurt 52, *53*
  Museum in Kornwestheim 52
Kollhoff/Ovaska 86
Koolhaas, Rem (OMA) 51, 63, 134, 147, 166, 170–76, 179, 219, 242, 248–51, 255
  cadavre exquis [exquisite corpse] 171
  CCTV Headquarters, Beijing 176, 248–50, *249*
  Congrexpo, Lille 174, *175*, 176
  Delirious New York (1978) 176
  Dutch Parliament Extension (competition with Zenghelis, E. and Hadid, Z.), The Hague 171, *172*
  Educatorium, University of Utrecht 174
  Euralille Master Plan, Lille 174, *175*, 176
  Exodus, or the Voluntary Prisoners of Architecture (competition with Zenghelis, E.) 171
  Jussieu, library at 174
  Kunsthal, Rotterdam 173–4, *173*
  Mutations (2001) 176
  S, M, L, XL (1995) 171, 176
  Seattle Central Library 176, 250–1, *250*, 259
  study of New York 171
  Villa Dall'Ava, Saint Cloud 171, 173
  Zeebrugge Terminal Building (competition) 174
Kraus, Karl 63
Krell, David Farrell 168
Krier, Rob, Léon 49–51, 77, 79, 85, 86
  Poundbury, new town 49, *50–51*
  Stadtraum (Urban Space) (1975) (Krier, R.) 49
Kuma, Kengo 103–5, 158
  Yunfeng Spa Resort, Yunnan 103
  Yusuhara market and hotel, Kochi 103, *104–5*
Kundoo, Anupama 107
  Nandalal Sewa Samithi Library, Pondicherry 107
  Wall House, Auroville 107
Kuznetsov, Sergey 224, 225
  Museum for Architectural Drawing (Tchoban, Kuznetsov) *224*, 225

Lasdun, Denys 17, 18
  Royal National Theatre, London 17, *18*
Le Corbusier 10, 11, 12, 16, 17, 18, 21, 29, 30, 38, 65, 76, 78, 106, 107, 114, 118, 131, 133, 142, 145, 160, 172, 174, 192, 219, 263
  Carpenter Center for the Visual Arts, Harvard University, Cambridge, Massachusetts 18, 21, *21*
  Millowners' Association Building, Ahmedabad 16, 21, 30
  Monastery of La Tourette, Lyon 16, 17
  Ronchamp, chapel in 76, 192
  Villa Cook, Paris 133
  Villa Savoye, Poissy 63, 65, 114, 173
  Villa Stein, Paris 133

Legorreta, Ricardo 98
  Camino Real Hotel, Mexico City (with Noguchi, I, and Goeritz, M.) 98, *98*
  Hamad Ben Khalifa University Student Center, Doha 98, *99*
Leonidov, Ivan 170, 171, 176
LeWitt, Sol 214–15
Libeskind, Daniel 44, 159, 167–9
  Jewish Museum addition to the Berlin Museum, Berlin 167–9, *168*
Lin, Maya 240–41
  Vietnam Veterans Memorial, Washington, DC 240, *241*
Longhi, Luis 98–9
  Pachacamac House, Lima 98–9
Loos, Adolf 41, 141, 145, 147, 225
Lootsma, Bart 176
Lyotard, Jean-François 62
  La Condition postmoderne (1979) 62

Macdonald, Angus 127
MAD Architects 202–4
  Culture Park, Shenzhen 204
  Harbin Opera House, Harbin *202–3*, 203–4
  Ordos Museum, Ordos 204, *204*
Maki, Fumihiko 134
Malevich, Kazimir 176, 179, 214
Märkli, Peter 222
  La Congiunta, Ticino 222, *222*
Martorell/Bohigas/Mackay 86
Maxwell, Robert 129
Mayne, Thom *see* Morphosis
Mecanoo 147, 148–9
  Delft University Library 147, 259
  Faculty of Economics and Management, Utrecht 147, *148–9*
Meier, Richard 131–5
  Atheneum, The, Indiana 133–4, *133*
  City Hall, The Hague 134, *134*
  Getty Center, Los Angeles 134–5, *135*
  Smith House, Darien, Connecticut *132*, 133
Melnikov, Konstantin 77
Mendelsohn, Erich 9, 10, 179, 192, 205, 209
Mendes da Rocha, Paulo 29–30, 131
  Brazilian Museum of Sculpture (MuBE), São Paulo 29–30, *30*
  Cais das Artes (pier of arts), Vitoria 30
Metabolism 31, 85
Mies van der Rohe, Ludwig/Miesian influence 9, 10, 76, 95, 114, 121, 129, 131, 135, 142, 147, 173, 215, 221, 225, 227, 251
  Barcelona Pavilion, International Exhibition (1929) 215
  Illinois Institute of Technology campus, Chicago 95
Minimalism/Minimalist 33, 38, 45, 47, 93, 96, 102, 145, 214–41, 251
  in art 45, 214–15, 217
  minimal art vs. minimalist architecture 215, 217
Miralles, Enric 189–90
  Community Centre and Assembly Hall, Barcelona (with Pinós, C.) 189

Olympic Archery Range, Barcelona (with Pinós, C.) 189
  Scottish Parliament, Edinburgh (with Tagliabue, B.) 189, *190*
Moneo, Rafael 89–91, 141, 142, 146–7, 203
  Auditorium of Barcelona 147
  Bank Inter, Madrid (with Bescos, R.) 146
  Kursaal, San Sebastian 146–7, *146*, 203
  Murcia Town Hall, Murcia 89, 91, *91*
  Museum of Roman Art, Merida 89, *90*, 91
Moore, Charles 63
  Piazza d'Italia, New Orleans 63
Moore, Lyndon, Turnbull and Whitaker 94–5
  Kresge College, Santa Cruz, California 94–5, *95*
  Sea Ranch Condominium, California 94
Moos, Stanislaus von 67
Mori, Toshiko 113
  Fass Elementary School 113
  Thread Artists' Residences and Cultural Center, Sinthian 113, *113*
Morphosis (Mayne, T. and Rotondi, M.) 179, 183, 186–8, 242
  2-4-6-8 House, Venice, CA 183
  72 Market Street Restaurant, Venice, CA 183, 186
  Artspark Performing Arts Pavilion (competition), Los Angeles 186–7, *187*
  Cooper Union Academic Center, New York 187
  Diamond Ranch High School, Pomona 187, *188*
  Venice III House, Los Angeles 183, *186*
  Yuzen Car Museum, Los Angeles (project) 186, *186*
Morris, Robert 214, 215
Moss, Eric Owen 179, 188–9
  Aronoff House, Tarzana, CA (project) 189
  Lawson/Westen House, Los Angeles 189
  Samitaur – Kodak company headquarters, Los Angeles 189
Moure, Gonzalo 147
  Alicante, Town Hall extension 147
Mumford, Lewis 87
Murcutt, Glenn 101–2
  Simpson-Lee House, NSW 102, *102*
Museum of Modern Art, New York 9, 12, 159
  Architecture without Architects, exhibition 12
  Deconstructivist Architecture, exhibition on (1988) 159, 169
  International Style, exhibition on (1930) 9
  Mies van der Rohe, exhibition on 215
Muthesius, Hermann 57, 192
MVRDV 87, 147, 150, 251, 259, 262, 266–67
  Silodam complex, Amsterdam 150
  Spijkenisse Public Library (Book Mountain) 266–7

INDEX

Tianjin Binhai Library 259, 262, *262*
WoZoCo Housing Complex, Osdorp 147, 150, *150*

Neo-Classicism/Neo-Classical 45, 49, 57, 63, 72, 78, 79, 85, 163, 169
Neo-Constructivism 170–76, 179, 183, 189, 191
Neo-Expressionism 192–213
Neo-Rationalism 39–61, 85, 188, 220
Neo-Suprematism 176–9, 191
Neutelings Riedijk 150, 151, 246–8
  Institute for Sound and Vision, Hilversum *246*, 247
  MAS Museum, Antwerp 150, *151*, 247–8, *247*
  Ornament and Identity (2018) 247
  Veenman Printing Works, Ede (with Karel Martens) 247, *247*
Neutra, Richard 87
New Brutalism 16, 77
New York Five 72, 131, 133, 158
Niemeyer, Oscar 29, 87, 95, 131, 136, 137
Nieto Sobejano Arquitectos 228–30
  Madinat-al-Zahra Museum, Córdoba 228, *229*
  San Telmo Museum Extension, San Sebastian (with Ferrán, L. and Otero, A.) 228, *229*, 230
Nishizawa, Ryue 240, 241
  Teshima Art Museum, Teshima Island (with artist Rei Naito) 240, *241*
  see also SANAA
Noguchi, Isamu 98
Norberg-Schulz, Christian 11, 12, 13–14
  Concept of Dwelling, The (1984) 14
  Genius Loci: Towards a Phenomenology of Architecture (1979) 13–14
Norris, Christopher 159
Nouvel, Jean 120, 121–122, 137, 138, 205, 208
  Arab World Institute, Paris *120*, 121
  Cartier Foundation, Paris 121, 121–2
  Lafayette Galleries, Berlin 121, 122
  Louvre Museum, Abu Dhabi 137, *138*
  Paris Philharmonic Concert Hall 205, *208*

O'Donnell + Tuomey 157
  Glucksman Gallery, University College Cork 157, *157*
Olgiati, Valerio 248
  Atelier Bardill (Olgiati) 248, *248*
OMA *see* Koolhaas, Rem
organic architecture 10–11

Palladio, Andrea 67
Papadakis, Andreas 159
  Academy Editions (Publisher) 159
Parametricism 262–3
Pawson, John 235
  Abbey of Nový Dvůr, Toužim 235
  Okinawa House, Okinawa Island 235
Paxton, Joseph 114, 115
  Crystal Palace 114, 115
Pei, I.M. 109, 135–6
  Museum of Islamic Art, Doha 109

National Gallery East Wing, Washington, DC 136, *136*
Perrault, Dominique 235, 266
  Bibliothèque nationale de France, Paris 235, *235*
  EWHA Womans University, Seoul 266, *266*
phenomenology in architecture 13–14, 15, 91, 109, 152, 220–21
Piano, Renzo 102–3, 115–21, 265–6
  Beyeler Foundation Museum, Riehen 118, 119, *119*
  California Academy of Sciences, San Francisco 265–6, *266*
  Centre Georges Pompidou, Paris 115, *115*, *116–17*, 118
  Isabella Stewart Gardner Museum addition, Boston 118, 119–20, *120*
  Jean-Marie Tjibaou Cultural Centre, Noumea, New Caledonia 102–3, *103*
  Kansai International Airport, Osaka 120–21
  Menil Collection, Texas 118–19, *118*
Pietilä, Reima and Raili 88–9
  Dipoli Student Residence in Otaniemi 88–9, *88*
Pinós, Carme 189–90
  Headquarters for the Delegations of 'Les Terres de l'Elbe', Tortosa 190
Polesello, Gianuggo 49
  University of Las Palmas, Canary Islands 49
Portoghesi, Paolo 63
  Postmodern: The Architecture of the Postindustrial Society 63
Portzamparc, Christian de 136–7
  Cidade das Artes, Rio de Janeiro 136–7, *137*
  Cité de la Musique, La Villette 136, *136*
Post-Modernism/Post-Modernist 9, 13, 14, 15, 33, 39, 57, 62–86, 87, 115, 124, 131, 133, 147, 159, 163, 169, 170, 183, 188, 192, 242, 247, 250, 262
Poundbury, new town (Krier, L.) 49, *50*, *51*
Predock, Antoine 93–4, 98
  American Heritage Center and Art Museum, Wyoming 94, *94*
  La Luz, housing settlement of, Albuquerque 93
  Nelson Fine Arts Center, Arizona State University 93–4
  Rio Grande Nature Center and Preserve, Albuquerque 93
Price, Cedric 129
Pruitt-Igoe housing complex 131
Pruscha, Carl 107
  Taragaon Hostel, Kathmandu 107

RCR Arquitectes 150
  Casa Rural, Girona 150
  Library and Senior Citizen Centre, Barcelona 152
Regional Modernism 87–113, 145, 263
Reidy, Alfonso Eduardo 29
Rella, Franco 161
Rice, Peter 115
Rogers, Ernesto 39, 47, 87

Rogers, Richard 115–18, 122–5, 263, 265, 267
  Centre Georges Pompidou, Paris 115, *115*, *116–17*, 118
  Cities for a Small Planet (1995) 263, 265
  Daimler Chrysler Residential, Berlin 124
  Law Courts of the City of Bordeaux 124–5, *124*, 265
  Lloyd's of London *122–3*, 124, 125, 265
  Nuevas Bodegas Protos winery, Peñafiel (with ABAA) 267, *267*
Rossi, Aldo 39–45, 47, 49, 85, 86
  Architecture of the City, The (Rossi) 39
  Bonnefanten Museum, Maastricht 44–5, *44*
  Elementary School, Fagnano Olona 41, *41*, 43
  Gallaratese, Milan *40*, 41, 43
  IBA project (Friedrichstadt Housing Block), Berlin 42–3, *43*
  'Mannerism and Modern Architecture' (1950) 142
  Schützenstrasse, Berlin 45, *46–7*
  Teatro del Mondo, Venice Biennale (1980) 43–4
Rowe, Colin 49, 77–8, 142
Rudolph, Paul 22, 27–8, 67, 122
  Boston Government Service Centre, Massachusetts 28, *28*
  Crawford Manor, Connecticut 67
  Yale School of Architecture, New Haven, Connecticut 27–8, *27*
Rudofsky, Bernard 12, 29
  Architecture without Architects (1964) 12, 29
Rykwert, Joseph 12
  The Idea of a Town, analysis of 12

Saarinen, Eero 179, 192, 205
Safdie, Moshe 28–9, 87
  Case for City Living, A 29
  Habitat 67, Montreal 28–9, *28*, 257
SANAA (Sejima, K. and Nishizawa, R.) 235, 238–40
  Museum of Contemporary Art in Kanazawa 238, *238*
  New Museum of Contemporary Art, New York 240, *240*
  Rolex Learning Center, Lausanne 238, *239*
Sauerbruch Hutton 265
  Federal Environment Agency, Dessau 265, *265*
Saussure, Ferdinand de 13, 39, 159, 160
Scandinavian Modernism 88–9
Scarpa, Carlo 63–5
  Banca Popolare di Verona 63, *64*, 65
  Castelvecchio, restoration of, Verona 65
Scharoun, Hans 10, 192–5, 205, 213
  Berlin Philharmonie 192–3, *193*, 209
  Berlin State Library (Staatsbibliothek) 192, 193, *194*
  Romeo and Juliet, Stuttgart 213
Schinkel, Karl Friedrich 59, 61, 78
Schneider and Lengauer 92–3
  Cemetery and Wake Room, East Tyrol *92*, 93

285

Schroeder House (Rietveld) 13
Schumacher, Patrik 166, 176, 179, 262–3
semiotics 13, 73
Sert, Josep Lluís 21
   Holyoke Center, Harvard University, Cambridge, Massachusetts 21, *21*
Shu, Wang (Amateur Architecture Studio) 33, 36, 103, 105–6
   Academy of Art in Hangzhou, The 105, *106*
   Ningbo History Museum, Ningbo 36, *36*
Silvestre, Fran 230
   House on the Castle Mountainside, Ayora 230, *230*
   Pati Blau House, Valencia 230
Siza, Álvaro 141–5, 152, 231, 270
   Antonio Carlos Siza House, Santo Tirso 142
   Borges and Irmão Bank, Vila do Conde 142
   Galician Centre for Contemporary Art, Santiago de Compostela 144–5, *145*
   Malagueira Social Housing, Evora 144
   Pinto and Sotto Mayor Bank, Oliveira de Azeméis 142
   Porto School of Architecture 142, *143*
   SAAL Bouça Social Housing Complex, Porto 144, *144*, 270
   Santa Maria church, Marco de Canaveses 145, *145*
   Serralves Museum, Porto 142, *143*
Smithson, Alison and Peter 11, 16
   Hunstanton School, Norfolk 16
   Robin Hood Gardens, London 16, *16*
   Sheffield University, competition for (unrealised) 16
Snøhetta 140–41
   Bibliotheca Alexandrina, Alexandria *140*, 141
   Norwegian National Opera and Ballet *140*, 141
Souto de Moura, Eduardo 145–6
   House in Bom Jesus 145
   House in Moledo 145
   Paula Rego, Casas das Historias 145–6
Spanish Mission style 75
Standard Architecture (Zhang Ke) 105–6, 158
   Tibet Namchabawa Visitor Centre, Pai Town, Linzhi 105–6
   Yarlung Boat Terminal, Linzhi 105, *106*
Stern, Robert 76, 79
   House on Lake Michigan, Chicago 76
   Wiseman House, Montauk, New York 76
Stirling, James 48, 63, 70, 76–8, 85, 134
   Dusseldorf, museum in 77
   Staatsgalerie, Stuttgart 63, 77–8, *78*
   University of Leicester Engineering building, Leicester 77, *77*
Strauven, Francis 11
structuralist influence on architecture 13, 39, 45, 47, 48, 159, 160, 165, 176
Studio Gang 211, 213
   Aqua Tower, Chicago 211, 213, *213*
   MIRA 213

Studio Mumbai (Bijoy Jain) *see* Jain, Bijoy
Suprematism 176–8, 191
   see also Neo-Suprematism
Surrealism 170, 171, 174, 176, 180, 248
sustainability in architecture 107, 114, 126–7, 130, 263–71
Sydney School 101

Tafuri, Manfredo 63
Taller de Arquitectura X *see* Kalach, Alberto
Taut, Bruno 180, 192
   Alpine Architektur (1917) 192
Tchoban, Sergei 224, 225
   Museum for Architectural Drawing (Tchoban, Kuznetsov) *224*, 225
Team 4 122, 124, 125, 129
   Reliance Controls factory, Swindon 122, 124, *125*
Team X 11
technological paradigm, the *see* High-Tech
Tendenza, La 39, 47, 49
Terragni, Giuseppe 147, 160
Testa, Clorindo 30, 31, 131
   Banco de Londres, Buenos Aires 30
Testa, Peter 142
Tiantian, Xu 158
Tod Williams Billie Tsien Architects 235, 237
   Barnes Foundation, Philadelphia 237, *237*
Tschumi, Bernard 137–8, 159, 164, 166–7
   Do-It-Yourself-City (project) 166
   Manhattan Transcripts (project) 167
   New Acropolis Museum, Athens 137–8, *138*
   Parc de la Villette, Paris 159, 164, 166–7, *166*, 205
Tukan, Jaafar 109
   SOS Children's Village, Aqaba 109, *109*
Tuñón, Emilio 60, 61
   Museum of Contemporary Art Helga de Alvear, Cáceres 60, *61*
Tzonis and Lefaivre 87, 88

UN Studio 262
   Mercedes-Benz Museum, Stuttgart 262, *262*
Ungers, Oswald Mathias 49, 51–2, 86
   Baden State Library, Karlsruhe 52, *52*
   Hotel Berlin 51
   Museum of Architecture, Frankfurt 51, *52*
Utzon, Jørn 89, 192
   Can Lis, Mallorca 89, *89*

Van de Velde, Henry 57, 192
Van den Broek and Bakema 17
   Delft University Auditorium, Delft 17, *17*
Vector Architects 33–6, 158
   Seashore Chapel, Beidaihe New District 33, 36
   Seashore Library, Beidaihe New District 33, *34–5*
Venezia, Francesco 215–16
   IUAV Materials Testing Laboratory, Venice 216
   Museum in Gibellina Nuova, restoration of 215–16

   Open Air Theatre, Salemi (with Collova and Aprile) 216
   pavilion for the XXI Triennale, Milan (2016) 216
Venturi, Robert 9, 63, 65–71, 85, 219, 242
   Complexity and Contradiction in Architecture (1966) (manifesto) 65
   Dixwell Fire Station, Connecticut *66*, 67
   Fire Station, Columbus, Indiana 67
   Gordon Wu Hall, Princeton University, NJ 67, *68–9*
   Guild House, Philadelphia 65, *66*, 67
   ISI Corporation, Philadelphia 242
   Lewis Thomas Laboratory, Princeton University, NJ 67, *70*
   Market Street building, Drexel University, Philadelphia 219
   Nurses Association, Philadelphia 65
   Ponte dell'Accademia, Venice 242
   Sainsbury Wing, National Gallery, London 67, 70, *70*, 71
   Vanna Venturi House, Philadelphia 65, *65*
Vidler, Anthony 77–8, 187, 238

Wandel Hoefer Lorch Architekten 223
   Ohel Jakob Synagogue, Munich 223, *223*, 225
Wei, Zhou *see* Atelier Z+
Weiss/Manfredi 258
   Krishna Singh Center for Nanotechnology, University of Pennsylvania 258, *258*
Werkbund exhibition, Cologne (1914) 55, 114, 192
Wigley, Mark 159, 169
   Deconstruction III – Architectural Design (1990) 169
Woolley, Ken 101
   Baudish House, Sydney, NSW 101
   Woolley House, Mosman, NSW 101
Wright, Frank Lloyd 9, 10, 14, 63, 65, 78, 87, 93

Yansong, Ma (MAD Architects) 158, 203
   see also MAD Architects

Zakarian and Navelet 33, 36–8
   Place du Village House (maison à Giens), Giens 36, *37*, 38
Zenghelis, Elia and Zoe 170–71
   see also Koolhaas, Rem
Zevi, Bruno 9, 10–11
   Modern Language of Architecture, The 10
   Towards an Organic Architecture 10
Zhang Ke *see* Standard Architecture
Zumthor, Peter 93, 215, 220–22
   Kunsthaus Bregenz 221, *221*
   Swiss Sound Pavilion, World Expo, Hannover 215
   Thermal Baths in Vals 220–21, *220*
   Bruder Klaus Field Chapel, Mechernich 221–2

Illustration Credits

2.1 Steve Cadman, Flickr, Creative Commons; 2.2 © Elie G. Haddad; 2.3 Ann Elliot, Wikimedia, Creative Commons; 2.4 (exterior and interior) © Thomas Kopf; 2.5 © Thomas Kopf; 2.6 © Elie G. Haddad; 2.7 © Elie G. Haddad; 2.8 Kristen Ruller, Wikimedia, Creative Commons; 2.9 Cecilia, Flickr, Creative Commons; 2.10 Jason Taellious, Flickr, Creative Commons; 2.11 M.D. Saiful Amin, Wikimedia, Creative Commons; 2.12 Beyond My Ken, Wikimedia Commons; 2.13 © Elie G. Haddad; 2.14 Gunnar Klack, Wikimedia, Creative Commons; 2.15 Ziko van Dijk, Wikimedia, Creative Commons; 2.16 Photo: Kazimierz Butelski; 2.17 © robert at made-by-architects.com; 2.18 Felipe Restrepo Acosta, Wikimedia, Creative Commons; 2.19 Photo: © Kentaro Tsukuba; 2.20 © Kentaro Tsukuba; 2.21 (exterior and interior) © Vector Architects, courtesy of Vector Architects; 2.22 钉钉, Wikimedia, Creative Commons; 2.23 Jaime Navarro, courtesy of Taller de Arquitectura X (Alberto Kalach); 2.24 © Sebastian van Damme, courtesy of KAAN Architecten; 2.25 (exterior and interior) © Stephane Chalmeau, courtesy of Zakarian-Navelet architectes urbanistes. 2.26 Adolf Bereuter, Wikimedia, Creative Commons; 3.1 © Elie G. Haddad; 3.2 © Elie G. Haddad; 3.3 © Barbara Burg and Oliver Schuh, www.palladium.de; 3.4 © Elie G. Haddad; 3.5 © Elie G. Haddad; 3.6 © Elie G. Haddad; 3.7 Corneille, Wikimedia, Creative Commons; 3.8 Alex Liivet, Flickr, Creative Commons; 3.9 © Elie G. Haddad; 3.10 Andreas Schwarzkopf, Wikimedia, Creative Commons; 3.11 © Laura Padgett; 3.12 © Alo Zanetta, courtesy of Mario Botta Architetti; 3.13 © Enrico Cano, courtesy of Mario Botta Architetti; 3.14 © Robert Canfield (11) and Pino Musi (9), courtesy of Mario Botta Architetti; 3.15 © Elie G. Haddad; 3.16 (exterior and interior) © Elie G. Haddad; 3.17 (exterior and interior) © Elie G. Haddad; 3.18 Chatchamp, Wikimedia, Creative Commons; 3.19 © Elie G. Haddad; 3.20 © Luis Asín, courtesy of Tuñón Arquitectos; 4.1 © Fabio Elia Sgarbi; 4.2 © Elie G. Haddad; 4.3 The Architectural Archives, University of Pennsylvania by the gift of Robert Venturi and Denise Scott Brown; 4.4 The Architectural Archives, University of Pennsylvania by the gift of Robert Venturi and Denise Scott Brown; 4.5 The Architectural Archives, University of Pennsylvania by the gift of Robert Venturi and Denise Scott Brown; 4.6 Daderot, Wikimedia, Creative Commons; 4.7 © Elie G. Haddad; 4.8 The Architectural Archives, University of Pennsylvania by the gift of Robert Venturi and Denise Scott Brown; 4.9 © courtesy of Michael Graves Architects; 4.10 © Norman McGrath, courtesy of Michael Graves Architects; 4.11 © courtesy of Michael Graves Architects; 4.12 © Peter Aaron, courtesy of Michael Graves Architects; 4.13 © Elie G. Haddad; 4.14 © Taisto H Makela; 4.15 Tom Parnell, Wikimedia, Creative Commons; 4.16 © Elie G. Haddad; 4.17 © Elie G. Haddad; 4.18 © courtesy of Ricardo Bofill Taller de Arquitectura; 4.19 © Gregori Civera, courtesy of Ricardo Bofill Taller de Arquitectura; 4.20 © courtesy of Ricardo Bofill Taller de Arquitectura; 4.21 © Gregori Civera, courtesy of Ricardo Bofill Taller de Arquitectura; 4.22 (photograph) 八幡鏡太郎, Wikimedia, Creative Commons; (axonometric drawing) © Arata Isozaki, courtesy of Arata Isozaki & Associates; 4.23 © Kentaro Tsukuba; 5.1 Ranerana, Wikimedia, Creative Commons; 5.2 © Julian Weyer; 5.3 © Michael Moran/OTTO, courtesy of Rafael Moneo Arquitecto; 5.4 © Michael Moran/OTTO, courtesy of Rafael Moneo Arquitecto; 5.5 © Kurt Hoerbst, courtesy of Schneider Lengauer Pühringer Architekten; 5.6 Carol McKinney Highsmith, Wikipedia, listed as part of public domain; 5.7 Ponderosapine210, Wikimedia, Creative Commons; 5.8 Šarūnas Burdulis, Flickr, Creative Commons; 5.9 Nicolás Boullosa, Flickr, Creative Commons; 5.10 Sam Agnew, Flickr, Creative Commons; 5.11 © Barclay & Crousse; 5.12 (exterior and interior) © Rafael Gamo, courtesy of Fernanda Canales Arquitectura; 5.13 © Jaime Navarro, courtesy of Taller de Arquitectura X (Alberto Kalach); 5.14 © Anthony Browell, courtesy Architecture Foundation Australia; 5.15 Fourrure, Flickr, Creative Commons; 5.16 © Kentaro Tsukuba; 5.17 Forgemind ArchiMedia, Flickr, Creative Commons; 5.18 © Studio Mumbai Architects; 5.19 © Studio Mumbai Architects; 5.20 © SOS Village, Jordan; 5.21 (exterior and interior) © Driss Kettani Architecte; 5.22 (both exteriors) © Driss Kettani Architecte; 5.23 © Gregori Civera, courtesy of Ricardo Bofill Taller de Arquitectura; 5.24 Helge Fahrnberger, Wikimedia, Creative Commons; 5.25 © Iwan Baan; 6.1 zoetnet, Flickr, Creative Commons; 6.2 Rob Oo, Flickr, Creative Commons; 6.3 Hester, Paul – Paul Hester Photography. © Fondazione Renzo Piano (Via P.P. Rubens 30A, 16158 Genova, Italy), 1981–87. The Menil Collection, Houston (Texas), USA. Client: The Menil Foundation. Piano & Fitzgerald, architects; 6.4 Christian Richters © RPBW – Renzo Piano Building Workshop Architects, 1991–1997. Beyeler Foundation Museum, Riehen (Basel), Switzerland. Client: Beyeler Foundation. Renzo Piano Building Workshop, architects in association with Burckhardt + Partner AG, Basel; 6.5 © Elie G. Haddad; 6.6 Arthur Weidmann, Wikimedia, Creative Commons; 6.7 © Philippe Ruault, courtesy of Ateliers Jean Nouvel; 6.8 (exterior) Cristian Bortes, Wikimedia, Creative Commons; (interior) Steve Cadman, Flickr, Creative Commons; 6.9 © Elie G. Haddad; 6.10 Ian Beales, Wikimedia, Creative Commons; 6.11 © Elie G. Haddad; 6.12 Wolfgang Staudt, Wikimedia, Creative Commons; 6.13 W & J, Flickr, Creative Commons; 6.14 © Elie G. Haddad; 6.15 Steve Cadman, Flickr, Creative Commons; 6.16 Valerian Guillot, Flickr, Creative Commons; 7.1 © Scott

Frances, courtesy of Richard Meier Architects; 7.2 Carol McKinney Highsmith, Wikipedia (listed as part of public domain); 7.3 GraphyArchy, Wikimedia, Creative Commons; 7.4 © Bassam Lahoud; 7.5 Elvert Barnes, Flickr, Creative Commons; 7.6 © Elie G. Haddad; 7.7 Cidade das Artes, Wikimedia, Creative Commons; 7.8 © Elie G. Haddad; 7.9 Jean Housen, Wikimedia, Creative Commons; 7.10 © Studio Majo, courtesy of EAA – Emre Arolat Architecture Archives; 7.11 Joakim Jardenburg, Flickr, Creative Commons; 7.12 Pudelek (Marcin Szala), Wikimedia, Creative Commons; 7.13 © Elie Michel Harfouche; 7.14 © Sabine Aoun; 7.15 © Elie G. Haddad; 7.16 © Sabine Aoun; 7.17 santiago lopez-pastor, Flickr, Creative Commons; 7.18 Santiago Lopez-Pastor, Flickr, Creative Commons; 7.19 © Michael Moran/OTTO, courtesy of Rafael Moneo Arquitecto; 7.20 © Christian Richters, courtesy of Mecanoo; 7.21 © Rob't Hart, courtesy of MVRDV; 7.22 © Sarah Blee, courtesy of Neutelings Riedijk Architecten; 7.23 © Andy Ryan, courtesy of Steven Holl Architects; 7.24 © Iwan Baan, courtesy of Steven Holl Architects; 7.25 John Lord, Flickr, Creative Commons; 7.26 Joachim Kohler, Wikimedia, Creative Commons; 7.27 © Nathalie Abou Reslan; 7.28 Paolo Gamba, Flickr, Creative Commons; 7.29 Glucksman2, Wikimedia, Creative Commons; 7.30 David Basulto, Flickr, Creative Commons; 8.1 © Elie G. Haddad; 8.2 Another Believer, Wikimedia, Creative Commons; 8.3 © Elie G. Haddad; 8.4 Xosema, Wikimedia, Creative Commons; 8.5 © Elie G. Haddad; 8.6 (exterior and interior) © Elie G. Haddad; 9.1 © OMA; 9.2 © Photograph by Delfino Sisto Legnani and Marco Cappelletti, courtesy of OMA; 9.3 © OMA; 9.4 © OMA; 9.5 © Zaha Hadid Foundation; 9.6 Marsupium, Wikimedia, Creative Commons; 9.7 © Elie G. Haddad; 9.8 © Coop Himmelb(l)au; 9.9 Kolossos, Wikimedia, Creative Commons; 9.10 Threebluro, listed as part of public domain; 9.11 (exterior) Diego Delso Wikimedia, Creative Commons; (interior) © Elie G. Haddad; 9.12 (exterior and interior) © Jean-Pierre El-Asmar; 9.13 © Morphosis Architects; 9.14 © Tom Bonner, courtesy of Morphosis Architects; 9.15 © Jasmine Park, courtesy of Morphosis Architects; 9.16 courtesy of Morphosis Architects, listed as part of public domain; 9.17 © ZAC and ZAC Photography, courtesy of EMBT Architects; 9.18 © DW5 BERNARD KHOURY; 9.19 © DW5 BERNARD KHOURY. Photo: WISSAM CHAAYA; 10.1 © Elie G. Haddad; 10.2 © Elie G. Haddad; 10.3 Aarp65, Wikimedia, Creative Commons; 10.4 André Corboz, Wikimedia, Creative Commons; 10.5 Phil Roeder, Flickr, Creative Commons; 10.6 LenaSevcikova, Wikimedia, Creative Commons; 10.7 © Elie G. Haddad; 10.8 Julio 535, Wikimedia, Creative Commons; 10.9 (exterior) Carol McKinney Highsmith, Wikimedia, listed as part of public domain; (interior) Daniel Hartwig, Flickr, Creative Commons; 10.10 © Elie G. Haddad; 10.11 © Zaha Hadid Foundation; 10.12 Jeremy Thompson, Flickr, Creative Commons; 10.13 Popolon, Wikimedia, Creative Commons; 10.14 Kuhnmi, Flickr, Creative Commons; 10.15 Gilles Messian, Wikimedia, Creative Commons; 10.16 fre3darchi, Flickr, Creative Commons; 10.17 © Thomas Kopf; 10.18 © Jörgens.mi, Wikimedia, Creative Commons; 10.19 DrKssn, Wikimedia, Creative Commons; 10.20 (interior) Julia Charles, courtesy of Durbach Block Jaggers/John Wardle Architects; (exterior) Trevor Mein, courtesy of Durbach Block Jaggers/John Wardle Architects; 10.21 Bs0u10e0, Flickr, Creative Commons; 10.22 Marion Schneider and Christoph Aistleitner, Wikimedia, listed as part of the public domain; 10.23 George Showman, Flickr, Creative Commons; 10.24 © Wassim Naghi; 11.1 © Kentaro Tsukuba; 11.2 Sarah Lou, Flickr, Creative Commons; 11.3 Till Niermann, Wikimedia, Creative Commons; 11.4 Immanuel Giel, Wikimedia, Creative Commons; 11.5 Micha L. Reiser, Wikimedia, Creative Commons; 11.6 Böhringer, Wikimedia, Creative Commons; 11.7 Jonathan Lin, Flickr, Creative Commons; 11.8 Brutarchitekt, Wikimedia, Creative Commons; 11.9 © Elie G. Haddad; 11.10 Ansgar Koreng, Wikimedia, Creative Commons; 11.11 © Hisao Suzuki, courtesy of Estudio Arquitectura Campo Baeza; 11.12 © Hisao Suzuki, courtesy of Estudio Arquitectura Campo Baeza; 11.13 © Javier Callejas, courtesy of Estudio Arquitectura Campo Baeza; 11.14 © Javier Callejas, courtesy of Estudio Arquitectura Campo Baeza; 11.15 © Roland Halbe, courtesy of Nieto Sobejano Arquitectos; 11.16 © Roland Halbe, courtesy of Nieto Sobejano Arquitectos; 11.17 Pcambal, Wikimedia, Creative Commons; 11.18 © Juan Rodriguez; 11.19 (exterior) Gzzz, Wikimedia, Creative Commons; (interior) Christophe95, Wikimedia, Creative Commons; 11.20 Jean-Pierre Dalbéra, Flickr, Creative Commons; 11.21 (exterior and interior) © Andy Ryan, courtesy of Steven Holl Architects; 11.22 © Elie G. Haddad; 11.23 金沢市, licensed under Creative Commons; 11.24 (exterior) Maarten Danial, Flickr, Creative Commons; (interior) Gabriel Garcia Marengo, Flickr, Creative Commons; 11.25 © Elie G. Haddad; 11.26 Forgemind ArchiMedia, Flickr, Creative Commons; 11.27 © Elie G. Haddad; 12.1 © Elie G. Haddad; 12.2 Lauren Manning, Flickr, Creative Commons; 12.3 Carol McKinney Highsmith, Wikimedia, listed as part of public domain; 12.4 Ron Cogswell, Flickr, Creative Commons; 12.5 (exterior and interior) © Scagliola Brakkee, courtesy of Neutelings Riedijk Architecten; 12.6 © Scagliola Brakkee, courtesy of Neutelings Riedijk Architecten; 12.7 Rick Ligthelm, Flickr, Creative Commons; 12.8 Christopher Mann McKay, Wikimedia, Creative Commons; 12.9 © Cindy Menassa; 12.10 © OMA; 12.11 © OMA; 12.12 © Sergio Pirrone, courtesy of Studio FUKSAS; 12.13 © Joel Rookwood, courtesy of Studio FUKSAS; 12.14 Jean-Pierre Dalbéra, Flickr, Creative Commons; 12.15 © Iwan Baan, courtesy of Bjarke Ingels Group; 12.16 © Jens Lindhe, courtesy of Bjarke Ingels Group; 12.17 © Rasmus Hjortshōj, courtesy of Bjarke Ingels Group; 12.18 © Max Touhey, courtesy of Bjarke Ingels Group; 12.19 © Elie G. Haddad; 12.20 Guilhem Vellut, Flickr, Creative Commons; 12.21 © Elie G. Haddad; 12.22 © Ossip van Duivenbode, courtesy of MVRDV; 12.23 © Elie G. Haddad; 12.24 © Commerzbank AG/CC-BY-SA 3.0 [DE]; 12.25 © Steffen Lehmann; 12.26 © Elie G. Haddad; 12.27 Alfred Twu, Wikimedia, in the public domain; 12.28 Christian Bolz, Wikimedia, Creative Commons; 12.29 Danidemanu, listed as part of public domain; 12.30 © Elie G. Haddad; 12.31 © Boeri Studio, photo by Dimitar Harizanov; 12.32 © Stefano Boeri Architetti China; 12.33 © Alejandro Aravena